HUMAN
NATURE

AND

CONDUCT

Titles on Ethics in Prometheus's Great Books in Philosophy Series

See the back of this volume for a complete list of titles in
Prometheus's Great Books in Philosophy and Great Minds series.

HUMAN NATURE

AND

CONDUCT

An Introduction to Social Psychology

JOHN DEWEY

GREAT BOOKS IN PHILOSOPHY

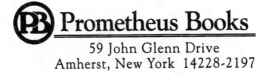 Prometheus Books

59 John Glenn Drive
Amherst, New York 14228-2197

Published 2002 by Prometheus Books
59 John Glenn Drive
Amherst, New York 14228–2197
VOICE: 716–691–0133, ext. 207
FAX: 716–564–2711
WWW.PROMETHEUSBOOKS.COM

Library of Congress Cataloging-in-Publication Data

Dewey, John, 1859–1952.
   Human nature and conduct : an introduction to social psychology / John
Dewey.
      p. cm.
   Originally published: New York : Henry Holt and Co., 1922.
   ISBN 1–59102–032–8 (alk. paper).
   1. Social psychology. 2. Habit. I. Title.

BF57 .D4 2002b
302—dc21   2002031852

Printed in the United States of America on acid-free paper

JOHN DEWEY was born near Burlington, Vermont, on October 20, 1859. Twenty years later, he graduated from the University of Vermont, after which he taught public school in Pennsylvania and Vermont. Having become interested in philosophical questions while still an undergraduate, Dewey continued his philosophical training at Johns Hopkins University. In 1884 he was awarded a doctorate in philosophy from that institution and soon thereafter he accepted a position in philosophy at the University of Michigan. Except for a one-year appointment as professor of philosophy at the University of Minnesota, Dewey remained at Michigan—serving a five-year term as chairman—until 1894 when he moved with his wife, Alice Chipman, to the University of Chicago and began his tenure as chairman of the philosophy department. It was at Chicago that Dewey received national recognition for his pioneering work in the field of education with the development of his laboratory school in which experimental approaches to teaching were explored. After a falling out with the University of Chicago over the administration of the school, Dewey left in 1904 and accepted a professorship in philosophy at Columbia University.

For the next twenty-six years, Dewey's academic position at Columbia served as a springboard for his many and varied interests— e.g., social questions, politics, education, and public affairs. His national and international reputation found him working with such groups as the American Philosophical Association, the American Association of University Professors (founder and first president), the Teacher's Union, and the American Civil Liberties Union, among others.

Unlike those who consider retirement a time to relax and enjoy the restful pleasures of later life, John Dewey dedicated his remaining years to sorting out the tough social questions facing America and the world. He joined organizations whose goal was to increase public education in the areas of domestic and international politics. One of Dewey's most famous public forums was his participation in the commission that met in Mexico City to inquire into the charges leveled against Leon Trotsky at his Moscow trial. The commission subsequently found Trotsky innocent of the charges. He was also one of several colleagues who publicly defended fellow philosopher Bertrand Russell when Russell was denied a teaching position at the City College of New York because of public criticism of his views on marriage and religion.

In developing his own unique philosophical stance, John Dewey overcame Hegelian idealism to embrace the pragmatic views of William James. Dewey's devotion to free inquiry and the scientific method found him spearheading the intellectual opposition against the belief that absolute knowledge can be attained in a world of variegated circumstances, discoveries, trailblazing research, and advances of all kinds. For Dewey, knowledge is not absolute, immutable, and eternal, but rather relative to the developmental interaction of man with his world as problems arise to present themselves for solution. This scientific approach, which allows one to declare the truth of a claim until—and only until—there is negative evidence sufficient to disconfirm the hypothesis, opens the mind to the need for a democratic approach to problem solving. Without cooperation and a rational tolerance for diverse points of view within a pluralistic community, society has no hope of mature development.

During his ninety-three years, John Dewey authored more than two dozen books and scores of articles in both scholarly and popular publications. His major works include: *School and Society* (1899), *Studies in Logical Theory* (1903), *How We Think* (1910), *Democracy and Education* (1916), *Reconstruction in Philosophy* (1920), *Human Nature and Conduct* (1922), *Experience and Nature* (1925), *The Quest for Certainty* (1929), *Art as Experience* (1934), *Liberalism and Social Action* (1935), *Logic: The Theory of Inquiry* (1938), *Experience and Education* (1938), and *Freedom and Culture* (1939). He is truly America's foremost philosopher, whose work will influence intellectuals throughout the world for many years to come.

John Dewey died in New York City on June 1, 1952.

PREFACE

In the spring of 1918 I was invited by Leland Stanford Junior University to give a series of three lectures upon the West Memorial Foundation. One of the topics included within the scope of the Foundation is Human Conduct and Destiny. This volume is the result, as, according to the terms of the Foundation, the lectures are to be published. The lectures as given have, however, been rewritten and considerably expanded. An Introduction and Conclusion have been added. The lectures should have been published within two years from delivery. Absence from the country rendered strict compliance difficult; and I am indebted to the authorities of the University for their indulgence in allowing an extension of time, as well as for so many courtesies received during the time when the lectures were given.

Perhaps the sub-title requires a word of explanation. The book does not purport to be a treatment of social psychology. But it seriously sets forth a belief that an understanding of habit and of different types of habit is the key to social psychology, while the operation of impulse and intelligence gives the key to individualized mental activity. But they are secondary to habit so that mind can be understood in the concrete only as a system of beliefs, desires and purposes which are formed in the interaction of biological aptitudes with a social environment.   **J. D.**

February, 1921.

CONTENTS

CONTENTS

INTRODUCTION

"Give a dog a bad name and hang him." Human nature has been the dog of professional moralists, and consequences accord with the proverb. Man's nature has been regarded with suspicion, with fear, with sour looks, sometimes with enthusiasm for its possibilities but only when these were placed in contrast with its actualities. It has appeared to be so evilly disposed that the business of morality was to prune and curb it; it would be thought better of if it could be replaced by something else. It has been supposed that morality would be quite superfluous were it not for the inherent weakness, bordering on depravity, of human nature. Some writers with a more genial conception have attributed the current blackening to theologians who have thought to honor the divine by disparaging the human. Theologians have doubtless taken a gloomier view of man than have pagans and secularists. But this explanation doesn't take us far. For after all these theologians are themselves human, and they would have been without influence if the human audience had not somehow responded to them.

Morality is largely concerned with controlling human nature. When we are attempting to control anything we are acutely aware of what resists us. So moralists were led, perhaps, to think of human nature as evil

1

because of its reluctance to yield to control, its rebel-
liousness under the yoke. But this explanation only
raises another question. Why did morality set up
rules so foreign to human nature? The ends it insisted
upon, the regulations it imposed, were after all outgrowths of human nature. Why then was human nature
so averse to them? Moreover rules can be obeyed and
ideals realized only as they appeal to something in human nature and awaken in it an active response. Moral
principles that exalt themselves by degrading human
nature are in effect committing suicide. Or else they
involve human nature in unending civil war, and treat
it as a hopeless mess of contradictory forces.

We are forced therefore to consider the nature and
origin of that control of human nature with which
morals has been occupied. And the fact which is forced
upon us when we raise this question is the existence
of classes. Control has been vested in an oligarchy.
Indifference to regulation has grown in the gap which
separates the ruled from the rulers. Parents, priests,
chiefs, social censors have supplied aims, aims which
were foreign to those upon whom they were imposed,
to the young, laymen, ordinary folk; a few have given
and administered rule, and the mass have in a passable
fashion and with reluctance obeyed. Everybody knows
that good children are those who make as little trouble
as possible for their elders, and since most of them
cause a good deal of annoyance they must be naughty
by nature. Generally speaking, good people have been
those who did what they were told to do, and lack of

eager compliance is a sign of something wrong in their nature.

But no matter how much men in authority have turned moral rules into an agency of class supremacy, any theory which attributes the origin of rule to deliberate design is false. To take advantage of conditions after they have come into existence is one thing; to create them for the sake of an advantage to accrue is quite another thing. We must go back of the bare fact of social division into superior and inferior. To say that accident produced social conditions is to perceive they were not produced by intelligence. Lack of understanding of human nature is the primary cause of disregard for it. Lack of insight always ends in despising or else unreasoned admiration. When men had no scientific knowledge of physical nature they either passively submitted to it or sought to control it magically. What cannot be understood cannot be managed intelligently. It has to be forced into subjection from without. The opaqueness of human nature to reason is equivalent to a belief in its intrinsic irregularity. Hence a decline in the authority of social oligarchy was accompanied by a rise of scientific interest in human nature. This means that the make-up and working of human forces afford a basis for moral ideas and ideals. Our science of human nature in comparison with physical sciences is rudimentary, and morals which are concerned with the health, efficiency and happiness of a development of human nature are correspondingly elementary. These pages are a discussion of some phases of the ethical change involved in positive respect for human nature when the latter is associated with scientific knowledge. We may anticipate the general nature of this change through considering the evils which have resulted from severing morals from the actualities of human physiology and psychology. There is a pathology of goodness as well as of evil; that is, of that sort of goodness which is nurtured by this separation. The badness of good people, for the most part recorded only in fiction, is the revenge taken by human nature for the injuries heaped upon it in the name of morality. In the first place, morals cut off from positive roots in man's nature is bound to be mainly negative. Practical emphasis falls upon avoidance, escape of evil, upon not doing things, observing prohibitions. Negative morals assume as many forms as there are types of temperament subject to it. Its commonest form is the protective coloration of a neutral respectability, an insipidity of character. For one man who thanks God that he is not as other men there are a thousand to offer thanks that they are as other men, sufficiently as others are to escape attention. Absence of social blame is the usual mark of goodness for it shows that evil has been avoided. Blame is most readily averted by being so much like everybody else that one passes unnoticed. Conventional morality is a drab morality, in which the only fatal thing is to be conspicuous. If there be flavor left in it, then some natural traits have somehow escaped being subdued. To be so good as to attract notice is to be priggish, too good for this world. The same psychology that brands the convicted criminal as forever a social outcast makes it the part of a gentleman not to obtrude virtues noticeably upon others.

The Puritan is never popular, not even in a society of Puritans. In case of a pinch, the mass prefer to be good fellows rather than to be good men. Polite vice is preferable to eccentricity and ceases to be vice. Morals that professedly neglect human nature end by emphasizing those qualities of human nature that are most commonplace and average; they exaggerate the herd instinct to conformity. Professional guardians of morality who have been exacting with respect to themselves have accepted avoidance of conspicuous evil as enough for the masses. One of the most instructive things in all human history is the system of concessions, tolerances, mitigations and reprieves which the Catholic Church with its official supernatural morality has devised for the multitude. Elevation of the spirit above everything natural is tempered by organized leniency for the frailties of flesh. To uphold an aloof realm of strictly ideal realities is admitted to be possible only for a few. Protestantism, except in its most zealous forms, has accomplished the same result by a sharp separation between religion and morality in which a higher justification by faith disposes at one stroke of daily lapses into the gregarious morals of average conduct.

There are always ruder forceful natures who cannot tame themselves to the required level of colorless conformity. To them conventional morality appears as an organized futility; though they are usually unconscious of their own attitude since they are heartily in favor of morality for the mass as making it easier to manage them. Their only standard is success, putting things over, getting things done. Being good is to them practically synonymous with ineffectuality; and accomplishment, achievement is its own justification. They know by experience that much is forgiven to those who succeed, and they leave goodness to the stupid, to those whom they qualify as boobs. Their gregarious nature finds sufficient outlet in the conspicuous tribute they pay to all established institutions as guardians of ideal interests, and in their denunciations of all who openly defy conventionalized ideals. Or they discover that they are the chosen agents of a higher morality and walk subject to specially ordained laws. Hypocrisy in the sense of a deliberate covering up of a will to evil by loud-voiced protestations of virtue is one of the rarest of occurrences. But the combination in the same person of an intensely executive nature with a love of popular approval is bound, in the face of conventional morality, to produce what the critical term hypocrisy.

Another reaction to the separation of morals from human nature is a romantic glorification of natural impulse as something superior to all moral claims. There are those who lack the persistent force of the executive will to break through conventions and to use them for their own purposes, but who unite sensitiveness with intensity of desire. Fastening upon the conventional element in morality, they hold that all morality is a conventionality hampering to the development of individuality. Although appetites are the commonest things in human nature, the least distinctive or individualized, they identify unrestraint in satisfaction of appetite with free realization of individuality. They treat subjection to passion as a manifestation of freedom in the degree in which it shocks the bourgeois. The urgent need for a transvaluation of morals is caricatured by the notion that an avoidance of the avoidances of conventional morals constitutes positive achievement. While the executive type keeps its eyes on actual conditions so as to manipulate them, this school abrogates objective intelligence in behalf of sentiment, and withdraws into little coteries of emancipated souls.

There are others who take seriously the idea of morals separated from the ordinary actualities of humanity and who attempt to live up to it. Some become engrossed in spiritual egotism. They are preoccupied with the state of their character, concerned for the purity of their motives and the goodness of their souls. The exaltation of conceit which sometimes accompanies this absorption can produce a corrosive inhumanity which exceeds the possibilities of any other known form of selfishness. In other cases, persistent preoccupation with the thought of an ideal realm breeds morbid discontent with surroundings, or induces a futile withdrawal into an inner world where all facts are fair to the eye. The needs of actual conditions are neglected, or dealt with in a half-hearted way, because in the light of the ideal they are so mean and sordid. To speak of evils, to strive seriously for change, shows a low mind. Or, again, the ideal becomes a refuge, an asylum, a way of escape from tiresome responsibilities. In varied ways men come to live in two worlds, one the actual, the other the ideal. Some are tortured by the sense of their irreconcilability. Others alternate between the two, compensating for the strains of renunciation involved in membership in the ideal realm by pleasureable excursions into the delights of the actual.

If we turn from concrete effects upon character to theoretical issues, we single out the discussion regarding freedom of will as typical of the consequences that come from separating morals from human nature. Men are wearied with bootless discussion, and anxious to dismiss it as a metaphysical subtlety. But nevertheless it contains within itself the most practical of all moral questions, the nature of freedom and the means of its achieving. The separation of morals from human nature leads to a separation of human nature in its moral aspects from the rest of nature, and from ordinary social habits and endeavors which are found in business, civic life, the run of companionships and recreations. These things are thought of at most as places where moral notions need to be applied, not as places where moral ideas are to be studied and moral energies generated. In short, the severance of morals from human nature ends by driving morals inwards from the public open out-of-doors air and light of day into the

obscurities and privacies of an inner life. The significance of the traditional discussion of free will is that
it reflects precisely a separation of moral activity from
nature and the public life of men.

One has to turn from moral theories to the general
human struggle for political, economic and religious
liberty, for freedom of thought, speech, assemblage and
creed, to find significant reality in the conception of
freedom of will. Then one finds himself out of the
stiflingly close atmosphere of an inner consciousness and
in the open-air world. The cost of confining moral
freedom to an inner region is the almost complete severance of ethics from politics and economics. The former is regarded as summed up in edifying exhortations,
and the latter as connected with arts of expediency
separated from larger issues of good.

In short, there are two schools of social reform. One
bases itself upon the notion of a morality which springs
from an inner freedom, something mysteriously cooped
up within personality. It asserts that the only way
to change institutions is for men to purify their own
hearts, and that when this has been accomplished,
change of institutions will follow of itself. The other
school denies the existence of any such inner power, and
in so doing conceives that it has denied all moral freedom. It says that men are made what they are by the
forces of the environment, that human nature is purely
malleable, and that till institutions are changed, nothing
can be done. Clearly this leaves the outcome as hopeless as does an appeal to an inner rectitude and benevo-

lence. For it provides no leverage for change of environment. It throws us back upon accident, usually disguised as a necessary law of history or evolution, and trusts to some violent change, symbolized by civil war, to usher in an abrupt millennium. There is an alternative to being penned in between these two theories. We can recognize that all conduct is *interaction* between elements of human nature and the environment, natural and social. Then we shall see that progress proceeds in two ways, and that freedom is found in that kind of interaction which maintains an environment in which human desire and choice count for something. There are in truth forces in man as well as without him. While they are infinitely frail in comparison with exterior forces, yet they may have the support of a foreseeing and contriving intelligence. When we look at the problem as one of an adjustment to be intelligently attained, the issue shifts from within personality to an engineering issue, the establishment of arts of education and social guidance.

The idea persists that there is something materialistic about natural science and that morals are degraded by having anything seriously to do with material things. If a sect should arise proclaiming that men ought to purify their lungs completely before they ever drew a breath it ought to win many adherents from professed moralists. For the neglect of sciences that deal specifically with facts of the natural and social environment leads to a side-tracking of moral forces into an unreal privacy of an unreal self. It is impossible to say how much of the remediable suffering of the world is due to the fact that physical science is looked upon as merely physical. It is impossible to say how much of the unnecessary slavery of the world is due to the conception that moral issues can be settled within conscience or human sentiment apart from consistent study of facts and application of specific knowledge in industry, law and politics. Outside of manufacturing and transportation, science gets its chance in war. These facts perpetuate war and the hardest, most brutal side of modern industry. Each sign of disregard for the moral potentialities of physical science drafts the conscience of mankind away from concern with the interactions of man and nature which must be mastered if freedom is to be a reality. It diverts intelligence to anxious preoccupation with the unrealities of a purely inner life, or strengthens reliance upon outbursts of sentimental affection. The masses swarm to the occult for assistance. The cultivated smile contemptuously. They might smile, as the saying goes, out of the other side of their mouths if they realized how recourse to the occult exhibits the practical logic of their own beliefs. For both rest upon a separation of moral ideas and feelings from knowable facts of life, man and the world.

It is not pretended that a moral theory based upon realities of human nature and a study of the specific connections of these realities with those of physical science would do away with moral struggle and defeat. It would not make the moral life as simple a matter as wending one's way along a well--lighted boulevard. All action is an invasion of the future, of the unknown. Conflict and uncertainty are ultimate traits. But morals based upon concern with facts and deriving guidance from knowledge of them would at least locate the points of effective endeavor and would focus available resources upon them. It would put an end to the impossible attempt to live in two unrelated worlds. It would destroy fixed distinction between the human and the physical, as well as that between the moral and the industrial and political. A morals based on study of human nature instead of upon disregard for it would find the facts of man continuous with those of the rest of nature and would thereby ally ethics with physics and biology. It would find the nature and activities of one person coterminous with those of other human beings, and therefore link ethics with the study of history, sociology, law and economics.

Such a morals would not automatically solve moral problems, nor resolve perplexities. But it would enable us to state problems in such forms that action could be courageously and intelligently directed to their solution. It would not assure us against failure, but it would render failure a source of instruction. It would not protect us against the future emergence of equally serious moral difficulties, but it would enable us to approach the always recurring troubles with a fund of growing knowledge which would add significant values to our conduct even when we overtly failed—as we should continue to do. Until the integrity of morals with human nature and of both with the environment is recognized, we shall be deprived of the aid of past experience to cope with the most acute and deep problems of life. Accurate and extensive knowledge will continue to operate only in dealing with purely technical problems. The intelligent acknowledgment of the continuity of nature, man and society will alone secure a growth of morals which will be serious without being fanatical, aspiring without sentimentality, adapted to reality without conventionality, sensible without taking the form of calculation of profits, idealistic without being romantic.

PART ONE

I

HABITS may be profitably compared to physiological functions, like breathing, digesting. The latter are, to be sure, involuntary, while habits are acquired. But important as is this difference for many purposes it should not conceal the fact that habits are like functions in many respects, and especially in requiring the cooperation of organism and environment. Breathing is an affair of the air as truly as of the lungs; digesting an affair of food as truly as of tissues of stomach. Seeing involves light just as certainly as it does the eye and optic nerve. Walking implicates the ground as well as the legs; speech demands physical air and human companionship and audience as well as vocal organs. We may shift from the biological to the mathematical use of the word function, and say that natural operations like breathing and digesting, acquired ones like speech and honesty, are functions of the surroundings as truly as of a person. They are things done *by* the environment by means of organic structures or acquired dispositions. The same air that under certain conditions ruffles the pool or wrecks buildings,

14

under other conditions purifies the blood and conveys thought. The outcome depends upon what air acts upon. The social environment acts through native impulses and speech and moral habitudes manifest themselves. There are specific good reasons for the usual attribution of acts to the person from whom they immediately proceed. But to convert this special reference into a belief of exclusive ownership is as misleading as to suppose that breathing and digesting are complete within the human body. To get a rational basis for moral discussion we must begin with recognizing that functions and habits are ways of using and incorporating the environment in which the latter has its say as surely as the former.

We may borrow words from a context less technical than that of biology, and convey the same idea by saying that habits are arts. They involve skill of sensory and motor organs, cunning or craft, and objective materials. They assimilate objective energies, and eventuate in command of environment. They require order, discipline, and manifest technique. They have a beginning, middle and end. Each stage marks progress in dealing with materials and tools, advance in converting material to active use. We should laugh at any one who said that he was master of stone working, but that the art was cooped up within himself and in no wise dependent upon support from objects and assistance from tools.

In morals we are however quite accustomed to such a fatuity. Moral dispositions are thought of as belonging exclusively to a self. The self is thereby isolated from natural and social surroundings. A whole school of morals flourishes upon capital drawn from restricting morals to character and then separating character from conduct, motives from actual deeds. Recognition of the analogy of moral action with functions and arts uproots the causes which have made morals subjective and " individualistic." It brings morals to earth, and if they still aspire to heaven it is to the heavens *of* the earth, and not to another world. Honesty, chastity, malice, peevishness, courage, triviality, industry, irresponsibility are not private possessions of a person. They are working adaptations of personal capacities with environing forces. All virtues and vices are habits which incorporate objective forces. They are interactions of elements contributed by the make-up of an individual with elements supplied by the out-door world. They can be studied as objectively as physiological functions, and they can be modified by change of either personal or social elements.

If an individual were alone in the world, he would form his habits (assuming the impossible, namely, that he would be able to form them) in a moral vacuum. They would belong to him alone, or to him only in reference to physical forces. Responsibility and virtue would be his alone. But since habits involve the support of environing conditions, a society or some specific group of fellow-men, is always accessory before and after the fact. Some activity proceeds from a man; then it sets up reactions in the surroundings. Others

approve, disapprove, protest, encourage, share and resist.   Even letting a man alone is a definite response.
Envy, admiration and imitation are complicities.   Neu-
trality is non-existent.   Conduct is always shared; this
is the difference between it and a physiological process.
It is not an ethical " ought " that conduct *should* be
social.   It *is* social, whether bad or good.

Washing one's hands of the guilt of others is a way
of sharing guilt so far as it encourages in others a
vicious way of action.   Non-resistance to evil which
takes the form of paying no attention to it is a way
of promoting it.   The desire of an individual to keep
his own conscience stainless by standing aloof from
badness may be a sure means of causing evil and thus
of creating personal responsibility for it.   Yet there are
circumstances in which passive resistance may be the
most effective form of nullification of wrong action,
or in which heaping coals of fire on the evil-doer may
be the most effective way of transforming conduct.   To
sentimentalize over a criminal—to " forgive " because
of a glow of feeling—is to incur liability for production
of criminals.   But to suppose that infliction of retribu-
tive suffering suffices, without reference to concrete
consequences, is to leave untouched old causes of criminality and to create new ones by fostering revenge and
brutality.   The abstract theory of justice which demands the " vindication " of law irrespective of instruction and reform of the wrong-doer is as much a
refusal to recognize responsibility as is the sentimental
gush which makes a suffering victim out of a criminal.

Courses of action which put the blame exclusively on a person as if his evil will were the sole cause of wrong-doing and those which condone offense on account of the share of social conditions in producing bad disposition, are equally ways of making an unreal separation of man from his surroundings, mind from the world. Causes for an act always exist, but causes are not excuses. Questions of causation are physical, not moral except when they concern future consequences. It is as causes of future actions that excuses and accusations alike must be considered. At present we give way to resentful passion, and then " rationalize " our surrender by calling it a vindication of justice. Our entire tradition regarding punitive justice tends to prevent recognition of social partnership in producing crime; it falls in with a belief in metaphysical free-will. By killing an evil-doer or shutting him up behind stone walls, we are enabled to forget both him and our part in creating him. Society excuses itself by laying the blame on the criminal; he retorts by putting the blame on bad early surroundings, the temptations of others, lack of opportunities, and the persecutions of officers of the law. Both are right, except in the wholesale character of their recriminations. But the effect on both sides is to throw the whole matter back into antecedent causation, a method which refuses to bring the matter to truly moral judgment. For morals has to do with acts still within our control, acts still to be performed. No amount of guilt on the part of the evil-doer absolves us from responsibility for the consequences upon him and others of our way of treating him, or from our continuing responsibility for the conditions under which persons develop perverse habits.

We need to discriminate between the physical and the moral question. The former concerns what *has* happened, and how it happened. To consider this question is indispensable to morals. Without an answer to it we cannot tell what forces are at work nor how to direct our actions so as to improve conditions. Until we know the conditions which have helped form the characters we approve and disapprove, our efforts to create the one and do away with the other will be blind and halting. But the moral issue concerns the future. It is prospective. To content ourselves with pronouncing judgments of merit and demerit without reference to the fact that our judgments are themselves facts which have consequences and that their value depends upon *their* consequences, is complacently to dodge the moral issue, perhaps even to indulge ourselves in pleasurable passion just as the person we condemn once indulged himself. The moral problem is that of modifying the factors which now influence future results. To change the working character or will of another we have to alter objective conditions which enter into his habits. Our own schemes of judgment, of assigning blame and praise, of awarding punishment and honor, are part of these conditions.

In practical life, there are many recognitions of the

part played by social factors in generating personal
traits. One of them is our habit of making social
classifications. We attribute distinctive characteristics
to rich and poor, slum-dweller and captain of industry,
rustic and suburbanite, officials, politicians, professors,
to members of races, sets and parties. These judgments are usually too coarse to be of much use. But
they show our practical awareness that personal traits
are functions of social situations. When we generalize
this perception and act upon it intelligently we are
committed by it to recognize that we change character
from worse to better only by changing conditions—
among which, once more, are our own ways of dealing
with the one we judge. We cannot change habit directly: that notion is magic. But we can change it
indirectly by modifying conditions, by an intelligent
selecting and weighting of the objects which engage
attention and which influence the fulfilment of desires.

A savage can travel after a fashion in a jungle.
Civilized activity is too complex to be carried on without smoothed roads. It requires signals and junction
points; traffic authorities and means of easy and rapid
transportation. It demands a congenial, antecedently
prepared environment. Without it, civilization would
relapse into barbarism in spite of the best of subjective
intention and internal good disposition. The eternal
dignity of labor and art lies in their effecting that permanent reshaping of environment which is the substantial foundation of future security and progress. In-

dividuals flourish and wither away like the grass of the fields. But the fruits of their work endure and make possible the development of further activities having fuller significance. It is of grace not of ourselves that we lead civilized lives. There is sound sense in the old pagan notion that gratitude is the root of all virtue. Loyalty to whatever in the established environment makes a life of excellence possible is the beginning of all progress. The best we can accomplish for posterity is to transmit unimpaired and with some increment of meaning the environment that makes it possible to maintain the habits of decent and refined life. Our individual habits are links in forming the endless chain of humanity. Their significance depends upon the environment inherited from our forerunners, and it is enhanced as we foresee the fruits of our labors in the world in which our successors live.

For however much has been done, there always remains more to do. We can retain and transmit our own heritage only by constant remaking of our own environment. Piety to the past is not for its own sake nor for the sake of the past, but for the sake of a present so secure and enriched that it will create a yet better future. Individuals with their exhortations, their preachings and scoldings, their inner aspirations and sentiments have disappeared, but their habits endure, because these habits incorporate objective conditions in themselves. So will it be with *our* activities. We may desire abolition of war, industrial justice, greater equality of opportunity for all. But no amount of preaching good will or the golden rule or cultivation of sentiments of love and equity will accomplish the results. There must be change in objective arrangements and institutions. We must work on the environment not merely on the hearts of men. To think otherwise is to suppose that flowers can be raised in a desert or motor cars run in a jungle. Both things can happen and without a miracle. But only by first changing the jungle and desert.

Yet the distinctively personal or subjective factors in habit count. Taste for flowers may be the initial step in building reservoirs and irrigation canals. The stimulation of desire and effort is one preliminary in the change of surroundings. While personal exhortation, advice and instruction is a feeble stimulus compared with that which steadily proceeds from the impersonal forces and depersonalized habitudes of the environment, yet they may start the latter going. Taste, appreciation and effort always spring from some accomplished objective situation. They have objective support; they represent the liberation of something formerly accomplished so that it is useful in further operation. A genuine appreciation of the beauty of flowers is not generated within a self-enclosed consciousness. It reflects a world in which beautiful flowers have already grown and been enjoyed. Taste and desire represent a prior objective fact recurring in action to secure perpetuation and extension. Desire for flowers comes after actual enjoyment of flowers. But it comes before the work that makes the desert blossom, it comes before *cultivation* of plants.   Every ideal is preceded by an actuality; but the ideal is more than a repetition in inner image of the actual.   It projects in securer and wider and fuller form some good which has been previously experienced in a precarious, accidental, fleeting way.

II

It is a significant fact that in order to appreciate the peculiar place of habit in activity we have to betake ourselves to bad habits, foolish idling, gambling, addiction to liquor and drugs. When we think of such habits, the union of habit with desire and with propulsive power is forced upon us. When we think of habits in terms of walking, playing a musical instrument, typewriting, we are much given to thinking of habits as technical abilities existing apart from our likings and as lacking in urgent impulsion. We think of them as passive tools waiting to be called into action from without. A bad habit suggests an inherent tendency to action and also a hold, command over us. It makes us do things we are ashamed of, things which we tell ourselves we prefer not to do. It overrides our formal resolutions, our conscious decisions. When we are honest with ourselves we acknowledge that a habit has this power because it is so intimately a part of ourselves. It has a hold upon us because we are the habit.

Our self-love, our refusal to face facts, combined perhaps with a sense of a possible better although unrealized self, leads us to eject the habit from the thought of ourselves and conceive it as an evil power which has somehow overcome us. We feed our conceit by recalling that the habit was not deliberately formed; we never intended to become idlers or gamblers or roués.

24

And how can anything be deeply ourselves which developed accidentally, without set intention? These traits of a bad habit are precisely the things which are most instructive about all habits and about ourselves. They teach us that all habits are affections, that all have projectile power, and that a predisposition formed by a number of specific acts is an immensely more intimate and fundamental part of ourselves than are vague, general, conscious choices. All habits are demands for certain kinds of activity; and they constitute the self. In any intelligible sense of the word will, they *are* will. They form our effective desires and they furnish us with our working capacities. They rule our thoughts, determining which shall appear and be strong and which shall pass from light into obscurity.

We may think of habits as means, waiting, like tools in a box, to be used by conscious resolve. But they are something more than that. They are active means, means that project themselves, energetic and dominating ways of acting. We need to distinguish between materials, tools and means proper. Nails and boards are not strictly speaking means of a box. They are only materials for making it. Even the saw and hammer are means only when they are employed in some actual making. Otherwise they are tools, or potential means. They are actual means only when brought in conjunction with eye, arm and hand in some specific operation. And eye, arm and hand are, correspondingly, means proper only when they are in active operation. And whenever they are in action they are cooperating with external materials and energies. Without support from beyond themselves the eye stares blankly and the hand moves fumblingly. They are means only when they enter into organization with things which independently accomplish definite results. These organizations are habits.

This fact cuts two ways. Except in a contingent sense, with an " if," neither external materials nor bodily and mental organs are in themselves means. They have to be employed in coordinated conjunction with one another to be actual means, or habits. This statement may seem like the formulation in technical language of a common-place. But belief in magic has played a large part in human history. And the essence of all hocus-pocus is the supposition that results can be accomplished without the joint adaptation to each other of human powers and physical conditions. A desire for rain may induce men to wave willow branches and to sprinkle water. The reaction is natural and innocent. But men then go on to believe that their act has immediate power to bring rain without the cooperation of intermediate conditions of nature. This is magic; while it may be natural or spontaneous, it is not innocent. It obstructs intelligent study of operative conditions and wastes human desire and effort in futilities.

Belief in magic did not cease when the coarser forms of superstitious practice ceased. The principle of magic is found whenever it is hoped to get results without intelligent control of means; and also when it is supposed that means can exist and yet remain inert and inoperative. In morals and politics such expectations still prevail, and in so far the most important phases of human action are still affected by magic. We think that by feeling strongly enough about something, by wishing hard enough, we can get a desirable result, such as virtuous execution of a good resolve, or peace among nations, or good will in industry. We slur over the necessity of the cooperative action of objective conditions, and the fact that this cooperation is assured only by persistent and close study. Or, on the other hand, we fancy we can get these results by external machinery, by tools or potential means, without a corresponding functioning of human desires and capacities. Often times these two false and contradictory beliefs are combined in the same person. The man who feels that *his* virtues are his own personal accomplishments is likely to be also the one who thinks that by passing laws he can throw the fear of God into others and make them virtuous by edict and prohibitory mandate.

Recently a friend remarked to me that there was one superstition current among even cultivated persons. They suppose that if one is told what to do, if the right *end* is pointed to them, all that is required in order to bring about the right act is will or wish on the part of the one who is to act. He used as an illustration the matter of physical posture; the assumption is that if a man is told to stand up straight, all that is further needed is wish and effort on his part, and the deed is done. He pointed out that this belief is on a par with primitive magic in its neglect of attention to the means which are involved in reaching an end. And he went on to say that the prevalence of this belief, starting with false notions about the control of the body and extending to control of mind and character, is the greatest bar to intelligent social progress. It bars the way because it makes us neglect intelligent inquiry to discover the means which will produce a desired result, and intelligent invention to procure the means. In short, it leaves out the importance of intelligently controlled habit.

We may cite his illustration of the real nature of a physical aim or order and its execution in its contrast with the current false notion.* A man who has a bad habitual posture tells himself, or is told, to stand up straight. If he is interested and responds, he braces himself, goes through certain movements, and it is assumed that the desired result is substantially attained; and that the position is retained at least as long as the man keeps the idea or order in his mind. Consider the assumptions which are here made. It is implied that the means or effective conditions of the realization of a purpose exist independently of established habit and even that they may be set in motion in opposition to habit. It is assumed that means are there, so that the failure to stand erect is wholly a matter of failure of purpose and desire. It needs paralysis or

* I refer to Alexander, "Man's Supreme Inheritance."

a broken leg or some other equally gross phenomenon to make us appreciate the importance of objective conditions.

Now in fact a man who *can* stand properly does so, and only a man who can, does. In the former case, fiats of will are unnecessary, and in the latter useless. A man who does not stand properly forms a habit of standing improperly, a positive, forceful habit. The common implication that his mistake is merely negative, that he is simply failing to do the right thing, and that the failure can be made good by an order of will is absurd. One might as well suppose that the man who is a slave of whiskey-drinking is merely one who fails to drink water. Conditions have been formed for producing a bad result, and the bad result will occur as long as those conditions exist. They can no more be dismissed by a direct effort of will than the conditions which create drought can be dispelled by whistling for wind. It is as reasonable to expect a fire to go out when it is ordered to stop burning as to suppose that a man can stand straight in consequence of a direct action of thought and desire. The fire can be put out only by changing objective conditions; it is the same with rectification of bad posture.

Of course something happens when a man acts upon his idea of standing straight. For a little while, he stands differently, but only a different kind of badly. He then takes the unaccustomed feeling which accompanies his unusual stand as evidence that he is now standing right. But there are many ways of standing badly, and he has simply shifted his usual way to a compensatory bad way at some opposite extreme. When we realize this fact, we are likely to suppose that it exists because control of the *body* is physical and hence is external to mind and will. Transfer the command inside character and mind, and it is fancied that an idea of an end and the desire to realize it will take immediate effect. After we get to the point of recognizing that habits must intervene between wish and execution in the case of bodily acts, we still cherish the illusion that they can be dispensed with in the case of mental and moral acts. Thus the net result is to make us sharpen the distinction between non-moral and moral activities, and to lead us to confine the latter strictly within a private, immaterial realm. But in fact, formation of ideas as well as their execution depends upon habit. *If* we could form a correct idea without a correct habit, then possibly we could carry it out irrespective of habit. But a wish gets definite form only in connection with an idea, and an idea gets shape and consistency only when it has a habit back of it. Only when a man can already perform an act of standing straight does he know what it is like to have a right posture and only then can he summon the idea required for proper execution. The act must come before the thought, and a habit before an ability to evoke the thought at will. Ordinary psychology reverses the actual state of affairs.

Ideas, thoughts of ends, are not spontaneously generated. There is no immaculate conception of meanings or purposes. Reason pure of all influence from prior habit is a fiction. But pure sensations out of which ideas can be framed apart from habit are equally fictitious. The sensations and ideas which are the " stuff " of thought and purpose are alike affected by habits manifested in the acts which give rise to sensations and meanings. The dependence of thought, or the more intellectual factor in our conceptions, upon prior experience is usually admitted. But those who attack the notion of thought pure from the influence of experience, usually identify experience with sensations impressed upon an empty mind. They therefore replace the theory of unmixed thoughts with that of pure unmixed sensations as the stuff of all conceptions, purposes and beliefs. But distinct and independent sensory qualities, far from being original elements, are the products of a highly skilled analysis which disposes of immense technical scientific resources. To be able to single out a definitive sensory element in any field is evidence of a high degree of previous training, that is, of well-formed habits. A moderate amount of observation of a child will suffice to reveal that even such gross discriminations as black, white, red, green, are the result of some years of active dealings with things in the course of which habits have been set up. It is not such a simple matter to have a clear-cut sensation. The latter is a sign of training, skill, habit.

Admission that the idea of, say, standing erect is dependent upon sensory materials is, therefore equivalent to recognition that it is dependent upon the habitual attitudes which govern concrete sensory materials. The medium of habit filters all the material that reaches our perception and thought. The filter is not, however, chemically pure. It is a reagent which adds new qualities and rearranges what is received. Our ideas truly depend upon experience, but so do our sensations. And the experience upon which they both depend is the operation of habits—originally of instincts. Thus our purposes and commands regarding action (whether physical or moral) come to us through the refracting medium of bodily and moral habits. Inability to think aright is sufficiently striking to have caught the attention of moralists. But a false psychology has led them to interpret it as due to a necessary conflict of flesh and spirit, not as an indication that our ideas are as dependent, to say the least, upon our habits as are our acts upon our conscious thoughts and purposes.

Only the man who can maintain a correct posture has the stuff out of which to form that idea of standing erect which can be the starting point of a right act. Only the man whose habits are already good can know what the good is. Immediate, seemingly instinctive, feeling of the direction and end of various lines of behavior is in reality the feeling of habits working below direct consciousness. The psychology of illusions of perception is full of illustrations of the distortion introduced by habit into observation of objects. The same fact accounts for the intuitive element in judgments of action, an element which is valuable or the reverse in accord with the quality of dominant habits. For, as Aristotle remarked, the untutored moral perceptions of a good man are usually trustworthy, those of a bad character, not. (But he should have added that the influence of social custom as well as personal habit has to be taken into account in estimating who is the good man and the good judge.)

What is true of the dependence of execution of an idea upon habit is true, then, of the formation and quality of the idea. Suppose that by a happy chance a right concrete idea or purpose—concrete, not simply correct in words—has been hit upon: What happens when one with an incorrect habit tries to act in accord with it? Clearly the idea can be carried into execution only with a mechanism already there. If this is defective or perverted, the best intention in the world will yield bad results. In the case of no other engine does one suppose that a defective machine will turn out good goods simply because it is invited to. Everywhere else we recognize that the design and structure of the agency employed tell directly upon the work done. Given a bad habit and the " will " or mental direction to get a good result, and the actual happening is a reverse or looking-glass manifestation of the usual fault—a compensatory twist in the opposite direction. Refusal to recognize this fact only leads to a separation of mind from body, and to supposing that mental or " psychical " mechanisms are different in kind from those of bodily operations and independent of them. So deep seated is this notion that even so " scientific " a theory as modern psycho-analysis thinks that mental habits can be straightened out by some kind of purely psychical manipulation without reference to the distortions of sensation and perception which are due to bad bodily sets. The other side of the error is found in the notion of " scientific " nerve physiologists that it is only necessary to locate a particular diseased cell or local lesion, independent of the whole complex of organic habits, in order to rectify conduct.

Means are means; they are intermediates, middle terms. To grasp this fact is to have done with the ordinary dualism of means and ends. The " end " is merely a series of acts viewed at a remote stage; and a means is merely the series viewed at an earlier one. The distinction of means and end arises in surveying the *course* of a proposed *line* of action, a connected series in time. The " end " is the last act thought of; the means are the acts to be performed prior to it in time. To *reach* an end we must take our mind off from it and attend to the act which is next to be performed. We must make that the end. The only exception to this statement is in cases where customary habit determines the course of the series. Then all that is wanted is a cue to set it off. But when the proposed end involves any deviation from usual action, or any rectification of it—as in the case of standing straight— then the main thing is to find some act which is different from the usual one. The discovery and performance of this unaccustomed act is the " end " to which we must devote all attention. Otherwise we shall simply do the old thing over again, no matter what is our conscious command. The only way of accomplishing this discovery is through a flank movement. We must stop even thinking of standing up straight. To think of it is fatal, for it commits us to the operation of an established habit of standing wrong. We must find an act within our power which is disconnected from any thought about standing. We must start to do another thing which on one side inhibits our falling into the customary bad position and on the other side is the beginning of a series of acts which may lead into the correct posture.* The hard-drinker who keeps thinking of not drinking is doing what he can to initiate the acts which lead to drinking. He is starting with the stimulus to his habit. To succeed he must find some positive interest or line of action which will inhibit the drinking series and which by instituting another course of action will bring him to his desired end. In short, the man's true aim is to discover some course of action, having nothing to do with the habit of drink or standing erect, which will take him where he wants to go. The discovery of this other series is at once his means and his end. Until one takes intermediate acts seriously enough to treat them as ends, one wastes one's time in any effort at change of habits. Of the intermediate acts, the most important is the *next* one. The first or earliest means is the most important *end* to discover.

* The technique of this process is stated in the book of Mr. Alexander already referred to, and the theoretical statement given is borrowed from Mr. Alexander's analysis.

Means and ends are two names for the same reality. The terms denote not a division in reality but a distinction in judgment. Without understanding this fact we cannot understand the nature of habits nor can we pass beyond the usual separation of the moral and non-moral in conduct. " End " is a name for a series of acts taken collectively—like the term army. " Means " is a name for the same series taken distributively—like this soldier, that officer. To think of the end signifies to extend and enlarge our view of the act to be performed. It means to look at the next act in perspective, not permitting it to occupy the entire field of vision. To bear the end in mind signifies that we should not stop thinking about our *next* act until we form some reasonably clear idea of the *course* of action to which it commits us. To attain a remote end means on the other hand to treat the end as a series of means. To say that an end is remote or distant, to say in fact that it is an end at all, is equivalent to saying that obstacles intervene between us and it. If, however, it remains a distant end, it becomes a *mere* end, that is a dream. As soon as we have projected it, we must begin to work backward in thought. We must change *what* is to be done into a *how*, the means whereby. The end thus re-appears as a series of " what nexts," and the what next of chief importance is the one nearest the present state of the one acting. Only as the end is converted into means is it definitely conceived, or intellectually defined, to say nothing of being executable. Just as end, it is vague, cloudy, impressionistic. We

do not *know* what we are really after until a *course* of
action is mentally worked out. Aladdin with his lamp
could dispense with translating ends into means, but no
one else can do so.

Now the thing which is closest to us, the means
within our power, is a habit. Some habit impeded by
circumstances is the source of the projection of the end.
It is also the primary means in its realization. The
habit is propulsive and moves anyway toward some end,
or result, whether it is projected as an end-in-view or
not. The man who can walk does walk; the man who
can talk does converse—if only with himself. How is
this statement to be reconciled with the fact that we
are not always walking and talking; that our habits
seem so often to be latent, inoperative? Such inactivity
holds only of *overt*, visibly obvious operation. In
actuality each habit operates all the time of waking
life; though like a member of a crew taking his turn
at the wheel, its operation becomes the dominantly
characteristic trait of an act only occasionally or
rarely.

The habit of walking is expressed in what a man
sees when he keeps still, even in dreams. The recognition of distances and directions of things from his
place at rest is the obvious proof of this statement.
The habit of locomotion is latent in the sense that it is
covered up, counteracted, by a habit of seeing which is
definitely at the fore. But counteraction is not suppression. Locomotion is a potential energy, not in
any metaphysical sense, but in the physical sense in

which potential energy as well as kinetic has to be taken account of in any scientific description. Everything that a man who has the habit of locomotion does and thinks he does and thinks differently on that account. This fact is recognized in current psychology, but is falsified into an association of sensations. Were it not for the continued operation of all habits in every act, no such thing as character could exist. There would be simply a bundle, an untied bundle at that, of isolated acts. Character is the interpenetration of habits. If each habit existed in an insulated compartment and operated without affecting or being affected by others, character would not exist. That is, conduct would lack unity being only a juxtaposition of disconnected reactions to separated situations. But since environments overlap, since situations are continuous and those remote from one another contain like elements, a continuous modification of habits by one another is constantly going on. A man may give himself away in a look or a gesture. Character can be read through the medium of individual acts.

Of course interpenetration is never total. It is most marked in what we call strong characters. Integration is an achievement rather than a datum. A weak, unstable, vacillating character is one in which different habits alternate with one another rather than embody one another. The strength, solidity of a habit is not its own possession but is due to reinforcement by the force of other habits which it absorbs into itself. Routine specialization always works against interpene-

tration. Men with "pigeon-hole" minds are not infrequent. Their diverse standards and methods of
judgment for scientific, religious, political matters testify to isolated compartmental habits of action. Character that is unable to undergo successfully the strain
of thought and effort required to bring competing
tendencies into a unity, builds up barriers between
different systems of likes and dislikes. The emotional
stress incident to conflict is avoided not by readjustment but by effort at confinement. Yet the exception
proves the rule. Such persons are successful in keeping
different ways of reacting apart from one another in
consciousness rather than in action. Their character
is marked by stigmata resulting from this division.

The mutual modification of habits by one another
enables us to define the nature of the moral situation.
It is not necessary nor advisable to be always considering the interaction of habits with one another, that
is to say the effect of a particular habit upon character—which is a name for the total interaction. Such
consideration distracts attention from the problem of
building up an effective habit. A man who is learning
French, or chess-playing or engineering has his hands
full with his particular occupation. He would be confused and hampered by constant inquiry into its effect
upon character. He would resemble the centipede who
by trying to think of the movement of each leg in relation to all the others was rendered unable to travel.
At any given time, certain habits must be taken for
granted as a matter of course. Their operation is not

a matter of moral judgment. They are treated as technical, recreational, professional, hygienic or economic or esthetic rather than moral. To lug in morals, or ulterior effect on character at every point, is to cultivate moral valetudinarianism or priggish posing. Nevertheless any act, even that one which passes ordinarily as trivial, may entail such consequences for habit and character as upon occasion to require judgment from the standpoint of the whole body of conduct. It then comes under moral scrutiny. To know when to leave acts without distinctive moral judgment and when to subject them to it is itself a large factor in morality. The serious matter is that this relative pragmatic, or intellectual, distinction between the moral and non-moral, has been solidified into a fixed and absolute distinction, so that some acts are popularly regarded as forever within and others forever without the moral domain. From this fatal error recognition of the relations of one habit to others preserves us. For it makes us see that character is the name given to the working interaction of habits, and that the cumulative effect of insensible modifications worked by a particular habit in the body of preferences may at any moment require attention.

The word habit may seem twisted somewhat from its customary use when employed as we have been using it. But we need a word to express that kind of human activity which is influenced by prior activity and in that sense acquired; which contains within itself a certain ordering or systematization of minor elements of action; which is projective, dynamic in quality, ready for overt manifestation; and which is operative in some subdued subordinate form even when not obviously dominating activity. Habit even in its ordinary usage comes nearer to denoting these facts than any other word. If the facts are recognized we may also use the words attitude and disposition. But unless we have first made clear to ourselves the facts which have been set forth under the name of habit, these words are more likely to be misleading than is the word habit. For the latter conveys explicitly the sense of operativeness, actuality. Attitude and, as ordinarily used, disposition suggest something latent, potential, something which requires a positive stimulus outside themselves to become active. If we perceive that they denote positive forms of action which are released merely through removal of some-counteracting "inhibitory" tendency, and then become overt, we may employ them instead of the word habit to denote subdued, non-patent forms of the latter.

In this case, we must bear in mind that the word disposition means predisposition, readiness to act overtly in a specific fashion whenever opportunity is presented, this opportunity consisting in removal of the pressure due to the dominance of some overt habit; and that attitude means some special case of a predisposition, the disposition waiting as it were to spring through an opened door. While it is admitted that the word habit has been used in a somewhat broader sense than is usual, we must protest against the tendency in psychological literature to limit its meaning to repetition. This usage is much less in accord with popular usage than is the wider way in which we have used the word. It assumes from the start the identity of habit with routine. Repetition is in no sense the essence of habit. Tendency to repeat acts is an incident of many habits but not of all. A man with the habit of giving way to anger may show his habit by a murderous attack upon some one who has offended. His act is nonetheless due to habit because it occurs only once in his life. The essence of habit is an acquired predisposition to *ways* or modes of response, not to particular acts except as, under special conditions, these express a way of behaving. Habit means special sensitiveness or accessibility to certain classes of stimuli, standing predilections and aversions, rather than bare recurrence of specific acts. It means will.

III

The dynamic force of habit taken in connection with the continuity of habits with one another explains the unity of character and conduct, or speaking more concretely of motive and act, will and deed. Moral theories have frequently separated these things from each other. One type of theory, for example, has asserted that only will, disposition, motive counts morally; that acts are external, physical, accidental; that moral good is different from goodness in act since the latter is measured by consequences, while moral good or virtue is intrinsic, complete in itself, a jewel shining by its own light—a somewhat dangerous metaphor however. The other type of theory has asserted that such a view is equivalent to saying that all that is necessary to be virtuous is to cultivate states of feeling; that a premium is put on disregard of the actual consequences of conduct, and agents are deprived of any objective criterion for the rightness and wrongness of acts, being thrown back on their own whims, prejudices and private peculiarities. Like most opposite extremes in philosophic theories, the two theories suffer from a common mistake. Both of them ignore the projective force of habit and the implication of habits in one another. Hence they separate a unified deed into two disjoined parts, an inner called motive and an outer called act.

The doctrine that the chief good of man is good will easily wins acceptance from honest men. For common-sense employs a juster psychology than either of the theories just mentioned. By will, common-sense understands something practical and moving. It understands the body of habits, of active dispositions which makes a man do what he does. Will is thus not something opposed to consequences or severed from them. It is a *cause* of consequences; it is causation in its personal aspect, the aspect immediately preceding action. It hardly seems conceivable to practical sense that by will is meant something which can be complete without reference to deeds prompted and results occasioned. Even the sophisticated specialist cannot prevent relapses from such an absurdity back into common-sense. Kant, who went the limit in excluding consequences from moral value, was sane enough to maintain that a society of men of good will would be a society which in fact would maintain social peace, freedom and cooperation. We take the will for the deed not as a substitute for doing, or a form of doing nothing, but in the sense that, other things being equal, the right disposition will produce the right deed. For a disposition means a tendency to act, a potential energy needing only opportunity to become kinetic and overt. Apart from such tendency a " virtuous " disposition is either hypocrisy or self-deceit.

Common-sense in short never loses sight wholly of the two facts which limit and define a moral situation. One is that consequences fix the moral quality of an act. The other is that upon the whole, or in the long run but not unqualifiedly, consequences are what they are because of the nature of desire and disposition. Hence there is a natural contempt for the morality of the " good " man who does not show his goodness in the results of his habitual acts. But there is also an aversion to attributing omnipotence to even the best of good dispositions, and hence an aversion to applying the criterion of consequences unreservedly. A holiness of character which is celebrated only on holy-days is unreal. A virtue of honesty, or chastity or benevolence which lives upon itself apart from definite results consumes itself and goes up in smoke. The separation of motive from motive-force in action accounts both for the morbidities and futilities of the professionally good, and for the more or less subconscious contempt for morality entertained by men of a strong executive habit with their preference for " getting things done."

Yet there is justification for the common assumption that deeds cannot be judged properly without taking their animating disposition as well as their concrete consequences into account. The reason, however, lies not in isolation of disposition from consequences, but in the need for viewing consequences broadly. *This* act is only one of a multitude of acts. If we confine ourselves to the consequences of this one act we shall come out with a poor reckoning. Disposition is habitual, persistent. It shows itself therefore in many acts and in many consequences. Only as we keep a running account, can we judge disposition, disentangling its tendency from accidental accompaniments. When once we have got a fair idea of its tendency, we are able to place the particular consequences of a single act in a wider context of continuing consequences. Thus we protect ourselves from taking as trivial a habit which is serious, and from exaggerating into momentousness an act which, viewed in the light of aggregate consequences, is innocent. There is no need to abandon common-sense which tells us in judging acts first to inquire into disposition; but there is great need that the estimate of disposition be enlightened by a scientific psychology. Our legal procedure, for example, wobbles between a too tender treatment of criminality and a viciously drastic treatment of it. The vacillation can be remedied only as we can analyze an act in the light of habits, and analyze habits in the light of education, environment and prior acts. The dawn of truly scientific criminal law will come when each individual case is approached with something corresponding to the complete clinical record which every competent physician attempts to procure as a matter of course in dealing with his subjects.

Consequences include effects upon character, upon confirming and weakening habits, as well as tangibly obvious results. To keep an eye open to these effects upon character may signify the most reasonable of precautions or one of the most nauseating of practices. It may mean concentration of attention upon personal rectitude in neglect of objective consequences, a practice which creates a wholly unreal rectitude. But it may mean that the survey of objective consequences is duly extended in time. An act of gambling may be judged, for example, by its immediate overt effects, consumption of time, energy, disturbance of ordinary monetary considerations, etc. It may also be judged by its consequences upon character, setting up an enduring love of excitement, a persistent temper of speculation, and a persistent disregard of sober, steady work. To take the latter effects into account is equivalent to taking a broad view of future consequences; for these dispositions affect future companionships, vocation and avocations, the whole tenor of domestic and public life.

For similar reasons, while common-sense does not run into that sharp opposition of virtues or moral goods and natural goods which has played such a large part in professed moralities, it does not insist upon an exact identity of the two. Virtues are ends because they are such important means. To be honest, courageous, kindly is to be in the way of producing specific natural goods or satisfactory fulfilments. Error comes into theories when the moral goods are separated from their consequences and also when the attempt is made to secure an exhaustive and unerring identification of the two. There is a reason, valid as far as it goes, for distinguishing virtue as a moral good resident in character alone, from objective consequences. As matter of fact, a desirable trait of character does not always produce desirable results while good things often happen with no assistance from good will. Luck, accident, contingency, plays its part. The act of a good character is deflected in operation, while a monomaniacal egotism may employ a desire for glory and power to perform acts which satisfy crying social needs. Reflection shows that we must supplement the conviction of the moral connection betweeen character or habit and consequences by two considerations.

One is the fact that we are inclined to take the notions of goodness in character and goodness in results in too fixed a way. Persistent disparity between virtuous disposition and actual outcome shows that we have misjudged either the nature of virtue or of success. Judgments of both motive and consequences are still, in the absence of methods of scientific analysis and continuous registration and reporting, rudimentary and conventional. We are inclined to wholesale judgments of character, dividing men into goats and sheep, instead of recognizing that all character is speckled, and that the problem of moral judgment is one of discriminating the complex of acts and habits into tendencies which are to be *specifically* cultivated and condemned. We need to study consequences more thoroughly and keep track of them more continuously before we shall be in a position where we can pass with reasonable assurance upon the good and evil in either disposition or results. But even when proper allowances are made, we are forcing the pace when we assume that there is or ever can be an exact equation of disposition and outcome. We have to admit the rôle of accident.

We cannot get beyond tendencies, and must perforce

content ourselves with judgments of tendency. The honest man, we are told, acts upon "principle" and not from considerations of expediency, that is, of particular consequences. The truth in this saying is that it is not safe to judge the worth of a proposed act by its probable consequences in an isolated case. The word "principle" is a eulogistic cover for the fact of *tendency*. The word "tendency" is an attempt to combine two facts, one that habits have a certain causal efficacy, the other that their outworking in any particular case is subject to contingencies, to circumstances which are unforeseeable and which carry an act one side of its usual effect. In cases of doubt, there is no recourse save to stick to "tendency," that is, to the probable effect of a habit in the long run, or as we say upon the whole. Otherwise we are on the lookout for exceptions which favor our immediate desire. The trouble is that we are not content with modest probabilities. So when we find that a good disposition may work out badly, we say, as Kant did, that the working-out, the consequence, has nothing to do with the moral quality of an act, or we strain for the impossible, and aim at some infallible calculus of consequences by which to measure moral worth in each specific case.

Human conceit has played a great part. It has demanded that the whole universe be judged from the standpoint of desire and disposition, or at least from that of the desire and disposition of the good man. The effect of religion has been to cherish this conceit by making men think that the universe invariably conspires to support the good and bring the evil to naught. By a subtle logic, the effect has been to render morals unreal and transcendental. For since the world of actual experience does not guarantee this identity of character and outcome, it is inferred that there must be some ulterior truer reality which enforces an equation that is violated in this life. Hence the common notion of another world in which vice and virtue of character produce their exact moral meed. The idea is equally found as an actuating force in Plato. Moral realities must be supreme. Yet they are flagrantly contradicted in a world where a Socrates drinks the hemlock of the criminal, and where the vicious occupy the seats of the mighty. Hence there must be a truer ultimate reality in which justice is only and absolutely justice. Something of the same idea lurks behind every aspiration for realization of abstract justice or equality or liberty. It is the source of all " idealistic " utopias and also of all wholesale pessimism and distrust of life.

Utilitarianism illustrates another way of mistreating the situation. Tendency is not good enough for the utilitarians. They want a mathematical equation of act and consequence. Hence they make light of the steady and controllable factor, the factor of disposition, and fasten upon just the things which are most subject to incalculable accident—pleasures and pains— and embark upon the hopeless enterprise of judging an act apart from character on the basis of definite results. An honestly modest theory will stick to the probabilities of tendency, and not import mathematics into morals. It will be alive and sensitive to consequences as they actually present themselves, because it knows that they give the only instruction we can procure as to the meaning of habits and dispositions. But it will never assume that a moral judgment which reaches certainty is possible. We have just to do the best we can with habits, the forces most under our control; and we shall have our hands more than full in spelling out their general tendencies without attempting an exact judgment upon each deed. For every habit incorporates within itself some part of the objective environment, and no habit and no amount of habits can incorporate the entire environment within itself or themselves. There will always be disparity between them and the results actually attained. Hence the work of intelligence in observing consequences and in revising and readjusting habits, even the best of good habits, can never be foregone. Consequences reveal unexpected potentialities in our habits whenever these habits are exercised in a different environment from that in which they were formed. The assumption of a stably uniform environment (even the hankering for one) expresses a fiction due to attachment to old habits. The utilitarian theory of equation of acts with consequences is as much a fiction of self-conceit as is the assumption of a fixed transcendental world wherein moral ideals are eternally and immutably real. Both of them deny in effect the relevancy of time, of change, to morals, while time is of the essence of the moral struggle.

We thus come, by an unexpected path, upon the old

question of the objectivity or subjectivity of morals.
Primarily they are objective. For will, as we have
seen, means, in the concrete, habits; and habits incorporate an environment within themselves. They are
adjustments *of* the environment, not merely *to* it. At
the same time, the environment is many, not one; hence
will, disposition, is plural. Diversity does not of itself
imply conflict, but it implies the possibility of conflict,
and this possibility is realized in fact. Life, for example, involves the habit of eating, which in turn involves a unification of organism and nature. But nevertheless this habit comes into conflict with other habits
which are also " objective," or in equilibrium with *their*
environments. Because the environment is not all of
one piece, man's house is divided within itself, against
itself. Honor or consideration for others or courtesy
conflict with hunger. Then the notion of the complete
objectivity of morals gets a shock. Those who wish
to maintain the idea unimpaired take the road which
leads to transcendentalism. The empirical world, they
say, is indeed divided, and hence any natural morality
must be in conflict with itself. This self-contradiction
however only points to a higher fixed reality with which
a true and superior morality is alone concerned. Objectivity is saved but at the expense of connection with
human affairs. Our problem is to see what objectivity
signifies upon a naturalistic basis; how morals are objective and yet secular and social. Then we may be
able to decide in what crisis of experience morals be-

come legitimately dependent upon character or self—
that is, " subjective."

Prior discussion points the way to the answer. A
hungry man could not conceive food as a good unless
he had actually experienced, with the support of environing conditions, food as good. The objective satisfaction comes first. But he finds himself in a situation where the good is denied in fact. It then lives in
imagination. The habit denied overt expression asserts
itself in idea. It sets up the thought, the ideal, of
food. This thought is not what is sometimes called
thought, a pale bloodless abstraction, but is charged
with the motor urgent force of habit. Food as a good
is now subjective, personal. But it has its source in
objective conditions and it moves forward to new objective conditions. For it works to secure a change of
environment so that food will again be present in fact.
Food is a " subjective " good during a temporary tran-
sitional stage from one object to another.

The analogy with morals lies upon the surface. A
habit impeded in overt operation continues nonetheless
to operate. It manifests itself in desireful thought,
that is in an ideal or imagined object which embodies
within itself the force of a frustrated habit. There is
therefore demand for a changed environment, a demand
which can be achieved only by some modification and
rearrangement of old habits. Even Plato preserves an
intimation of the natural function of ideal objects when
he insists upon their value as patterns for use in re-

organization of the actual scene. The pity is that he could not see that patterns exist only within and for the sake of reorganization, so that they, rather than empirical or natural objects, are the instrumental affairs. Not seeing this, he converted a function of reorganization into a metaphysical reality. If we essay a technical formulation we shall say that morality becomes legitimately subjective or personal when activities which once included objective factors in their operation temporarily lose support from objects, and yet strive to change existing conditions until they regain a support which has been lost. It is all of a kind with the doings of a man, who remembering a prior satisfaction of thirst and the conditions under which it occurred, digs a well. For the time being water in reference to his activity exists in imagination not in fact. But this imagination is not a self-generated, self-enclosed, psychical existence. It is the persistent operation of a prior object which has been incorporated in effective habit. There is no miracle in the fact that an object in a new context operates in a new way.

Of transcendental morals, it may at least be said that they retain the intimation of the objective character of purposes and goods. Purely subjective morals arise when the incidents of the temporary (though recurrent) crisis of reorganization are taken as complete and final in themselves. A self having habits and attitudes formed with the cooperation of objects runs ahead of immediately surrounding objects to effect a new equilibration. Subjective morals substitutes a self

always set over against objects and generating its
ideals independently of objects, and in permanent, not
transitory, opposition to them. Achievement, any
achievement, is to it a negligible second best, a cheap
and poor substitute for ideals that live only in the
mind, a compromise with actuality made from physical
necessity not from moral reasons. In truth, there is
but a temporal episode. For a time, a self, a person,
carries in his own habits against the forces of the immediate environment, a good which the existing environment denies. For this self moving temporarily, in
isolation from objective conditions, between a good, a
completeness, that has been and one that it is hoped
to restore in some new form, subjective theories have
substituted an erring soul wandering hopelessly between
a Paradise Lost in the dim past and a Paradise to be
Regained in a dim future. In reality, even when a
person is in some respects at odds with his environment
and so has to act for the time being as the sole agent
of a good, he in many respects is still supported by
objective conditions and is in possession of undisturbed
goods and virtues. Men do die from thirst at times,
but upon the whole in their search for water they are
sustained by other fulfilled powers. But subjective
morals taken wholesale sets up a solitary self without
objective ties and sustenance. In fact, there exists a
shifting mixture of vice and virtue. Theories paint a
world with a God in heaven and a Devil in hell. Moralists in short have failed to recall that a severance of
moral desire and purpose from immediate actualities

is an inevitable phase of activity when habits persist while the world which they have incorporated alters. Back of this failure lies the failure to recognize that in a changing world, old habits must perforce need modification, no matter how good they have been.

Obviously any such change can be only experimental. The lost objective good persists in habit, but it can recur in objective form only through some condition of affairs which has not been yet experienced, and which therefore can be anticipated only uncertainly and inexactly. The essential point is that anticipation should at least guide as well as stimulate effort, that it should be a working hypothesis corrected and developed by events as action proceeds. There was a time when men believed that each object in the external world carried its nature stamped upon it as a form, and that intelligence consisted in simply inspecting and reading off an intrinsic self-enclosed complete nature. The scientific revolution which began in the seventeenth century came through a surrender of this point of view. It began with recognition that every natural object is in truth an event continuous in space and time with other events; and is to be *known* only by experimental inquiries which will exhibit a multitude of complicated, obscure and minute relationships. Any observed form or object is but a challenge. The case is not otherwise with ideals of justice or peace or human brotherhood, or equality, or order. They too are not things self-enclosed to be known by introspection, as objects were once supposed to be known by rational insight. Like thunderbolts and tubercular disease and the rainbow they can be known only by extensive and minute observation of consequences incurred in action. A false psychology of an isolated self and a subjective morality shuts out from morals the things important to it, acts and habits in their objective consequences. At the same time it misses the point characteristic of the personal subjective aspect of morality: the significance of desire and thought in breaking down old rigidities of habit and preparing the way for acts that re-create an environment.

IV

We often fancy that institutions, social custom, collective habit, have been formed by the consolidation of individual habits. In the main this supposition is false to fact. To a considerable extent customs, or widespread uniformities of habit, exist because individuals face the same situation and react in like fashion. But to a larger extent customs persist because individuals form their personal habits under conditions set by prior customs. An individual usually acquires the morality as he inherits the speech of his social group. The activities of the group are already there, and some assimilation of his own acts to their pattern is a prerequisite of a share therein, and hence of having any part in what is going on. Each person is born an infant, and every infant is subject from the first breath he draws and the first cry he utters to the attentions and demands of others. These others are not just persons in general with minds in general. They are beings with habits, and beings who upon the whole esteem the habits they have, if for no other reason than that, having them, their imagination is thereby limited. The nature of habit is to be assertive, insistent, self-perpetuating. There is no miracle in the fact that if a child learns any language he learns the language that those about him speak and teach, especially since his ability to speak that language is a pre-condition of his entering into effective connection with them, making wants known and getting them satisfied. Fond parents and relatives frequently pick up a few of the child's spontaneous modes of speech and for a time at least they are portions of the speech of the group. But the ratio which such words bear to the total vocabulary in use gives a fair measure of the part played by purely individual habit in forming custom in comparison with the part played by custom in forming individual habits. Few persons have either the energy or the wealth to build private roads to travel upon. They find it convenient, " natural," to use the roads that are already there; while unless their private roads connect at some point with the high-way they cannot build them even if they would.

These simple facts seem to me to give a simple explanation of matters that are often surrounded with mystery. To talk about the priority of " society " to *the* individual is to indulge in nonsensical metaphysics. But to say that some pre-existent association of human beings is prior to every particular human being who is born into the world is to mention a commonplace. These associations are definite modes of interaction of persons with one another; that is to say they form customs, institutions. There is no problem in all history so artificial as that of how " individuals " manage to form " society." The problem is due to the pleasure taken in manipulating concepts, and discussion goes on because concepts are kept from inconvenient contact with facts. The facts of infancy and sex have

only to be called to mind to see how manufactured are
the conceptions which enter into this particular
problem.

The problem, however, of how those established
and more or less deeply grooved systems of interaction
which we call social groups, big and small, modify the
activities of individuals who perforce are caught-up
within them, and how the activities of component individuals remake and redirect previously established customs is a deeply significant one. Viewed from the standpoint of custom and its priority to the formation of
habits in human beings who are born babies and gradually grow to maturity, the facts which are now usually
assembled under the conceptions of collective minds,
group-minds, national-minds, crowd-minds, etc., etc.,
lose the mysterious air they exhale when mind is
thought of (as orthodox psychology teaches us to think
of it) as something which precedes action. It is difficult to see that collective mind means anything more
than a custom brought at some point to explicit, emphatic consciousness, emotional or intellectual.*

* Mob psychology comes under the same principles, but in a
negative aspect. The crowd and mob express a disintegration of
habits which releases impulse and renders persons susceptible
to immediate stimuli, rather than such a functioning of habits
as is found in the mind of a club or school of thought or a
political party. Leaders of an organization, that is of an interaction having settled habits, may, however, in order to put over
some schemes deliberately resort to stimuli which will break
through the crust of ordinary custom and release impulses on
such a scale as to create a mob psychology. Since fear is a
normal reaction to the unfamiliar, dread and suspicion are the
forces most played upon to accomplish this result, together with
vast vague contrary hopes. This is an ordinary technique in
excited political campaigns, in starting war, etc. But an assimi-

The family into which one is born is a family in a village or city which interacts with other more or less integrated systems of activity, and which includes a diversity of groupings within itself, say, churches, political parties, clubs, cliques, partnerships, trade-unions, corporations, etc. If we start with the traditional notion of mind as something complete in itself, then we may well be perplexed by the problem of how a common mind, common ways of feeling and believing and purposing, comes into existence and then forms these groups. The case is quite otherwise if we recognize that in any case we must start with grouped action, that is, with some fairly settled system of interaction among individuals. The problem of origin and development of the various groupings, or definite customs, in existence at any particular time in any particular place is not solved by reference to psychic causes, elements, forces. It is to be solved by reference to facts of action, demand for food, for houses, for a

lation like that of Le Bon of the psychology of democracy to the psychology of a crowd in overriding individual judgment shows lack of psychological insight. A political democracy exhibits an overriding of thought like that seen in any convention or institution. That is, thought is submerged in habit. In the crowd and mob, it is submerged in undefined emotion. China and Japan exhibit crowd psychology more frequently than do western democratic countries. Not in my judgment because of any essentially Oriental psychology but because of a nearer background of rigid and solid customs conjoined with the phenomena of a period of transition. The introduction of many novel stimuli creates occasions where habits afford no ballast. Hence great waves of emotion easily sweep through masses. Sometimes they are waves of enthusiasm for the new; sometimes of violent reaction against it—both equally undiscriminating. The war has left behind it a somewhat similar situation in western countries.

mate, for some one to talk to and to listen to one talk, for control of others, demands which are all intensified by the fact already mentioned that each person begins a helpless, dependent creature. I do not mean of course that hunger, fear, sexual love, gregariousness, sympathy, parental love, love of bossing and of being ordered about, imitation, etc., play no part. But I do mean that these words do not express elements or forces which are psychic or mental in their first intention. They denote *ways of behavior*. These ways of behaving involve interaction, that is to say, and prior groupings. And to understand the existence of organized ways or habits we surely need to go to physics, chemistry and physiology rather than to psychology.

There is doubtless a great mystery as to why any such thing as being conscious should exist at all. But *if* consciousness exists at all, there is no mystery in its being connected with what it is connected with. That is to say, if an activity which is an interaction of various factors, or a grouped activity, comes to consciousness it seems natural that it should take the form of an emotion, belief or purpose that reflects the interaction, that it should be an " our " consciousness or a " my " consciousness. And by this is meant both that it will be shared by those who are implicated in the associative custom, or more or less alike in them all, and that it will be felt or thought to concern others as well as one's self. A family-custom or organized habit of action comes into contact and conflict for example with that of some other family. The emotions of ruffled pride, the belief about superiority or being " as good as other people," the intention to hold one's own are naturally *our* feeling and idea of *our* treatment and position.   Substitute the Republican party or the American nation for the family and the general situation remains the same.   The conditions which determine the nature and extent of the particular grouping in question are matters of supreme import.   But they are not as such subject-matter of psychology, but of the history of politics, law, religion, economics, invention, the technology of communication and intercourse.   Psychology comes in as an indispensable tool. But it enters into the matter of understanding these various special topics, not into the question of what psychic forces form a collective mind and therefore a social group.   That way of stating the case puts the cart a long way before the horse, and naturally gathers obscurities and mysteries to itself.   In short, the primary facts of social psychology center about collective habit, custom.   In addition to the general psychology of habit—which *is* general not individual in any intelligible sense of that word—we need to find out just how different customs shape the desires, beliefs, purposes of those who are affected by them.   The problem of social psychology is not how either individual or collective mind forms social groups and customs, but how different customs, established interacting arrangements, form and nurture different minds.   From this general statement we return to our special problem, which is how the rigid character of past custom has unfavorably influenced beliefs, emotions and purposes having to do with morals.

We come back to the fact that individuals begin their career as infants. For the plasticity of the young presents a temptation to those having greater experience and hence greater power which they rarely resist. It seems putty to be molded according to current designs. That plasticity also means power to change prevailing custom is ignored. Docility is looked upon not as ability to learn whatever the world has to teach, but as subjection to those instructions of others which reflect *their* current habits. To be truly docile is to be eager to learn all the lessons of active, inquiring, expanding experience. The inert, stupid quality of current customs perverts learning into a willingness to follow where others point the way, into conformity, constriction, surrender of scepticism and experiment. When we think of the docility of the young we first think of the stocks of information adults wish to impose and the ways of acting they want to reproduce. Then we think of the insolent coercions, the insinuating briberies, the pedagogic solemnities by which the freshness of youth can be faded and its vivid curiosities dulled. Education becomes the art of taking advantage of the helplessness of the young; the forming of habits becomes a guarantee for the maintenance of hedges of custom.

Of course it is not wholly forgotten that habits are abilities, arts. Any striking exhibition of acquired skill in physical matters, like that of an acrobat or billiard-player, arouses universal admiration. But we like to have innovating power limited to technical matters and reserve our admiration for those manifestations that display virtuosity rather than virtue. In moral matters it is assumed that it is enough if some ideal has been exemplified in the life of a leader, so that it is now the part of others to follow and reproduce. For every branch of conduct, there is a Jesus or Buddha, a Napoleon or Marx, a Froebel or Tolstoi, whose pattern of action, exceeding our own grasp, is reduced to a practicable copy-size by passage through rows and rows of lesser leaders.

The notion that it suffices if the idea, the end, is present in the mind of some authority dominates formal schooling. It permeates the unconscious education derived from ordinary contact and intercourse. Where following is taken to be normal, moral originality is pretty sure to be eccentric. But if independence were the rule, originality would be subjected to severe, experimental tests and be saved from cranky eccentricity, as it now is in say higher mathematics. The regime of custom assumes that the outcome is the same whether an individual understands what he is about or whether he goes through certain motions while mouthing the words of others—repetition of formulæ being esteemed of greater importance, upon the whole, than repetition of deeds. To say what the sect or clique or class says is the way of proving that one also understands and approves what the clique clings to. In theory, democracy should be a means of stimulating original thought,

and of evoking action deliberately adjusted in advance
to cope with new forces. In fact it is still so immature
that its main effect is to multiply occasions for imitation. If progress in spite of this fact is more rapid
than in other social forms, it is by accident, since the
diversity of models conflict with one another and
thus give individuality a chance in the resulting chaos
of opinions. Current democracy acclaims success more
boisterously than do other social forms, and surrounds
failure with a more reverberating train of echoes. But
the prestige thus given excellence is largely adventi-
tious. The achievement of thought attracts others not
so much intrinsically as because of an eminence due to
multitudinous advertising and a swarm of imitators.

Even liberal thinkers have treated habit as essentially, not because of the character of existing customs,
conservative. In fact only in a society dominated by
modes of belief and admiration fixed by past custom is
habit any more conservative than it is progressive. It
all depends upon its quality. Habit is an ability, an
art, formed through past experience. But whether an
ability is limited to repetition of past acts adopted to
past conditions or is available for new emergencies
depends wholly upon what kind of habit exists. The
tendency to think that only "bad" habits are dis-
serviceable and that bad habits are conventionally
enumerable, conduces to make all habits more or less
bad. For what makes a habit bad is enslavement to
old ruts. The common notion that enslavement to good
ends converts mechanical routine into good is a

negation of the principle of moral goodness. It identifies morality with what *was* sometime rational, possibly in some prior experience of one's own, but more probably in the experience of some one else who is now blindly set up as a final authority. The genuine heart of reasonableness (and of goodness in conduct) lies in effective mastery of the conditions which *now* enter into action. To be satisfied with repeating, with traversing the ruts which in other conditions led to good, is the surest way of creating carelessness about present and actual good.

Consider what happens to thought when habit is merely power to repeat acts without thought. Where does thought exist and operate when it is excluded from habitual activities? Is not such thought of necessity shut out from effective power, from ability to control objects and command events? Habits deprived of thought and thought which is futile are two sides of the same fact. To laud habit as conservative while praising thought as the main spring of progress is to take the surest course to making thought abstruse and irrelevant and progress a matter of accident and catastrophe. The concrete fact behind the current separation of body and mind, practice and theory, actualities and ideals, is precisely this separation of habit and thought. Thought which does not exist within ordinary habits of action lacks means of execution. In lacking application, it also lacks test, criterion. Hence it is condemned to a separate realm. If we try to act upon it, our actions are clumsy, forced. In fact, contrary

habits (as we have already seen) come into operation
and betray our purpose. After a few such experiences,
it is subconsciously decided that thought is too precious
and high to be exposed to the contingencies of action.
It is reserved for separate uses; thought feeds only
thought not action. Ideals must not run the risk of
contamination and perversion by contact with actual
conditions. Thought then either resorts to specialized
and technical matters influencing action in the library
or laboratory alone, or else it becomes sentimentalized.

Meantime there are certain " practical " men who
combine thought and habit and who are effectual. Their
thought is about their own advantage; and their habits
correspond. They dominate the actual situation. They
encourage routine in others, and they also subsidize
such thought and learning as are kept remote from
affairs. This they call sustaining the standard of the
ideal. Subjection they praise as team-spirit, loyalty,
devotion, obedience, industry, law-and-order. But they
temper respect for law—by which they mean the order
of the existing status—on the part of others with most
skilful and thoughtful manipulation of it in behalf of
their own ends. While they denounce as subversive
anarchy signs of independent thought, of thinking for
themselves, on the part of others lest such thought
disturb the conditions by which they profit, they think
quite literally *for* themselves, that is, *of* themselves.
This is the eternal game of the practical men. Hence
it is only by accident that the separate and endowed

" thought " of professional thinkers leaks out into action and affects custom.

For thinking cannot itself escape the influence of habit, any more than anything else human. If it is not a part of ordinary habits, then it is a separate habit, habit alongside other habits, apart from them, as isolated and indurated as human structure permits. Theory is a possession of the theorist, intellect of the intellectualist. The so-called separation of theory and practice means in fact the separation of two kinds of practice, one taking place in the outdoor world, the other in the study. The habit of thought commands some materials (as every habit must do) but the materials are technical, books, words. Ideas are objectified in action but speech and writing monopolize their field of action. Even then subconscious pains are taken to see that the words used are not too widely understood. Intellectual habits like other habits demand an environment, but the environment is the study, library, laboratory and academy. Like other habits they produce external results, possessions. Some men acquire ideas and knowledge as other men acquire monetary wealth. While practising thought for their own special ends they deprecate it for the untrained and unstable masses for whom " habits," that is unthinking routines, are necessities. They favor popular education—up to the point of disseminating as matter of authoritative information for the many what the few have established by thought, and up to the point of

converting an original docility to the new into a docility
to repeat and to conform.

Yet all habit involves mechanization. Habit is impossible without setting up a mechanism of action,
physiologically engrained, which operates " spontaneously," automatically, whenever the cue is given. But
mechanization is not of necessity *all* there is to habit.
Consider the conditions under which the first serviceable
abilities of life are formed. When a child begins to
walk he acutely observes, he intently and intensely experiments. He looks to see what is going to happen
and he keeps curious watch on every incident. What
others do, the assistance they give, the models they set,
operate not as limitations but as encouragements to his
own acts, reinforcements of personal perception and
endeavor. The first toddling is a romantic adventuring into the unknown; and every gained power is a
delightful discovery of one's own powers and of the
wonders of the world. We may not be able to retain
in adult habits this zest of intelligence and this
freshness of satisfaction in newly discovered powers.
But there is surely a middle term between a normal
exercise of power which includes some excursion into
the unknown, and a mechanical activity hedged within
a drab world. Even in dealing with inanimate machines
we rank that invention higher which adapts its movements to varying conditions.

All life operates through a mechanism, and the
higher the form of life the more complex, sure and
flexible the mechanism. This fact alone should save

us from opposing life and mechanism, thereby reducing the latter to unintelligent automatism and the former to an aimless splurge. How delicate, prompt, sure and varied are the movements of a violin player or an engraver! How unerringly they phrase every shade of emotion and every turn of idea! Mechanism is indispensable. If each act has to be consciously searched for at the moment and intentionally performed, execution is painful and the product is clumsy and halting. Nevertheless the difference between the artist and the mere technician is unmistakeable. The artist is a masterful technician. The technique or mechanism is fused with thought and feeling. The " mechanical " performer permits the mechanism to dictate the performance. It is absurd to say that the latter exhibits habit and the former not. We are confronted with two kinds of habit, intelligent and routine. All life has its élan, but only the prevalence of dead habits deflects life into mere élan.

Yet the current dualism of mind and body, thought and action, is so rooted that we are taught (and science is said to support the teaching) that the art, the habit, of the artist is acquired by previous mechanical exercises of repetition in which skill apart from thought is the aim, until suddenly, magically, this soulless mechanism is taken possession of by sentiment and imagination and it becomes a flexible instrument of mind. The fact, the scientific fact, is that even in his exercises, his practice *for* skill, an artist uses an art he already has. He acquires greater skill because practice *of* skill is more important to him than practice *for* skill. Otherwise natural endowment would count for nothing, and sufficient mechanical exercise would make any one an expert in any field. A flexible, sensitive habit grows more varied, more adaptable by practice and use. We do not as yet fully understand the physiological factors concerned in mechanical routine on one hand and artistic skill on the other, but we do know that the latter is just as much habit as is the former. Whether it concerns the cook, musician, carpenter, citizen, or statesman, the intelligent or artistic habit is the desirable thing, and the routine the undesirable thing:—or, at least, desirable and undesirable from every point of view except one.

Those who wish a monopoly of social power find desirable the separation of habit and thought, action and soul, so characteristic of history. For the dualism enables them to do the thinking and planning, while others remain the docile, even if awkward, instruments of execution. Until this scheme is changed, democracy is bound to be perverted in realization. With our present system of education—by which something much more extensive than schooling is meant—democracy multiplies occasions for imitation not occasions for thought in action. If the visible result is rather a messy confusion than an ordered discipline of habits, it is because there are so many models of imitation set up that they tend to cancel one another, so that individuals have the advantage neither of uniform training nor of intelligent adaptation. Whence an intellectualist, the one with whom thinking is itself a segregated habit, infers that the choice is between muss-and-muddling and a bureaucracy. He prefers the latter, though under some other name, usually an aristocracy of talent and intellect, possibly a dictatorship of the proletariat.

It has been repeatedly stated that the current philosophical dualism of mind and body, of spirit and mere outward doing, is ultimately but an intellectual reflex of the social divorce of routine habit from thought, of means from ends, practice from theory. One hardly knows whether most to admire the acumen with which Bergson has penetrated through the accumulation of historic technicalities to this essential fact, or to deplore the artistic skill with which he has recommended the division and the metaphysical subtlety with which he has striven to establish its necessary and unchangeable nature. For the latter tends to confirm and sanction the dualism in all its obnoxiousness. In the end, however, detection, discovery, is the main thing. To envisage the relation of spirit, life, to matter, body, as in effect an affair of a force which outruns habit while it leaves a trail of routine habits behind it, will surely turn out in the end to imply the acknowledgment of the need of a continuous unification of spirit and habit, rather than to be a sanction of their divorce. And when Bergson carries the implicit logic to the point of a clear recognition that upon this basis concrete intelligence is concerned with the habits which incorporate and deal with objects, and that noth-

ing remains to spirit, pure thought, except a blind onward push or impetus, the net conclusion is surely the
need of revision of the fundamental premiss of separation of soul and habit. A blind creative force is as
likely to turn out to be destructive as creative; the vital
élan may delight in war rather than in the laborious
arts of civilization, and a mystic intuition of an ungoing
splurge be a poor substitute for the detailed work of an
intelligence embodied in custom and institution, one
which creates by means of flexible continuous contrivances of reorganization. For the eulogistic qualities
which Bergson attributes to the *élan vital* flow not from
its nature but from a reminiscence of the optimism of
romanticism, an optimism which is only the reverse side
of pessimism about actualities. A spiritual life which
is nothing but a blind urge separated from thought
(which is said to be confined to mechanical manipulation of material objects for personal uses) is
likely to have the attributes of the Devil in spite of its
being ennobled with the name of God.

V

For practical purposes morals mean customs, folkways, established collective habits. This is a commonplace of the anthropologist, though the moral theorist generally suffers from an illusion that his own place and day is, or ought to be, an exception. But always and everywhere customs supply the standards for personal activities. They are the pattern into which individual activity must weave itself. This is as true today as it ever was. But because of present mobility and interminglings of customs, an individual is now offered an enormous range of custom-patterns, and can exercise personal ingenuity in selecting and rearranging their elements. In short he can, if he will, intelligently adapt customs to conditions, and thereby remake them. Customs in any case constitute moral standards. For they are active demands for certain ways of acting. Every habit creates an unconscious expectation. It forms a certain outlook. What psychologists have laboriously treated under the caption of association of ideas has little to do with ideas and everything to do with the influence of habit upon recollection and perception. A habit, a routine habit, when interfered with generates uneasiness, sets up a protest in favor of restoration and a sense of need of some expiatory act, or else it goes off in casual reminiscence. It is the essence of routine to insist upon its own continuation. Breach of it is violation of right. Deviation from it is transgression.

All that metaphysics has said about the nisus of Being to conserve its essence and all that a mythological psychology has said about a special instinct of self-preservation is a cover for the persistent self-assertion of habit. Habit is energy organized in certain channels. When interfered with, it swells as resentment and as an avenging force. To say that it will be obeyed, that custom makes law, that *nomos* is lord of all, is after all only to say that habit is habit. Emotion is a perturbation from clash or failure of habit, and reflection, roughly speaking, is the painful effort of disturbed habits to readjust themselves. It is a pity that Westermarck in his monumental collection of facts which show the connection of custom with morals* is still so much under the influence of current subjective psychology that he misstates the point of his data. For although he recognizes the objectivity of custom, he treats sympathetic resentment and approbation as distinctive inner feelings or conscious states which give rise to acts. In his anxiety to displace an unreal rational source of morals he sets up an equally unreal emotional basis. In truth, feelings as well as reason spring up within action. Breach of custom or habit is the source of sympathetic resentment, while overt approbation goes out to fidelity to custom maintained under exceptional circumstances.

* "The Origin and Development of Moral Ideas."

Those who recognize the place of custom in lower social forms generally regard its presence in civilized society as a mere survival. Or, like Sumner, they fancy that to recognize its abiding place is equivalent to the denial of all rationality and principle to morality; equivalent to the assertion of blind, arbitrary forces in life. In effect, this point of view has already been dealt with. It overlooks the fact that the real opposition is not between reason and habit but between routine, unintelligent habit, and intelligent habit or art. Even a savage custom may be reasonable in that it is adapted to social needs and uses. Experience may add to such adaptation a conscious recognition of it, and then the custom of rationality is added to a prior custom.

External reasonableness or adaptation to ends precedes reasonableness of mind. This is only to say that in morals as well as in physics things have to be there before we perceive them, and that rationality of mind is not an original endowment but is the offspring of intercourse with objective adaptations and relations— a view which under the influence of a conception of knowing the like by the like has been distorted into Platonic and other objective idealisms. Reason as observation of an adaptation of acts to valuable results is not however a mere idle mirroring of pre-existent facts. It is an additional event having its own career. It sets up a heightened emotional appreciation and provides a new motive for fidelities previously blind. It sets up an attitude of criticism, of inquiry, and

makes men sensitive to the brutalities and extravagancies of customs. In short, it becomes a custom of
expectation and outlook, an active demand for reasonableness in other customs. The reflective disposition is
not self-made nor a gift of the gods. It arises in some
exceptional circumstance out of social customs, as we
see in the case of the Greeks. But when it has been
generated it establishes a new custom, which is capable
of exercising the most revolutionary influence upon
other customs.

Hence the growing importance of personal rationality or intelligence, in moral theory if not in practice.
That current customs contradict one another, that
many of them are unjust, and that without criticism
none of them is fit to be the guide of life was the discovery with which the Athenian Socrates initiated conscious moral theorizing. Yet a dilemma soon presented
itself, one which forms the burden of Plato's ethical
writings. How shall thought which is personal arrive
at standards which hold good for all, which, in modern
phrase, are objective? The solution found by Plato
was that reason is itself objective, universal, cosmic
and makes the individual soul its vehicle. The result,
however, was merely to substitute a metaphysical or
transcendental ethics for the ethics of custom. If Plato
had been able to see that reflection and criticism express
a conflict of customs, and that their purport and office
is to re-organize, re-adjust customs, the subsequent
course of moral theory would have been very different.
Custom would have provided needed objective and sub-

stantial ballast, and personal rationality or reflective intelligence been treated as the necessary organ of experimental initiative and creative invention in re-making custom.

We have another difficulty to face: a greater wave rises to overwhelm us. It is said that to derive moral standards from social customs is to evacuate the latter of all authority. Morals, it is said, imply the subordination of fact to ideal consideration, while the view presented makes morals secondary to bare fact, which is equal to depriving them of dignity and jurisdiction. The objection has the force of the custom of moral theorists behind it; and therefore in its denial of custom avails itself of the assistance of the notion it attacks. The criticism rests upon a false separation. It argues in effect that either ideal standards antecede customs and confer their moral quality upon them, or that in being subsequent to custom and evolved from them, they are mere accidental by-products. But how does the case stand with language? Men did not intend language; they did not have social objects consciously in view when they began to talk, nor did they have grammatical and phonetic principles before them by which to regulate their efforts at communication. These things come after the fact and because of it. Language grew out of unintelligent babblings, instinctive motions called gestures, and the pressure of circumstance. But nevertheless language once called into existence is language and operates as language. It operates not to perpetuate the forces which produced it but to modify and redirect them. It has such transcendent importance that pains are taken with its use. Literatures are produced, and then a vast apparatus of grammar, rhetoric, dictionaries, literary criticism, reviews, essays, a derived literature *ad lib*. Education, schooling, becomes a necessity; literacy an end. In short language when it is produced meets old needs and opens new possibilities. It creates demands which take effect, and the effect is not confined to speech and literature, but extends to the common life in communication, counsel and instruction.

What is said of the institution of language holds good of every institution. Family life, property, legal forms, churches and schools, academies of art and science did not originate to serve conscious ends nor was their generation regulated by consciousness of principles of reason and right. Yet each institution has brought with its development demands, expectations, rules, standards. These are not mere embellishments of the forces which produced them, idle decorations of the scene. They are additional forces. They reconstruct. They open new avenues of endeavor and impose new labors. In short they are civilization, culture, morality.

Still the question recurs: What authority have standards and ideas which have originated in this way? What claim have they upon us? In one sense the question is unanswerable. In the same sense, however, the question is unanswerable whatever origin and sanction is ascribed to moral obligations and loyalties. Why attend to metaphysical and transcendental ideal realities even if we concede they are the authors of moral standards? Why do this act if I feel like doing something else? Any moral question may reduce itself to this question if we so choose. But in an empirical sense the answer is simple. The authority is that of life. Why employ language, cultivate literature, acquire and develop science, sustain industry, and submit to the refinements of art? To ask these questions is equivalent to asking: Why live? And the only answer is that if one is going to live one must live a life of which these things form the substance. The only question having sense which can be asked is *how* we are going to use and be used by these things, not whether we are going to use them. Reason, moral principles, cannot in any case be shoved behind these affairs, for reason and morality grow out of them. But they have grown into them as well as out of them. They are there as part of them. No one can escape them if he wants to. He cannot escape the problem of *how* to engage in life, since in any case he must engage in it in some way or other—or else quit and get out. In short, the choice is not between a moral authority outside custom and one within it. It is between adopting more or less intelligent and significant customs.

Curiously enough, the chief practical effect of refusing to recognize the connection of custom with moral standards is to deify some special custom and treat it as eternal, immutable, outside of criticism and revision.

This consequence is especially harmful in times of rapid social flux. For it leads to disparity between nominal standards, which become ineffectual and hypocritical in exact ratio to their theoretical exaltation, and actual habits which have to take note of existing conditions. The disparity breeds disorder. Irregularity and confusion are however practically intolerable, and effect the generation of a new rule of some sort or other. Only such complete disturbance of the physical bases of life and security as comes from plague and starvation can throw society into utter disorder. No amount of intellectual transition can seriously disturb the main tenor of custom, or morals. Hence the greater danger which attends the attempt in period of social change to maintain the immutability of old standards is not general moral relaxation. It is rather social clash, an irreconciled conflict of moral standards and purposes, the most serious form of class warfare.

For segregated classes develop their own customs, which is to say their own working morals. As long as society is mainly immobile these diverse principles and ruling aims do not clash. They exist side by side in different strata. Power, glory, honor, magnificence, mutual faith here; industry, obedience, abstinence, humility, and reverence there: noble and plebeian virtues. Vigor, courage, energy, enterprise here; submission, patience, charm, personal fidelity there: the masculine and feminine virtues. But mobility invades society. War, commerce, travel, communication, contact with the thoughts and desires of other classes, new inventions in productive industry, disturb the settled distribution of customs. Congealed habits thaw out, and a flood mixes things once separated.

Each class is rigidly sure of the rightness of its own ends and hence not overscrupulous about the means of attaining them. One side proclaims the ultimacy of order—that of some old order which conduces to its own interest. The other side proclaims its rights to freedom, and identifies justice with its submerged claims. There is no common ground, no moral understanding, no agreed upon standard of appeal. Today such a conflict occurs between propertied classes and those who depend upon daily wage; between men and women; between old and young. Each appeals to its own standard of right, and each thinks the other the creature of personal desire, whim or obstinacy. Mobility has affected peoples as well. Nations and races face one another, each with its own immutable standards. Never before in history have there existed such numerous contacts and minglings. Never before have there been such occasions for conflict which are the more significant because each side feels that it is supported by moral principles. Customs relating to what has been and emotions referring to what may come to be go their independent ways. The demand of each side treats its opponent as a wilful violator of moral principles, an expression of self-interest or superior might. Intelligence which is the only possible messenger of reconciliation dwells in a far land of abstractions or comes after the event to record accomplished facts.

VI

The prior discussion has tried to show why the psychology of habit is an objective and social psychology. Settled and regular action must contain an adjustment of environing conditions; it must incorporate them in itself. For human beings, the environing affairs directly important are those formed by the activities of other human beings. This fact is accentuated and made fundamental by the fact of infancy—the fact that each human being begins life completely dependent upon others. The net outcome accordingly is that what can be called distinctively individual in behavior and mind is not, contrary to traditional theory, an original datum. Doubtless physical or physiological individuality always colors responsive activity and hence modifies the form which custom assumes in its personal reproductions. In forceful energetic characters this quality is marked. But it is important to note that it is a quality of habit, not an element or force existing apart from adjustment of the environment and capable of being termed a separate individual mind. Orthodox psychology starts however from the assumption of precisely such independent minds. However much different schools may vary in their definitions of mind, they agree in this premiss of separateness and priority. Hence social psychology

is confused by the effort to render its facts in the terms
characteristic of old psychology, when the distinctive
thing about it is that it implies an abandonment of that
psychology.

The traditional psychology of the original separate
soul, mind or consciousness is in truth a reflex of conditions which cut human nature off from its natural
objective relations. It implies first the severance of
man from nature and then of each man from his fellows. The isolation of man from nature is duly manifested in the split between mind and body—since body
is clearly a connected part of nature. Thus the instrument of action and the means of the continuous modification of action, of the cumulative carrying forward
of old activity into new, is regarded as a mysterious
intruder or as a mysterious parallel accompaniment.
It is fair to say that the psychology of a separate and
independent consciousness began as an intellectual
formulation of those facts of morality which treated
the most important kind of action as a private concern, something to be enacted and concluded within
character as a purely personal possession. The religious and metaphysical interests which wanted the
ideal to be a separate realm finally coincided with a
practical revolt against current customs and institutions to enforce current psychological individualism.
But this formulation (put forth in the name of science)
reacted to confirm the conditions out of which it arose,
and to convert it from a historic episode into an essential truth. Its exaggeration of individuality is largely

a compensatory reaction against the pressure of institutional rigidities.

Any moral theory which is seriously influenced by current psychological theory is bound to emphasize states of consciousness, an inner private life, at the expense of acts which have public meaning and which incorporate and exact social relationships. A psychology based upon habits (and instincts which become elements in habits as soon as they are acted upon) will on the contrary fix its attention upon the objective conditions in which habits are formed and operate. The rise at the present time of a clinical psychology which revolts at traditional and orthodox psychology is a symptom of ethical import. It is a protest against the futility, as a tool of understanding and dealing with human nature in the concrete, of the psychology of conscious sensations, images and ideas. It exhibits a sense for reality in its insistence upon the profound importance of unconscious forces in determining not only overt conduct but desire, judgment, belief, idealization.

Every moment of reaction and protest, however, usually accepts some of the basic ideas of the position against which it rebels. So the most popular forms of the clinical psychology, those associated with the founders of psycho-analysis, retain the notion of a separate psychic realm or force. They add a statement pointing to facts of the utmost value, and which is equivalent to practical recognition of the dependence of mind upon habit and of habit upon social conditions. This is the statement of the existence and operation of the " unconscious," of complexes due to contacts and conflicts with others, of the social censor. But they still cling to the idea of the separate psychic realm and so in effect talk about unconscious consciousness. They get their truths mixed up in theory with the false psychology of original individual consciousness, just as the school of social psychologists does upon its side. Their elaborate artificial explanations, like the mystic collective mind, consciousness, over-soul, of social psychology, are due to failure to begin with the facts of habit and custom.

What then is meant by individual mind, by mind *as* individual? In effect the reply has already been given. Conflict of habits releases impulsive activities which in their manifestation require a modification of habit, of custom and convention. That which was at first the individualized color or quality of habitual activity is abstracted, and becomes a center of activity aiming to reconstruct customs in accord with some desire which is rejected by the immediate situation and which therefore is felt to belong to one's self, to be the mark and possession of an individual in partial and temporary opposition to his environment. These general and necessarily vague statements will be made more definite in the further discussion of impulse and intelligence. For impulse when it asserts itself deliberately against an existing custom is the beginning of individuality in mind. This beginning is developed and consolidated in the observations, judgments, inventions which try to transform the environment so that a variant, deviating impulse may itself in turn become incarnated in objective habit.

PART TWO

I

Habits as organized activities are secondary and acquired, not native and original. They are outgrowths of unlearned activities which are part of man's endowment at birth. The order of topics followed in our discussion may accordingly be questioned. Why should what is derived and therefore in some sense artificial in conduct be discussed before what is primitive, natural and inevitable? Why did we not set out with an examination of those instinctive activities upon which the acquisition of habits is conditioned?

The query is a natural one, yet it tempts to flinging forth a paradox. In conduct the acquired is the primitive. Impulses although first in time are never primary in fact; they are secondary and dependent. The seeming paradox in statement covers a familiar fact. In the life of the individual, instinctive activity comes first. But an individual begins life as a baby, and babies are dependent beings. Their activities could continue at most for only a few hours were it not for the presence and aid of adults with their formed habits. And babies owe to adults more than procreation, more

89

than the continued food and protection which preserve life. They owe to adults the opportunity to express their native activities in ways which have meaning. Even if by some miracle original activity could continue without assistance from the organized skill and art of adults, it would not amount to anything. It would be mere sound and fury.

In short, the *meaning* of native activities is not native; it is acquired. It depends upon interaction with a matured social medium. In the case of a tiger or eagle, anger may be identified with a serviceable life-activity, with attack and defense. With a human being it is as meaningless as a gust of wind on a mudpuddle apart from a direction given it by the presence of other persons, apart from the responses they make to it. It is a physical spasm, a blind dispersive burst of wasteful energy. It gets quality, significance, when it becomes a smouldering sullenness, an annoying interruption, a peevish irritation, a murderous revenge, a blazing indignation. And although these phenomena which have a meaning spring from original native reactions to stimuli, yet they depend also upon the responsive behavior of others. They and all similar human displays of anger are not pure impulses; they are habits formed under the influence of association with others who have habits already and who show their habits in the treatment which converts a blind physical discharge into a significant anger.

After ignoring impulses for a long time in behalf of sensations, modern psychology now tends to start out with an inventory and description of instinctive activities. This is an undoubted improvement. But when it tries to explain complicated events in personal and social life by direct reference to these native powers, the explanation becomes hazy and forced. It is like saying the flea and the elephant, the lichen and the redwood, the timid hare and the ravening wolf, the plant with the most inconspicuous blossom and the plant with the most glaring color are alike products of natural selection. There may be a sense in which the statement is true; but till we know the specific environing conditions under which selection took place we really know nothing. And so we need to know about the social conditions which have educated original activities into definite and significant dispositions before we can discuss the psychological element in society. This is the true meaning of social psychology.

At some place on the globe, at some time, every kind of practice seems to have been tolerated or even praised. How is the tremendous diversity of institutions (including moral codes) to be accounted for? The native stock of instincts is practically the same everywhere. Exaggerate as much as we like the native differences of Patagonians and Greeks, Sioux Indians and Hindoos, Bushmen and Chinese, their original differences will bear no comparison to the amount of difference found in custom and culture. Since such a diversity cannot be attributed to an original identity, the development of native impulse must be stated in terms of acquired habits, not the growth of customs in terms of instincts.

The wholesale human sacrifices of Peru and the tenderness of St. Francis, the cruelties of pirates and the philanthropies of Howard, the practice of Suttee and the cult of the Virgin, the war and peace dances of the Comanches and the parliamentary institutions of the British, the communism of the southsea islander and the proprietary thrift of the Yankee, the magic of the medicine man and the experiments of the chemist in his laboratory, the non-resistance of Chinese and the aggressive militarism of an imperial Prussia, monarchy by divine right and government by the people; the countless diversity of habits suggested by such a random list springs from practically the same capital-stock of native instincts.

It would be pleasant if we could pick and choose those institutions which we like and impute them to human nature, and the rest to some devil; or those we like to our kind of human nature, and those we dislike to the nature of despised foreigners on the ground they are not really " native " at all.   It would appear to be simpler if we could point to certain customs, saying that they are the unalloyed products of certain instincts, while those other social arrangements are to be attributed wholly to other impulses.   But such methods are not feasible.   The same original fears, angers, loves and hates are hopelessly entangled in the most opposite institutions.   The thing we need to know is how a native stock has been modified by interaction with different environments.

Yet it goes without saying that original, unlearned

activity has its distinctive place and that an important one in conduct. Impulses are the pivots upon which the re-organization of activities turn, they are agencies of deviation, for giving new directions to old habits and changing their quality. Consequently whenever we are concerned with understanding social transition and flux or with projects for reform, personal and collective, our study must go to analysis of native tendencies. Interest in progress and reform is, indeed, the reason for the present great development of scientific interest in primitive human nature. If we inquire why men were so long blind to the existence of powerful and varied instincts in human beings, the answer seems to be found in the lack of a conception of orderly progress. It is fast becoming incredible that psychologists disputed as to whether they should choose between innate ideas and an empty, passive, wax-like mind. For it seems as if a glance at a child would have revealed that the truth lay in neither doctrine, so obvious is the surging of specific native activities. But this obtuseness to facts was evidence of lack of interest in what could be done with impulses, due, in turn, to lack of interest in modifying existing institutions. It is no accident that men became interested in the psychology of savages and babies when they became interested in doing away with old institutions.

A combination of traditional individualism with the recent interest in progress explains why the discovery of the scope and force of instincts has led many psychologists to think of them as the fountain head of all

conduct, as occupying a place before instead of after
that of habits. The orthodox tradition in psychology
is built upon isolation of individuals from their surroundings. The soul or mind or consciousness was
thought of as self-contained and self-enclosed. Now in
the career of an individual if it is regarded as complete in itself instincts clearly come before habits. Generalize this individualistic view, and we have an assumption that all customs, all significant episodes in the life
of individuals can be carried directly back to the operation of instincts.

But, as we have already noted, if an individual be
isolated in this fashion, along with the fact of primacy
of instinct we find also the fact of death. The inchoate
and scattered impulses of an infant do not coordinate
into serviceable powers except through social dependencies and companionships. His impulses are merely
starting points for assimilation of the knowledge and
skill of the more matured beings upon whom he depends.
They are tentacles sent out to gather that nutrition
from customs which will in time render the infant capable of independent action. They are agencies for
transfer of existing social power into personal ability;
they are means of reconstructive growth. Abandon an
impossible individualistic psychology, and we arrive at
the fact that native activities are organs of re-organization and re-adjustment. The hen precedes the egg.
But nevertheless this particular egg may be so treated
as to modify the future type of hen.

II

In the case of the young it is patent that impulses are highly flexible starting points for activities which are diversified according to the ways in which they are used. Any impulse may become organized into almost any disposition according to the way it interacts with surroundings. Fear may become abject cowardice, prudent caution, reverence for superiors or respect for equals; an agency for credulous swallowing of absurd superstitions or for wary scepticism. A man may be chiefly afraid of the spirits of his ancestors, of officials, of arousing the disapproval of his associates, of being deceived, of fresh air, or of Bolshevism. The actual outcome depends upon how the impulse of fear is interwoven with other impulses. This depends in turn upon the outlets and inhibitions supplied by the social environment.

In a definite sense, then, a human society is always starting afresh. It is always in process of renewing, and it endures only because of renewal. We speak of the peoples of southern Europe as Latin peoples. Their existing languages depart widely from one another and from the Latin mother tongue. Yet there never was a day when this alteration of speech was intentional or explicit. Persons always meant to reproduce the speech they heard from their elders and supposed they were succeeding. This fact may stand as a kind of symbol of the reconstruction wrought in habits because of the fact that they can be transmitted and be made to endure only through the medium of the crude activities of the young or through contact with persons having different habits.

For the most part, this continuous alteration has been unconscious and unintended. Immature, undeveloped activity has succeeded in modifying adult organized activity accidentally and surreptitiously. But with the dawn of the idea of progressive betterment and an interest in new uses of impulses, there has grown up some consciousness of the extent to which a future new society of changed purposes and desires may be created by a deliberate humane treatment of the impulses of youth. This is the meaning of education; for a truly humane education consists in an intelligent direction of native activities in the light of the possibilities and necessities of the social situation. But for the most part, adults have given training rather than education. An impatient, premature mechanization of impulsive activity after the fixed pattern of adult habits of thought and affection has been desired. The combined effect of love of power, timidity in the face of the novel and a self-admiring complacency has been too strong to permit immature impulse to exercise its reorganizing potentialities. The younger generation has hardly even knocked frankly at the door of adult customs, much less been invited in to rectify through better education the brutalities and inequities established in adult habits. Each new generation has crept blindly and furtively through such chance gaps as have happened to be left open. Otherwise it has been modeled after the old.

We have already noted how original plasticity is warped and docility is taken mean advantage of. It has been used to signify not capacity to learn liberally and generously, but willingness to learn the customs of adult associates, ability to learn just those special things which those having power and authority wish to teach. Original modifiability has not been given a fair chance to act as a trustee for a better human life. It has been loaded with convention, biased by adult convenience. It has been practically rendered into an equivalent of non-assertion of originality, a pliant accommodation to the embodied opinions of others.

Consequently docility has been identified with imitativeness, instead of with power to re-make old habits, to re-create. Plasticity and originality have been opposed to each other. That the most precious part of plasticity consists in ability to form habits of independent judgment and of inventive initiation has been ignored. For it demands a more complete and intense docility to form flexible easily re-adjusted habits than it does to acquire those which rigidly copy the ways of others. In short, among the native activities of the young are some that work towards accommodation, assimilation, reproduction, and others that work toward exploration, discovery and creation. But the weight of adult custom has been thrown upon retaining and strengthening tendencies toward conformity, and against those which make for variation and independence. The habits of the growing person are jealously kept within the limit of adult customs. The delightful originality of the child is tamed. Worship of institutions and personages themselves lacking in imaginative foresight, versatile observation and liberal thought, is enforced.

Very early in life sets of mind are formed without attentive thought, and these sets persist and control the mature mind. The child learns to avoid the shock of unpleasant disagreement, to find the easy way out, to appear to conform to customs which are wholly mysterious to him in order to get his own way—that is to display some natural impulse without exciting the unfavorable notice of those in authority. Adults distrust the intelligence which a child has while making upon him demands for a kind of conduct that requires a high order of intelligence, if it is to be intelligent at all. The inconsistency is reconciled by instilling in him "moral" habits which have a maximum of emotional empressment and adamantine hold with a minimum of understanding. These habitudes, deeply engrained before thought is awake and even before the day of experiences which can later be recalled, govern conscious later thought. They are usually deepest and most unget-at-able just where critical thought is most needed —in morals, religion and politics. These "infantalisms" account for the mass of irrationalities that prevail among men of otherwise rational tastes. These personal " hang-overs " are the cause of what the student of culture calls survivals. But unfortunately these survivals are much more numerous and pervasive than the anthropologist and historian are wont to admit. To list them would perhaps oust one from " respectable " society.

And yet the intimation never wholly deserts us that there is in the unformed activities of childhood and youth the possibilities of a better life for the community as well as for individuals here and there. This dim sense is the ground of our abiding idealization of childhood. For with all its extravagancies and uncertainties, its effusions and reticences, it remains a standing proof of a life wherein growth is normal not an anomaly, activity a delight not a task, and where habit-forming is an expansion of power not its shrinkage. Habit and impulse may war with each other, but it is a combat between the habits of adults and the impulses of the young, and not, as with the adult, a civil warfare whereby personality is rent asunder. Our usual measure for the " goodness " of children is the amount of trouble they make for grownups, which means of course the amount they deviate from adult habits and expectations. Yet by way of expiation we envy children their love of new experiences, their intentness in extracting the last drop of significance from each situation, their vital seriousness in things that to us are outworn.

We compensate for the harshness and monotony of our present insistence upon formed habits by imagining a future heaven in which we too shall respond freshly and generously to each incident of life. In consequence of our divided attitude, our ideals are self-contradictory. On the one hand, we dream of an attained perfection, an ultimate static goal, in which effort shall cease, and desire and execution be once and for all in complete equilibrium. We wish for a character which shall be steadfast, and we then conceive this desired faithfulness as something immutable, a character exactly the same yesterday, today and forever. But we also have a sneaking sympathy for the courage of an Emerson in declaring that consistency should be thrown to the winds when it stands between us and the opportunities of present life. We reach out to the opposite extreme of our ideal of fixity, and under the guise of a return to nature dream of a romantic freedom, in which *all* life is plastic to impulse, a continual source of improvised spontaneities and novel inspirations. We rebel against all organization and all stability. If modern thought and sentiment is to escape from this division in its ideals, it must be through utilizing released impulse as an agent of steady reorganization of custom and institutions.

While childhood is the conspicuous proof of the renewing of habit rendered possible by impulse, the latter never wholly ceases to play its refreshing rôle in adult life. If it did, life would petrify, society stagnate. Instinctive reactions are sometimes too intense to be woven into a smooth pattern of habits. Under ordinary circumstances they appear to be tamed to obey their master, custom. But extraordinary crises release them and they show by wild violent energy how superficial is the control of routine. The saying that civilization is only skin deep, that a savage persists beneath the clothes of a civilized man, is the common acknowledgment of this fact. At critical moments of unusual stimuli the emotional outbreak and rush of instincts dominating all activity show how superficial is the modification which a rigid habit has been able to effect.

When we face this fact in its general significance, we confront one of the ominous aspects of the history of man. We realize how little the progress of man has been the product of intelligent guidance, how largely it has been a by-product of accidental upheavals, even though by an apologetic interest in behalf of some privileged institution we later transmute chance into providence. We have depended upon the clash of war, the stress of revolution, the emergence of heroic individuals, the impact of migrations generated by war and famine, the incoming of barbarians, to change established institutions. Instead of constantly utilizing unused impulse to effect continuous reconstruction, we have waited till an accumulation of stresses suddenly breaks through the dikes of custom.

It is often supposed that as old persons die, so must old peoples. There are many facts in history to support the belief. Decadence and degeneration seems to be the rule as age increases. An irruption of some uncivilized horde has then provided new blood and fresh life—so much so that history has been defined as a process of rebarbarization. In truth the analogy between a person and a nation with respect to senescence and death is defective. A nation is always renewed by the death of its old constituents and the birth of those who are as young and fresh as ever were any individuals in the hey-day of the nation's glory. Not the nation but its customs get old. Its institutions petrify into rigidity; there is social arterial sclerosis. Then some people not overburdened with elaborate and stiff habits take up and carry on the moving process of life. The stock of fresh peoples is, however, approaching exhaustion. It is not safe to rely upon this expensive method of renewing civilization. We need to discover how to rejuvenate it from within. A normal perpetuation becomes a fact in the degree in which impulse is released and habit is plastic to the transforming touch of impulse. When customs are flexible and youth is educated as youth and not as premature adulthood, no nation grows old.

There always exists a goodly store of non-functioning impulses which may be drawn upon. Their manifestation and utilization is called conversion or regeneration when it comes suddenly. But they may be drawn upon continuously and moderately. Then we call it learning or educative growth. Rigid custom signifies not that there are no such impulses but that they are not organically taken advantage of. As matter of fact, the stiffer and the more encrusted the customs, the larger is the number of instinctive activities that find no regular outlet and that accordingly merely await a chance to get an irregular, uncoordinated manifestation. Routine habits never take up all the slack. They apply only where conditions remain the same or recur in uniform ways. They do not fit the unusual and novel.

Consequently rigid moral codes that attempt to lay down definite injunctions and prohibitions for every occasion in life turn out in fact loose and slack. Stretch ten commandments or any other number as far as you will by ingenious exegesis, yet acts unprovided for by them will occur. No elaboration of statute law can forestall variant cases and the need of interpretation *ad hoc*. Moral and legal schemes that attempt the impossible in the way of definite formulation compensate for explicit strictness in some lines by implicit looseness in others. The only truly severe code is the one which foregoes codification, throwing responsibility for judging each case upon the agents concerned, imposing upon them the burden of discovery and adaptation.

The relation which actually exists between undirected instinct and over-organized custom is illustrated in the two views that are current about savage life. The popular view looks at the savage as a wild man; as one who knows no controlling principles or rules of action, who freely follows his own impulse, whim or desire whenever it seizes him and wherever it takes him. Anthropologists are given to the opposed notion. They view savages as bondsmen to custom.

They note the network of regulations that order his risings-up and his sittings-down, his goings-out and his comings-in. They conclude that in comparison with civilized man the savage is a slave, governed by many inflexible tribal habitudes in conduct and ideas.

The truth about savage life lies in a combination of these two conceptions. Where customs exist they are of one pattern and binding on personal sentiment and thought to a degree unknown in civilized life. But since they cannot possibly exist with respect to all the changing detail of daily life, whatever is left uncovered by custom is free from regulation. It is therefore left to appetite and momentary circumstance. Thus enslavement to custom and license of impulse exist side by side. Strict conformity and unrestrained wildness intensify each other. This picture of life shows us in an exaggerated form the psychology current in civilized life whenever customs harden and hold individuals enmeshed. Within civilization, the savage still exists. He is known in his degree by oscillation between loose indulgence and stiff habit.

Impulse in short brings with itself the possibility but not the assurance of a steady reorganization of habits to meet new elements in new situations. The moral problem in child and adult alike as regards impulse and instinct is to utilize them for formation of new habits, or what is the same thing, the modification of an old habit so that it may be adequately serviceable under novel conditions. The place of impulse in conduct as a pivot of re-adjustment, re-organization, in habits may be defined as follows: On one side, it is marked off from the territory of arrested and encrusted habits. On the other side, it is demarcated from the region in which impulse is a law unto itself.* Generalizing these distinctions, a valid moral theory contrasts with all those theories which set up static goals (even when they are called perfection), and with those theories which idealize raw impulse and find in its spontaneities an adequate mode of human freedom. Impulse is a source, an indispensable source, of liberation; but only as it is employed in giving habits pertinence and freshness does it liberate power.

* The use of the words instinct and impulse as practical equivalents is intentional, even though it may grieve critical readers. The word instinct taken alone is still too laden with the older notion that an instinct is always definitely organized and adapted —which for the most part is just what it is not in human beings. The word impulse suggests something primitive, yet loose, undirected, initial. Man can progress as beasts cannot, precisely because he has so many 'instincts' that they cut across one another, so that most serviceable actions must be *learned*. In learning habits it is possible for man to learn the habit of learning. Then betterment becomes a conscious principle of life.

III

Incidentally we have touched upon a most far-reaching problem: The alterability of human nature. Early reformers, following John Locke, were inclined to minimize the significance of native activities, and to emphasize the possibilities inherent in practice and habit-acquisition. There was a political slant to this denial of the native and a priori, this magnifying of the accomplishments of acquired experience. It held out a prospect of continuous development, of improvement without end. Thus writers like Helvetius made the idea of the complete malleability of a human nature which originally is wholly empty and passive, the basis for asserting the omnipotence of education to shape human society, and the ground of proclaiming the infinite perfectibility of mankind.

Wary, experienced men of the world have always been sceptical of schemes of unlimited improvement. They tend to regard plans for social change with an eye of suspicion. They find in them evidences of the proneness of youth to illusion, or of incapacity on the part of those who have grown old to learn anything from experience. This type of conservative has thought to find in the doctrine of native instincts a scientific support for asserting the practical unalterability of human nature. Circumstances may change but human nature remains from age to age the same. Heredity is more potent than environment, and human heredity is untouched by human intent. Effort for a serious alteration of human institutions is utopian. As things have been so they will be. The more they change the more they remain the same.

Curiously enough both parties rest their case upon just the factor which when it is analyzed weakens their respective conclusions. That is to say, the radical reformer rests his contention in behalf of easy and rapid change upon the psychology of habits, of institutions in shaping raw nature, and the conservative grounds his counter-assertion upon the psychology of instincts. As matter of fact, it is precisely custom which has greatest inertia, which is least susceptible of alteration; while instincts are most readily modifiable through use, most subject to educative direction. The conservative who begs scientific support from the psychology of instincts is the victim of an outgrown psychology which derived its notion of instinct from an exaggeration of the fixity and certainty of the operation of instincts among the lower animals. He is a victim of a popular zoology of the bird, bee and beaver, which was largely framed to the greater glory of God. He is ignorant that instincts in the animals are less infallible and definite than is supposed, and also that the human being differs from the lower animals in precisely the fact that his native activities lack the complex ready-made organization of the animals' original abilities.

But the short-cut revolutionist fails to realize the

full force of the things about which he talks most, namely institutions as embodied habits. Any one with knowledge of the stability and force of habit will hesitate to propose or prophesy rapid and sweeping social changes. A social revolution may effect abrupt and deep alterations in external customs, in legal and political institutions. But the habits that are behind these institutions and that have, willy-nilly, been shaped by objective conditions, the habits of thought and feeling, are not so easily modified. They persist and insensibly assimilate to themselves the outer innovations —much as American judges nullify the intended changes of statute law by interpreting legislation in the light of common law. The force of lag in human life is enormous.

Actual social change is never so great as is apparent change. Ways of belief, of expectation, of judgment and attendant emotional dispositions of like and dislike, are not easily modified after they have once taken shape. Political and legal institutions may be altered, even abolished; but the bulk of popular thought which has been shaped to their pattern persists. This is why glowing predictions of the immediate coming of a social millennium terminate so uniformly in disappointment, which gives point to the standing suspicion of the cynical conservative about radical changes. Habits of thought outlive modifications in habits of overt action. The former are vital, the latter, without the sustaining life of the former, are muscular tricks. Consequently as a rule the moral effects of even great political revolutions, after a few years of outwardly conspicuous alterations, do not show themselves till after the lapse of years. A new generation must come upon the scene whose habits of mind have been formed under the new conditions. There is pith in the saying that important reforms cannot take real effect until after a number of influential persons have died. Where general and enduring moral changes do accompany an external revolution it is because appropriate habits of thought have previously been insensibly matured. The external change merely registers the removal of an external superficial barrier to the operation of existing intellectual tendencies.

Those who argue that social and moral reform is impossible on the ground that the Old Adam of human nature remains forever the same, attribute however to native activities the permanence and inertia that in truth belong only to acquired customs. To Aristotle slavery was rooted in aboriginal human nature. Native distinctions of quality exist such that some persons are by nature gifted with power to plan, command and supervise, and others possess merely capacity to obey and execute. Hence slavery is natural and inevitable. There is error in supposing that because domestic and chattel slavery has been legally abolished, therefore slavery as conceived by Aristotle has disappeared. But matters have at least progressed to a point where it is clear that slavery is a social state not a psychological necessity. Nevertheless the worldlywise Aristotles of today assert that the institutions of war and the present wage-system are so grounded in immutable human nature that effort to change them is foolish.

Like Greek slavery or feudal serfdom, war and the existing economic regime are social patterns woven out of the stuff of instinctive activities. Native human nature supplies the raw materials, but custom furnishes the machinery and the designs. War would not be possible without anger, pugnacity, rivalry, self-display, and such like native tendencies. Activity inheres in them and will persist under every condition of life. To imagine they can be eradicated is like supposing that society can go on without eating and without union of the sexes. But to fancy that they must eventuate in war is as if a savage were to believe that because he uses fibers having fixed natural properties in order to weave baskets, therefore his immemorial tribal patterns are also natural necessities and immutable forms.

From a humane standpoint our study of history is still all too primitive. It is possible to study a multitude of histories, and yet permit history, the record of the transitions and transformations of human activities, to escape us. Taking history in separate doses of this country and that, we take it as a succession of isolated finalities, each one in due season giving way to another, as supernumeraries succeed one another in a march across the stage. We thus miss the fact of history and also its lesson; the diversity of institutional forms and customs which the same human nature may produce and employ. An infantile logic, now happily expelled from physical science, taught that opium put men to sleep because of its dormitive potency. We follow the same logic in social matters when we believe that war exists because of bellicose instincts; or that a particular economic regime is necessary because of acquisitive and competitive impulses which must find expression.

Pugnacity and fear are no more native than are pity and sympathy. The important thing morally is the way these native tendencies interact, for their interaction may give a chemical transformation not a mechanical combination. Similarly, no social institution stands alone as a product of one dominant force. It is a phenomenon or function of a multitude of social factors in their mutual inhibitions and reinforcements. If we follow an infantile logic we shall reduplicate the unity of result in an assumption of unity of force behind it—as men once did with natural events, employing teleology as an exhibition of causal efficiency. We thus take the same social custom twice over: once as an existing fact and then as an original force which produced the fact, and utter sage platitudes about the unalterable workings of human nature or of race. As we account for war by pugnacity, for the capitalistic system by the necessity of an incentive of gain to stir ambition and effort, so we account for Greece by power of esthetic observation, Rome by administrative ability, the middle ages by interest in religion and so on. We have constructed an elaborate political zoology as mythological and not nearly as poetic as the other zoology of phœnixes, griffins and unicorns. Native racial spirit, the spirit of the people or of the time, national destiny are familiar figures in this social zoo. As names for effects, for existing customs, they are sometimes useful. As names for explanatory forces they work havoc with intelligence.

An immense debt is due William James for the mere title of his essay: The Moral Equivalents of War. It reveals with a flash of light the true psychology. Clans, tribes, races, cities, empires, nations, states have made war. The argument that this fact proves an ineradicable belligerent instinct which makes war forever inevitable is much more respectable than many arguments about the immutability of this and that social tradition. For it has the weight of a certain empirical generality back of it. Yet the suggestion of an *equivalent* for war calls attention to the medley of impulses which are casually bunched together under the caption of belligerent impulse; and it calls attention to the fact that the elements of this medley may be woven together into many differing types of activity, some of which may function the native impulses in much better ways than war has ever done.

Pugnacity, rivalry, vainglory, love of booty, fear, suspicion, anger, desire for freedom from the conventions and restrictions of peace, love of power and hatred of oppression, opportunity for novel displays, love of home and soil, attachment to one's people and to the altar and the hearth, courage, loyalty, opportunity to make a name, money or a career, affection, piety to ancestors and ancestral gods—all of these

things and many more make up the war-like force. To
suppose there is some one unchanging native force which
generates war is as naive as the usual assumption that
our enemy is actuated solely by the meaner of the tendencies named and we only by the nobler. In earlier
days there was something more than a verbal connection between pugnacity and fighting; anger and fear
moved promptly through the fists. But between a
loosely organized pugilism and the highly organized
warfare of today there intervenes a long economic,
scientific and political history. Social conditions
rather than an old and unchangeable Adam have generated wars; the ineradicable impulses that are utilized
in them are capable of being drafted into many other
channels. The century that has witnessed the triumph
of the scientific doctrine of the convertibility of natural
energies ought not to balk at the lesser miracle of
social equivalences and substitutes.

It is likely that if Mr. James had witnessed the world
war, he would have modified his mode of treatment. So
many new transformations entered into the war, that
the war seems to prove that though an equivalent has
not been found for war, the psychological forces traditionally associated with it have already undergone
profound changes. We may take the Iliad as a classic
expression of war's traditional psychology as well as
the source of the literary tradition regarding its motives and glories. But where are Helen, Hector and
Achilles in modern warfare? The activities that evoke
and incorporate a war are no longer personal love,

love of glory, or the soldier's love of his own privately
amassed booty, but are of a collective, prosaic political
and economic nature.

Universal conscription, the general mobilization of
all agricultural and industrial forces of the folk not
engaged in the trenches, the application of every conceivable scientific and mechanical device, the mass
movements of soldiery regulated from a common center
by a depersonalized general staff: these factors relegate
the traditional psychological apparatus of war to a
now remote antiquity. The motives once appealed to
are out of date; they do not now induce war. They
simply are played upon after war has been brought
into existence in order to keep the common soldiers
keyed up to their task. The more horrible a depersonalized scientific mass war becomes, the more necessary it is to find universal ideal motives to justify it.
Love of Helen of Troy has become a burning love for
all humanity, and hatred of the foe symbolizes a hatred
of all the unrighteousness and injustice and oppression
which he embodies. The more prosaic the actual causes,
the more necessary is it to find glowingly sublime
motives.

Such considerations hardly prove that war is to be
abolished at some future date. But they destroy that
argument for its necessary continuance which is based
on the immutability of specified forces in original human
nature. Already the forces that once caused wars have
found other outlets for themselves; while new provoca-
tions, based on new economic and political conditions,

have come into being. War is thus seen to be a function of social institutions, not of what is natively fixed in human constitution. The last great war has not, it must be confessed, made the problem of finding social equivalents simpler and easier. It is now naive to attribute war to specific isolable human impulses for which separate channels of expression may be found, while the rest of life is left to go on about the same. A general social re-organization is needed which will redistribute forces, immunize, divert and nullify. Hinton was doubtless right when he wrote that the only way to abolish war was to make peace heroic. It now appears that the heroic emotions are not anything which may be specialized in a side-line, so that the war-impulses may find a sublimation in special practices and occupations. They have to get an outlet in all the tasks of peace.

The argument for the abiding necessity of war turns out, accordingly, to have this much value. It makes us wisely suspicious of all cheap and easy equivalencies. It convinces us of the folly of striving to eliminate war by agencies which leave other institutions of society pretty much unchanged. History does not prove the inevitability of war, but it does prove that customs and institutions which organize native powers into certain patterns in politics and economics will also generate the war-pattern. The problem of war is difficult because it is serious. It is none other than the wider problem of the effective moralizing or humanizing of native impulses in times of peace.

The case of economic institutions is as suggestive as that of war. The present system is indeed much more recent and more local than is the institution of war. But no system has ever as yet existed which did not in some form involve the exploitation of some human beings for the advantage of others. And it is argued that this trait is unassailable because it flows from the inherent, immutable qualities of human nature. It is argued, for example, that economic inferiorities and disabilities are incidents of an institution of private property which flows from an original proprietary instinct; it is contended they spring from a competitive struggle for wealth which in turn flows from the absolute need of profit as an inducement to industry. The pleas are worth examination for the light they throw upon the place of impulses in organized conduct.

No unprejudiced observer will lightly deny the existence of an original tendency to assimilate objects and events to the self, to make them part of the " me." We may even admit that the " me " cannot exist without the " mine." The self gets solidity and form through an appropriation of things which identifies them with whatever we call myself. Even a workman in a modern factory where depersonalization is extreme gets to have " his " machine and is perturbed at a change. Possession shapes and consolidates the " I " of philosophers. " I own, therefore I am " expresses a truer psychology than the Cartesian " I think, therefore I am." A man's deeds are imputed to him as their owner, not merely as their creator. That he cannot disown them when the moment of their occurrence passes is the root of responsibility, moral as well as legal.

But these same considerations evince the versatility of possessive activity. My worldly goods, my good name, my friends, my honor and shame all depend upon a possessive tendency. The need for appropriation has had to be satisfied; but only a calloused imagination fancies that the institution of private property as it exists A. D. 1921 is the sole or the indispensable means of its realization. Every gallant life is an experiment in different ways of fulfilling it. It expends itself in predatory aggression, in forming friendships, in seeking fame, in literary creation, in scientific production. In the face of this elasticity, it requires an arrogant ignorance to take the existing complex system of stocks and bonds, of wills and inheritance, a system supported at every point by manifold legal and political arrangements, and treat it as the sole legitimate and baptized child of an instinct of appropriation. Sometimes, even now, a man most accentuates the fact of ownership when he gives something away; use, consumption, is the normal end of possession. We can conceive a state of things in which the proprietary impulse would get full satisfaction by holding goods as mine in just the degree in which they were visibly administered for a benefit in which a corporate community shared.

Does the case stand otherwise with the other psychological principle appealed to, namely, the need of an incentive of personal profit to keep men engaged in useful work? We need not content ourselves with pointing out the elasticity of the idea of gain, and possible equivalences for pecuniary gain, and the possibility of a state of affairs in which only those things would be counted personal gains which profit a group. It will advance the discussion if we instead subject to analysis the whole conception of incentive and motive.

There is doubtless some sense in saying that every conscious act has an incentive or motive. But this sense is as truistic as that of the not dissimilar saying that every event has a cause. Neither statement throws any light on any particular occurrence. It is at most a maxim which advises us to search for some other fact with which the one in question may be correlated. Those who attempt to defend the necessity of existing economic institutions as manifestations of human nature convert this suggestion of a concrete inquiry into a generalized truth and hence into a definitive falsity. They take the saying to mean that nobody would do anything, or at least anything of use to others, without a prospect of some tangible reward. And beneath this false proposition there is another assumption still more monstrous, namely, that man exists naturally in a state of rest so that he requires some external force to set him into action.

The idea of a thing intrinsically wholly inert in the sense of absolutely passive is expelled from physics and has taken refuge in the psychology of current economics. In truth man acts anyway, he can't help acting. In every fundamental sense it is false that a man requires a motive to make him do something. To a

healthy man inaction is the greatest of woes. Any one
who observes children knows that while periods of rest
are natural, laziness is an acquired vice—or virtue.
While a man is awake he will do something, if only to
build castles in the air. If we like the form of words
we may say that a man eats only because he is
" moved " by hunger. The statement is nevertheless
mere tautology. For what does hunger mean except
that one of the things which man does naturally, instinctively, is to search for food—that his activity naturally turns that way? Hunger primarily names an
act or active process not a motive to an act. It is an
act if we take it grossly, like a babe's blind hunt for the
mother's breast; it is an activity if we take it minutely
as a chemico-physiological occurrence.

The whole concept of motives is in truth extra-
psychological. It is an outcome of the attempt of men
to influence human action, first that of others, then of
a man to influence his own behavior. No sensible person
thinks of attributing the acts of an animal or an idiot
to a motive. We call a biting dog ugly, but we don't
look for his motive in biting. If however we were able
to direct the dog's action by inducing him to reflect
upon his acts, we should at once become interested in
the dog's motives for acting as he does, and should
endeavor to get him interested in the same subject. It
is absurd to ask what induces a man to activity generally speaking. He is an active being and that is all
there is to be said on that score. But when we want
to get him to act in this specific way rather than in

that, when we want to direct his activity that is to say in a specified channel, then the question of motive is pertinent. A motive is then that element in the total complex of a man's activity which, if it can be sufficiently stimulated, will result in an act having specified consequences. And part of the process of intensifying (or reducing) certain elements in the total activity and thus regulating actual consequence is to impute these elements to a person as his actuating motives.

A child naturally grabs food. But he does it in our presence. His manner is socially displeasing and we attribute to his act, up to this time wholly innocent, the motive of greed or selfishness. Greediness simply means the quality of his act as socially observed and disapproved. But by attributing it to him as his motive for acting in the disapproved way, we induce him to refrain. We analyze his total act and call his attention to an obnoxious element in its outcome. A child with equal spontaneity, or thoughtlessness, gives way to others. We point out to him with approval that he acted considerately, generously. And this quality of action when noted and encouraged becomes a reinforcing stimulus of that factor which will induce similar acts in the future. An element in an act viewed as a tendency to produce such and such consequences is a motive. A motive does not exist prior to an act and produce it. It is an act *plus* a judgment upon some element of it, the judgment being made in the light of the consequences of the act.

At first, as was said, others characterize an act with favorable or condign qualities which they impute to an agent's character. They react in this fashion in order to encourage him in future acts of the same sort, or in order to dissuade him—in short to build or destroy a habit. This characterization is part of the technique of influencing the development of character and conduct. It is a refinement of the ordinary reactions of praise and blame. After a time and to some extent, a person teaches himself to think of the results of acting in this way or that before he acts. He recalls that if he acts this way or that some observer, real or imaginary, will attribute to him noble or mean disposition, virtuous or vicious motive. Thus he learns to influence his own conduct. An inchoate activity taken in this forward-looking reference to results, especially results of approbation and condemnation, constitutes a motive. Instead then of saying that a man requires a motive in order to induce him to act, we should say that when a man is going to act he needs to know *what* he is going to do—what the quality of his act is in terms of consequences to follow. In order to act properly he needs to view his act as others view it; namely, as a manifestation of a character or will which is good or bad according as it is bent upon specific things which are desirable or obnoxious. There is no call to furnish a man with incentives to activity in general. But there is every need to induce him to guide his own action by an intelligent perception of its results. For in the long run this is the most effective way of influencing activity to take this desirable direction rather than that objectionable one.

A motive in short is simply an impulse viewed as a constituent in a habit, a factor in a disposition. In general its meaning is simple. But in fact motives are as numerous as are original impulsive activities multiplied by the diversified consequences they produce as they operate under diverse conditions. How then does it come about that current economic psychology has so tremendously oversimplified the situation? Why does it recognize but one type of motive, that which concerns personal gain. Of course part of the answer is to be found in the natural tendency in all sciences toward a substitution of artificial conceptual simplifications for the tangles of concrete empirical facts. But the significant part of the answer has to do with the social conditions under which work is done, conditions which are such as to put an unnatural emphasis upon the prospect of reward. It exemplifies again our leading proposition that social customs are not direct and necessary consequences of specific impulses, but that social institutions and expectations shape and crystallize impulses into dominant habits.

The social peculiarity which explains the emphasis put upon profit as an inducement to productive serviceable work stands out in high relief in the identification of work with labor. For labor means in economic theory something painful, something so onerously disagreeable or " costly " that every individual avoids it if he can, and engages in it only because of the promise of an overbalancing gain. Thus the question we are invited to consider is what the social condition is which makes productive work uninteresting and toilsome. Why is the psychology of the industrialist so different from that of inventor, explorer, artist, sportsman, scientific investigator, physician, teacher? For the latter we do not assert that activity is such a burdensome sacrifice that it is engaged in only because men are bribed to act by hope of reward or are coerced by fear of loss.

The social conditions under which " labor " is undertaken have become so uncongenial to human nature that it is not undertaken because of intrinsic meaning. It is carried on under conditions which render it immediately irksome. The alleged need of an incentive to stir men out of quiescent inertness is the need of an incentive powerful enough to overcome contrary stimuli which proceed from the social conditions. Circumstances of productive service now shear away direct satisfaction from those engaging in it. A real and important fact is thus contained in current economic psychology, but it is a fact about existing industrial conditions and not a fact about native, original activity.

It is " natural " for activity to be agreeable. It tends to find fulfillment, and finding an outlet is itself satisfactory, for it marks partial accomplishment. If productive activity has become so inherently unsatisfactory that men have to be artificially induced to engage in it, this fact is ample proof that the conditions under which work is carried on balk the complex of activities instead of promoting them, irritate and frustrate natural tendencies instead of carrying them forward to fruition. Work then becomes labor, the consequence of some aboriginal curse which forces man to do what he would not do if he could help it, the outcome of some original sin which excluded man from a paradise in which desire was satisfied without industry, compelling him to pay for the means of livelihood with the sweat of his brow. From which it follows naturally that Paradise Regained means the accumulation of investments such that a man can live upon their return without labor. There is, we repeat, too much truth in this picture. But it is not a truth concerning original human nature and activity. It concerns the form human impulses have taken under the influence of a specific social environment. If there are difficulties in the way of social alteration—as there certainly are—they do not lie in an original aversion of human nature to serviceable action, but in the historic conditions which have differentiated the work of the laborer for wage from that of the artist, adventurer, sportsman, soldier, administrator and speculator.

IV

War and the existing economic regime have not been discussed primarily on their own account. They are crucial cases of the relation existing between original impulse and acquired habit. They are so fraught with evil consequences that any one who is disposed can heap up criticisms without end. Nevertheless they persist. This persistence constitutes the case for the conservative who argues that such institutions are rooted in an unalterable human nature. A truer psychology locates the difficulty elsewhere. It shows that the trouble lies in the inertness of established habit. No matter how accidental and irrational the circumstances of its origin, no matter how different the conditions which now exist to those under which the habit was formed, the latter persists until the environment obstinately rejects it. Habits once formed perpetuate themselves, by acting unremittingly upon the native stock of activities. They stimulate, inhibit, intensify, weaken, select, concentrate and organize the latter into their own likeness. They create out of the formless void of impulses a world made in their own image. Man is a creature of habit, not of reason nor yet of instinct.

Recognition of the correct psychology locates the problem but does not guarantee its solution. Indeed, at first sight it seems to indicate that every attempt to solve the problem and secure fundamental reorganizations is caught in a vicious circle. For the direction of native activity depends upon acquired habits, and yet acquired habits can be modified only by redirection of impulses. Existing institutions impose their stamp, their superscription, upon impulse and instinct. They embody the modifications the latter have undergone. How then can we get leverage for changing institutions? How shall impulse exercise that re-adjusting office which has been claimed for it? Shall we not have to depend in the future as in the past upon upheaval and accident to dislocate customs so as to release impulses to serve as points of departure for new habits?

The existing psychology of the industrial worker for example is slack, irresponsible, combining a maximum of mechanical routine with a maximum of explosive, unregulated impulsiveness. These things have been bred by the existing economic system. But they exist, and are formidable obstacles to social change. We cannot breed in men the desire to get something for as nearly nothing as possible and in the end not pay the price. We satisfy ourselves cheaply by preaching the charm of productivity and by blaming the inherent selfishness of human nature, and urging some great moral and religious revival. The evils point in reality to the necessity of a change in economic institutions, but meantime they offer serious obstacles to the change. At the same time, the existing economic system has enlisted in behalf of its own perpetuity the managerial and the technological abilities which must serve the cause of the laborer if he is to be emancipated. In the face of these difficulties other persons seek an equally cheap satisfaction in the thought of universal civil war and revolution.

Is there any way out of the vicious circle? In the first place, there are possibilities resident in the education of the young which have never yet been taken advantage of. The idea of universal education is as yet hardly a century old, and it is still much more of an idea than a fact, when we take into account the early age at which it terminates for the mass. Also, thus far schooling has been largely utilized as a convenient tool of the existing nationalistic and economic regimes. Hence it is easy to point out defects and perversions in every existing school system. It is easy for a critic to ridicule the religious devotion to education which has characterized for example the American republic. It is easy to represent it as zeal without knowledge, fanatical faith apart from understanding. And yet the cold fact of the situation is that the chief means of continuous, graded, economical improvement and social rectification lies in utilizing the opportunities of educating the young to modify prevailing types of thought and desire.

The young are not as yet as subject to the full impact of established customs. Their life of impulsive activity is vivid, flexible, experimenting, curious. Adults have their habits formed, fixed, at least comparatively. They are the subjects, not to say victims, of an environment which they can directly change only

by a maximum of effort and disturbance. They may
not be able to perceive clearly the needed changes, or
be willing to pay the price of effecting them. Yet they
wish a different life for the generation to come. In
order to realize that wish they may create a special
environment whose main function is education. In
order that education of the young be efficacious in inducing an improved society, it is not necessary for
adults to have a formulated definite ideal of some better
state. An educational enterprise conducted in this
spirit would probably end merely in substituting one
rigidity for another. What is necessary is that habits
be formed which are more intelligent, more sensitively
percipient, more informed with foresight, more aware
of what they are about, more direct and sincere, more
flexibly responsive than those now current. Then they
will meet their own problems and propose their own
improvements.

Educative development of the young is not the only
way in which the life of impulse may be employed to
effect social ameliorations, though it is the least expensive and most orderly. No adult environment is all of
one piece. The more complex a culture is, the more
certain it is to include habits formed on differing, even
conflicting patterns. Each custom may be rigid, unintelligent in itself, and yet this rigidity may cause it to
wear upon others. The resulting attrition may release
impulse for new adventures. The present time is conspicuously a time of such internal frictions and liber-
ations. Social life seems chaotic, unorganized, rather

than too fixedly regimented. Political and legal institutions are now inconsistent with the habits that dominate friendly intercourse, science and art. Different institutions foster antagonistic impulses and form contrary dispositions.

If we had to wait upon exhortations and unembodied "ideals" to effect social alterations, we should indeed wait long. But the conflict of patterns involved in institutions which are inharmonious with one another is already producing great changes. The significant point is not whether modifications shall continue to occur, but whether they shall be characterized chiefly by uneasiness, discontent and blind antagonistic struggles, or whether intelligent direction may modulate the harshness of conflict, and turn the elements of disintegration into a constructive synthesis. At all events, the social situation in "advanced" countries is such as to impart an air of absurdity to our insistence upon the rigidity of customs. There are plenty of persons to tell us that the real trouble lies in lack of fixity of habit and principle; in departure from immutable standards and structures constituted once for all. We are told that we are suffering from an excess of instinct, and from laxity of habit due to surrender to impulse as a law of life. The remedy is said to be to return from contemporary fluidity to the stable and spacious patterns of a classic antiquity that observed law and proportion: for somehow antiquity is always classic. When instability, uncertainty, erratic change are diffused throughout the situation, why dwell upon the

evils of fixed habit and the need of release of impulse
as an initiator of reorganizations? Why not rather
condemn impulse and exalt habits of reverencing order
and fixed truth?

The question is natural, but the remedy suggested
is futile. It is not easy to exaggerate the extent to
which we now pass from one kind of nurture to
another as we go from business to church, from science
to the newspaper, from business to art, from companionship to politics, from home to school. An individual is now subjected to many conflicting schemes of
education. Hence habits are divided against one another, personality is disrupted, the scheme of conduct
is confused and disintegrated. But the remedy lies in
the development of a new morale which can be attained
only as released impulses are intelligently employed to
form harmonious habits adapted to one another in a
new situation. A laxity due to decadence of old habits
cannot be corrected by exhortations to restore old
habits in their former rigidity. Even though it were
abstractly desirable it is impossible. And it is not desirable because the inflexibility of old habits is precisely
the chief cause of their decay and disintegration.
Plaintive lamentations at the prevalence of change and
abstract appeals for restoration of senile authority are
signs of personal feebleness, of inability to cope with
change. It is a " defense reaction."

V

We may sum up the discussion in a few generalized statements. In the first place, it is unscientific to try to restrict original activities to a definite number of sharply demarcated classes of instincts. And the practical result of this attempt is injurious. To classify is, indeed, as useful as it is natural. The indefinite multitude of particular and changing events is met by the mind with acts of defining, inventorying and listing, reducing to common heads and tying up in bunches. But these acts like other intelligent acts are performed for a purpose, and the accomplishment of purpose is their only justification. Speaking generally, the purpose is to facilitate our dealings with unique individuals and changing events. When we assume that our clefts and bunches represent fixed separations and collections *in rerum natura,* we obstruct rather than aid our transactions with things. We are guilty of a presumption which nature promptly punishes. We are rendered incompetent to deal effectively with the delicacies and novelties of nature and life. Our thought is hard where facts are mobile; bunched and chunky where events are fluid, dissolving.

The tendency to forget the office of distinctions and classifications, and to take them as marking things in themselves, is the current fallacy of scientific specialism. It is one of the conspicuous traits of high-browism, the essence of false abstractionism. This attitude which once flourished in physical science now governs theorizing about human nature. Man has been resolved into a definite collection of primary instincts which may be numbered, catalogued and exhaustively described one by one. Theorists differ only or chiefly as to their number and ranking. Some say one, self-love; some two, egoism and altruism; some three, greed, fear and glory; while today writers of a more empirical turn run the number up to fifty and sixty. But in fact there are as many specific reactions to differing stimulating conditions as there is time for, and our lists are only classifications for a purpose.

One of the great evils of this artificial simplification is its influence upon social science. Complicated provinces of life have been assigned to the jurisdiction of some special instinct or group of instincts, which has reigned despotically with the usual consequences of despotism. Politics has replaced religion as the set of phenomena based upon fear; or after having been the fruit of a special Aristotelian political faculty, has become the necessary condition of restraining man's self-seeking impulse. All sociological facts are disposed of in a few fat volumes as products of imitation and invention, or of cooperation and conflict. Ethics rest upon sympathy, pity, benevolence. Economics is the science of phenomena due to one love and one aversion —gain and labor. It is surprising that men can engage in these enterprises without being reminded of their ex-

act similarity to natural science before scientific method
was discovered in the seventeenth century. Just now
another simplification is current. All instincts go back
to the sexual, so that *cherchez la femme* (under multitudinous symbolic disguises) is the last word of science
with respect to the analysis of conduct.

Some sophisticated simplifications which once had
great influence are now chiefly matters of historic moment. Even so they are instructive. They show how
social conditions put a heavy load on certain tendencies,
so that in the end an acquired disposition is treated
as if it were an original, and almost the only original
activity. Consider, for example, the burden of causal
power placed by Hobbes upon the reaction of fear. To
a man living with reasonable security and comfort today, Hobbes' pervasive consciousness of fear seems like
the idiosyncrasy of an abnormally timid temperament.
But a survey of the conditions of his own time, of the
disorders which bred general distrust and antagonism,
which led to brutal swashbuckling and disintegrating
intrigue, puts the matter on a different footing. The
social situation conduced to fearfulness. As an account
of the psychology of the natural man his theory is un-
sound. As a report of contemporary social conditions there is much to be said for it.

Something of the same sort may be said regarding
the emphasis of eighteenth century moralists upon
benevolence as the inclusive moral spring to action, an
emphasis represented in the nineteenth century by
Comte's exaltation of altruism. The load was excessive.

But it testifies to the growth of a new philanthropic spirit. With the breaking down of feudal barriers and a consequent mingling of persons previously divided, a sense of responsibility for the happiness of others, for the mitigation of misery, grew up. Conditions were not ripe for its translation into political action. Hence the importance attached to the private disposition of voluntary benevolence.

If we venture into more ancient history, Plato's threefold division of the human soul into a rational element, a spirited active one, and an appetitive one, aiming at increase or gain, is immensely illuminating. As is well known, Plato said that society is the human soul writ large. In society he found three classes: the philosophic and scientific, the soldier-citizenry, and the traders and artisans. Hence the generalization as to the three dominating forces in human nature. Read the other way around, we perceive that trade in his days appealed especially to concupiscence, citizenship to a generous *élan* of self-forgetting loyalty, and scientific study to a disinterested love of wisdom that seemed to be monopolized by a small isolated group. The distinctions were not in truth projected from the breast of the natural individual into society, but they were cultivated in classes of individuals by force of social custom and expectation.

Now the prestige that once attached to the " instinct " of self-love has not wholly vanished. The case is still worth examination. In its " scientific " form, start was taken from an alleged instinct of self-preservation, characteristic of man as well as of other animals. From this seemingly innocuous assumption, a mythological psychology burgeoned. Animals, including man, certainly perform many acts whose consequence is to protect and preserve life. If their acts did not upon the whole have this tendency, neither the individual or the species would long endure. The acts that spring from life also in the main conserve life. Such is the undoubted fact. What does the statement amount to? Simply the truism that life is life, that life is a continuing activity as long as it is life at all. But the self-love school converted the fact that life tends to maintain life into a separate and special force which somehow lies back of life and accounts for its various acts. An animal exhibits in its life-activity a multitude of acts of breathing, digesting, secreting, excreting, attack, defense, search for food, etc., a multitude of specific responses to specific stimulations of the environment. But mythology comes in and attributes them all to a nisus for self-preservation. Thence it is but a step to the idea that all conscious acts are prompted by self-love. This premiss is then elaborated in ingenious schemes, often amusing when animated by a cynical knowledge of the " world," tedious when of a would-be logical nature, to prove that every act of man including his apparent generosities is a variation played on the theme of self-interest.

The fallacy is obvious. Because an animal cannot live except as it is alive, except that is as its acts have the result of sustaining life, it is concluded that all its

acts are instigated by an impulse to self-preservation.
Since all acts affect the well-being of their agent in one
way or another, and since when a person becomes reflective he prefers consequences in the way of weal to
those of woe, therefore all his acts are due to self-love.
In actual substance, one statement says that life is life;
and the other says that a self is a self. One says that
special acts are acts of a living creature and the other
that they are acts of a self. In the biological statement
the concrete diversity between the acts of say a clam
and of a dog are covered up by pointing out that the
acts of each tend to self-preservation, ignoring the
somewhat important fact that in one case it is the life
of a clam and in the other the life of a dog which is
continued. In morals, the concrete differences between
a Jesus, a Peter, a John and a Judas are covered up
by the wise remark that after all they are all selves and
all act as selves. In every case, a result or " end " is
treated as an actuating cause.

The fallacy consists in transforming the (truistic)
fact of acting *as* a self into the fiction of acting always
for self. Every act, truistically again, tends to a certain fulfilment or satisfaction of some habit which is
an undoubted element in the structure of character.
Each satisfaction is qualitatively what it is because of
the disposition fulfilled in the object attained, treachery
or loyalty, mercy or cruelty. But theory comes in and
blankets the tremendous diversity in the quality of the
satisfactions which are experienced by pointing out that
they are all satisfactions. The harm done is then com-

pleted by transforming this artificial unity of result
into an original love of satisfaction as the force that
generates all acts alike. Because a Nero and a Peabody
both get satisfaction in acting as they do it is inferred
that the satisfaction of each is the same in quality, and
that both were actuated by love of the same objective.
In reality the more we concretely dwell upon the common fact of fulfilment, the more we realize the difference in the kinds of selves fulfilled. In pointing out
that both the north and the south poles are poles we
do not abolish the difference of north from south; we
accentuate it.

The explanation of the fallacy is however too easy
to be convincing. There must have been some material,
empirical reason why intelligent men were so easily en-
trapped by a fairly obvious fallacy. That material
error was a belief in the fixity and simplicity of the
self, a belief which had been fostered by a school far
removed from the one in question, the theologians with
their dogma of the unity and ready-made completeness
of the soul. We arrive at true conceptions of motiva-
tion and interest only by the recognition that selfhood
(except as it has encased itself in a shell of routine)
is in process of making, and that any self is capable of
including within itself a number of inconsistent selves,
of unharmonized dispositions. Even a Nero may be
capable upon occasion of acts of kindness. It is even
conceivable that under certain circumstances he may be
appalled by the consequences of cruelty, and turn to the
fostering of kindlier impulses. A sympathetic person is

not immune to harsh arrogances, and he may find himself involved in so much trouble as a consequence of a kindly act, that he allows his generous impulses to shrivel and henceforth governs his conduct by the dictates of the strictest worldly prudence. Inconsistencies and shiftings in character are the commonest things in experience. Only the hold of a traditional conception of the singleness and simplicity of soul and self blinds us to perceiving what they mean: the relative fluidity and diversity of the constituents of selfhood. There is no one ready-made self behind activities. There are complex, unstable, opposing attitudes, habits, impulses which gradually come to terms with one another, and assume a certain consistency of configuration, even though only by means of a distribution of inconsistencies which keeps them in water-tight compartments, giving them separate turns or tricks in action.

Many good words get spoiled when the word self is prefixed to them: Words like pity, confidence, sacrifice, control, love. The reason is not far to seek. The word self infects them with a fixed introversion and isolation. It implies that the act of love or trust or control is turned back upon a self which already is in full existence and in whose behalf the act operates. Pity fulfils and creates a self when it is directed outward, opening the mind to new contacts and receptions. Pity for self withdraws the mind back into itself, rendering its subject unable to learn from the buffetings of fortune. Sacrifice may enlarge a self by bringing about surrender of acquired possessions to requirements of new growth. Self-sacrifice means a self-maiming which asks for compensatory pay in some later possession or indulgence. Confidence as an outgoing act is directness and courage in meeting the facts of life, trusting them to bring instruction and support to a developing self. Confidence which terminates in the self means a smug complacency that renders a person obtuse to instruction by events. Control means a command of resources that enlarges the self; self-control denotes a self which is contracting, concentrating itself upon its own achievements, hugging them tight, and thereby estopping the growth that comes when the self is generously released; a self-conscious moral athleticism that ends in a disproportionate enlargement of some organ.

What makes the difference in each of these cases is the difference between a self taken as something already made and a self still making through action. In the former case, action has to contribute profit or security or consolation *to* a self. In the latter, impulsive action becomes an adventure in discovery of a self which is possible but as yet unrealized, an experiment in creating a self which shall be more inclusive than the one which exists. The idea that only those impulses have moral validity which aim at the welfare of others, or are altruistic, is almost as one-sided a doctrine as the dogma of self-love. Yet altruism has one marked superiority; it at least suggests a generosity of outgoing action, a liberation of power as against the close, pent in, protected atmosphere of a ready-made ego.

The reduction of all impulses to forms of self-love

is worth investigation because it gives an opportunity to say something about self as an ongoing process. The doctrine itself is faded, its advocates are belated. The notion is too tame to appeal to a generation that has experienced romanticism and has been intoxicated by imbibing from the streams of power released by the industrial revolution. The fashionable unification of today goes by the name of the will to power.

In the beginning, this is hardly more than a name for a quality of all activity. Every fulfilled activity terminates in added control of conditions, in an art of administering objects. Execution, satisfaction, realization, fulfilment are all names for the fact that an activity implies an accomplishment which is possible only by subduing circumstance to serve as an accomplice of achievement. Each impulse or habit is thus a will to its *own* power. To say this is to clothe a truism in a figure. It says that anger or fear or love or hate is successful when it effects some change outside the organism which measures its force and registers its efficiency. The achieved outcome marks the difference between action and a cooped-up sentiment which is expended upon itself. The eye hungers for light, the ear for sound, the hand for surfaces, the arm for things to reach, throw and lift, the leg for distance, anger for an enemy to destroy, curiosity for something to shiver and cower before, love for a mate. Each impulse is a demand for an object which will enable it to function. Denied an object in reality it tends to create one in fancy, as pathology shows.

So far we have no generalized will to power, but only the inherent pressure of every activity for an adequate manifestation. It is not so much a demand for power as search for an opportunity to use a power already existing. If opportunities corresponded to the need, a desire *for* power would hardly arise: power would be used and satisfaction would accrue. But impulse is balked. If conditions are right for an educative growth, the snubbed impulse will be " sublimated." That is, it will become a contributory factor in some more inclusive and complex activity, in which it is reduced to a subordinate yet effectual place. Sometimes however frustration dams activity up, and intensifies it. A longing for satisfaction at any cost is engendered. And when social conditions are such that the path of least resistance lies through subjugation of the energies of others, the will to power bursts into flower.

This explains why we attribute a will to power to others but not to ourselves, except in the complimentary sense that being strong we naturally wish to exercise our strength. Otherwise for ourselves we only want what we want when we want it, not being overscrupulous about the means we take to get it. This psychology is naive but it is truer to facts than the supposition that there exists by itself as a separate and original thing a will to power. For it indicates that the real fact is some existing power which demands outlet, and which becomes self-conscious only when it is too weak to overcome obstacles. Conventionally the will to power is imputed only to a comparatively small number of ambitious and ruthless men. They are probably upon the whole quite unconscious of any such will, being mastered by specific intense impulses that find their realization most readily by bending others to serve as tools of their aims. Self-conscious will to power is found mainly in those who have a so-called inferiority complex, and who would compensate for a sense of personal disadvantage (acquired early in childhood) by making a striking impression upon others, in the reflex of which they feel their strength appreciated. The literateur who has to take his action out in imagination is much more likely to evince a will to power than a Napoleon who sees definite objects with extraordinary clearness and who makes directly for them. Explosive irritations, naggings, the obstinacy of weak persons, dreams of grandeur, the violence of those usually submissive are the ordinary marks of a will to power.

Discussion of the false simplification involved in this doctrine suggests another unduly fixed and limited classification. Critics of the existing economic regime have divided instincts into the creative and the acquisitive, and have condemned the present order because it embodies the latter at the expense of the former. The division is convenient, yet mistaken. Convenient because it sums up certain facts of the present system, mistaken because it takes social products for psychological originals. Speaking roughly we may say that native activity is both creative and acquisitive, creative as a process, acquisitive in that it terminates as a rule in some tangible product which brings the process to consciousness of itself.

Activity is creative in so far as it moves to its own enrichment as activity, that is, bringing along with itself a release of further activities. Scientific inquiry, artistic production, social companionship possess this trait to a marked degree; some amount of it is a normal accompaniment of all successfully coordinated action. While from the standpoint of what precedes it is a fulfilment, it is a liberative expansion with respect to what comes after. There is here no antagonism between creative expression and the production of results which endure and which give a sense of accomplishment. Architecture at its best, for example, would probably appear to most persons to be *more* creative, not less, than dancing at its best. There is nothing in industrial production which of necessity excludes creative activity. The fact that it terminates in tangible utilities no more lowers its status than the uses of a bridge exclude creative art from a share in its design and construction. What requires explanation is why process is so definitely subservient to product in so much of modern industry:—that is, why later use rather than present achieving is the emphatic thing. The answer seems to be twofold.

An increasingly large portion of economic work is done with machines. As a rule, these machines are not under the personal control of those who operate them. The machines are operated for ends which the worker has no share in forming and in which as such, or apart from his wage, he has no interest. He neither understands the machines nor cares for their purpose. He is engaged in an activity in which means are cut off from ends, instruments from what they achieve. Highly mechanized activity tends as Emerson said to turn men into spiders and needles. But if men understand what they are about, if they see the whole process of which their special work is a necessary part, and if they have concern, care, for the whole, then the mechanizing effect is counteracted. But when a man is only the tender of a machine, he can have no insight and no affection; creative activity is out of the question.

What remains to the workman is however not so much acquisitive desires as love of security and a wish for a good time. An excessive premium on security springs from the precarious conditions of the workman; desire for a good time, so far as it needs any explanation, from demand for relief from drudgery, due to the absence of culturing factors in the work done. Instead of acquisition being a primary end, the net effect of the process is rather to destroy sober care for materials and products; to induce careless wastefulness, so far as that can be indulged in without lessening the weekly wage. From the standpoint of orthodox economic theory, the most surprising thing about modern industry is the small number of persons who have any effective interest in acquisition of wealth. This disregard for acquisition makes it easier for a few who do want to have things their own way, and who monopolize what is amassed. If an acquisitive impulse were only more evenly developed, more of a real fact, than it is, it it quite possible that things would be better than they are.

Even with respect to men who succeed in accumulating wealth it is a mistake to suppose that acquisitiveness plays with most of them a large rôle, beyond getting control of the tools of the game. Acquisition is necessary as an outcome, but it arises not from love of accumulation but from the fact that without a large stock of possessions one cannot engage effectively in modern business. It is an incident of love of power, of desire to impress fellows, to obtain prestige, to secure influence, to manifest ability, to " succeed " in short under the conditions of the given regime. And if we are to shove a mythological psychology of instincts behind modern economics, we should do better to invent instincts for security, a good time, power and success than to rely upon an acquisitive instinct. We should have also to give much weight to a peculiar sporting instinct. Not acquiring dollars, but chasing them, hunting them is the important thing. Acquisition has its part in the big game, for even the most devoted sportsman prefers, other things being equal, to bring home the fox's brush. A tangible result is the mark to one's self and to others of success in sport.

Instead of dividing sharply an acquisitive impulse manifested in business and a creative instinct displayed in science, art and social fellowship, we should rather first inquire why it is that so much of creative activity is in our day diverted into business, and then ask why it is that opportunity for exercise of the creative capacity in business is now restricted to such a small class, those who have to do with banking, finding a market, and manipulating investments; and finally ask why creative activity is perverted into an over-specialized and frequently inhumane operation. For after all it is not the bare fact of creation but its quality which counts.

That captains of industry are creative artists of a sort, and that industry absorbs an undue share of the creative activity of the present time cannot be denied. To impute to the leaders of industry and commerce simply an acquisitive motive is not merely to lack insight into their conduct, but it is to lose the clew to bettering conditions. For a more proportionate distribution of creative power between business and other occupations, and a more humane, wider use of it in business depend upon grasping aright the forces actually at work. Industrial leaders combine interest in making far-reaching plans, large syntheses of conditions based upon study, mastery of refined and complex technical skill, control over natural forces and events, with love of adventure, excitement and mastery of fellow-men. When these interests are reinforced with actual command of all the means of luxury, of display and procuring admiration from the less fortunate, it is not surprising that creative force is drafted largely into business channels, and that competition for an opportunity to display power becomes brutal.

The strategic question, as was said, is to understand

how and why political, legal, scientific and educational conditions of society for the last centuries have stimulated and nourished such a one-sided development of creative activities. To approach the problem from this point of view is much more hopeful, though infinitely more complex intellectually, than the approach which sets out with a fixed dualism between acquisitive and creative impulses. The latter assumes a complete split of higher and lower in the original constitution of man. Were this the case, there would be no organic remedy. The sole appeal would be to sentimental exhortation to men to wean themselves from devotion to the things which are beloved by their lower and material nature. And if the appeal were moderately successful the social result would be a fixed class division. There would remain a lower class, superciliously looked down upon by the higher, consisting of those in whom the acquisitive instinct remains stronger and who do the necessary work of life, while the higher " creative " class devotes itself to social intercourse, science and art.

Since the underlying psychology is wrong, the problem and its solution assumes in fact a radically different form. There are an indefinite number of original or instinctive activities, which are organized into interests and dispositions according to the situations to which they respond. To increase the creative phase and the humane quality of these activities is an affair of modifying the social conditions which stimulate, select, intensify, weaken and coordinate native activities.

The first step in dealing with it is to increase our detailed scientific knowledge. We need to know exactly the selective and directive force of each social situation; exactly how each tendency is promoted and retarded. Command of the physical environment on a large and deliberate scale did not begin until belief in gross forces and entities was abandoned. Control of physical energies is due to inquiry which establishes specific correlations between minute elements. It will not be otherwise with social control and adjustment. Having the knowledge we may set hopefully at work upon a course of social invention and experimental engineering. A study of the educative effect, the influence upon habit, of each definite form of human intercourse, is prerequisite to effective reform.

VI

In spite of what has been said, it will be asserted that there are definite, independent, original instincts which manifest themselves in specific acts in a one-to-one correspondence. Fear, it will be said, is a reality, and so is anger, and rivalry, and love of mastery of others, and self-abasement, maternal love, sexual desire, gregariousness and envy, and each has its own appropriate deed as a result. Of course they are realities. So are suction, rusting of metals, thunder and lightning and lighter-than-air flying machines. But science and invention did not get on as long as men indulged in the notion of special forces to account for such phenomena. Men tried that road, and it only led them into learned ignorance. They spoke of nature's abhorrence of a vacuum; of a force of combustion; of intrinsic nisus toward this and that; of heaviness and levity as forces. It turned out that these " forces " were only the phenomena over again, translated from a specific and concrete form (in which they were at least actual) into a generalized form in which they were verbal. They converted a problem into a solution which afforded a simulated satisfaction.

Advance in insight and control came only when the mind turned squarely around. After it had dawned upon inquirers that their alleged causal forces were only

names which condensed into a duplicate form a variety
of complex occurrences, they set about breaking up
phenomena into minute detail and searching for correlations, that is, for elements in other gross phenomena
which also varied.   Correspondence of variations of
elements took the place of large and imposing forces.
The psychology of behavior is only beginning to undergo similar treatment.   It is probable that the vogue
of sensation-psychology was due to the fact that it
seemed to promise a similar detailed treatment of personal phenomena.   But as yet we tend to regard sex,
hunger, fear, and even much more complex active interests as if they were lump forces, like the combustion
or gravity of old-fashioned physical science.

It is not hard to see how the notion of a single and
separate tendency grew up in the case of simpler acts
like hunger and sex.   The paths of motor outlet or discharge are comparatively few and are fairly well defined.   Specific bodily organs are conspicuously involved.   Hence there is suggested the notion of a correspondingly separate psychic force or impulse.   There
are two fallacies in this assumption.   The first consists in ignoring the fact that no activity (even one
that is limited by routine habit) is confined to the
channel which is most flagrantly involved in its execution.   The whole organism is concerned in every act to
some extent and in some fashion, internal organs as
well as muscular, those of circulation, secretion, etc.
Since the total state of the organism is never exactly
twice alike, in so far the phenomena of hunger and sex

are never twice the same in fact. The difference may be negligible for some purposes, and yet give the key for the purposes of a psychological analysis which shall terminate in a correct judgment of value. Even physiologically the context of organic changes accompanying an act of hunger or sex makes the difference between a normal and a morbid phenomenon.

In the second place, the environment in which the act takes place is never twice alike. Even when the overt organic discharge is substantially the same, the acts impinge upon a different environment and thus have different consequences. It is impossible to regard these differences of objective result as indifferent to the quality of the acts. They are immediately sensed if not clearly perceived; and they are the only *components of the meaning* of the act. When feelings, dwelling antecedently in the soul, were supposed to be the causes of acts, it was natural to suppose that each psychic element had its own inherent quality which might be directly read off by introspection. But when we surrender this notion, it becomes evident that the only way of telling what an organic act is like is by the sensed or perceptible changes which it occasions. Some of these will be intra-organic, and (as just indicated) they will vary with every act. Others will be external to the organism, and these consequences are more important than the intra-organic ones for determining the quality of the act. For they are consequences in which others are concerned and which evoke reactions of favor and disfavor as well as cooperative and resisting activities of a more indirect sort.

Most so-called self-deception is due to employing immediate organic states as criteria of the value of an act. To say that it feels good or yields direct satisfaction is to say that it gives rise to a comfortable internal state. The judgment based upon this experience may be entirely different from the judgment passed by others upon the basis of its objective or social consequences. As a matter of even the most rudimentary precaution, therefore, every person learns to recognize to some extent the quality of an act on the basis of its consequences in the acts of others. But even without this judgment, the exterior changes produced by an act are immediately sensed, and being associated with the act become a part of its quality. Even a young child sees the smash of things occasionally by his anger, and the smash may compete with his satisfied feeling of discharged energy as an index of value.

A child gives way to what, grossly speaking, we call anger. Its felt or appreciated quality depends in the first place upon the condition of his organism at the time, and this is never twice alike. In the second place, the act is at once modified by the environment upon which it impinges so that different consequences are immediately reflected back to the doer. In one case, anger is directed say at older and stronger playmates who immediately avenge themselves upon the offender, perhaps cruelly. In another case, it takes effect upon weaker and impotent children, and the reflected appreciated consequence is one of achievement, victory, power and a knowledge of the means of having one's own way. The notion that anger still remains a single force is a lazy mythology. Even in the cases of hunger and sex, where the channels of action are fairly demarcated by antecedent conditions (or "nature"), the actual content and feel of hunger and sex, are indefinitely varied according to their social contexts. Only when a man is starving, is hunger an unqualified natural impulse; as it approaches this limit, it tends to lose, moreover, its psychological distinctiveness and to become a raven of the entire organism.

The treatment of sex by psycho-analysts is most instructive, for it flagrantly exhibits both the consequences of artificial simplification and the transformation of social results into psychic causes. Writers, usually male, hold forth on the psychology of woman, as if they were dealing with a Platonic universal entity, although they habitually treat men as individuals, varying with structure and environment. They treat phenomena which are peculiarly symptoms of the civilization of the West at the present time as if they were the necessary effects of fixed native impulses of human nature. Romantic love as it exists today, with all the varying perturbations it occasions, is as definitely a sign of specific historic conditions as are big battle ships with turbines, internal-combustion engines, and electrically driven machines. It would be as sensible to treat the latter as effects of a single psychic cause as to attribute the phenomena of disturbance and con-

flict which accompany present sexual relations as manifestations of an original single psychic force or *Libido*.
Upon this point at least a Marxian simplification is
nearer the truth than that of Jung.

Again it is customary to suppose that there is
a single instinct of fear, or at most a few well-defined
sub-species of it. In reality, when one is afraid the
whole being reacts, and this entire responding organism
is never twice the same. In fact, also, every reaction
takes place in a different environment, and its meaning
is never twice alike, since the difference in environment
makes a difference in consequences. It is only mythology which sets up a single, identical psychic force
which " causes " all the reactions of fear, a force beginning and ending in itself. It is true enough that in
all cases we are able to identify certain more or less
separable characteristic acts—muscular contractions,
withdrawals, evasions, concealments. But in the latter
words we have already brought in an environment. Such
terms as withdrawal and concealment have no meaning
except as attitudes toward objects. There is no such
thing as an environment in general; there are specific
changing objects and events. Hence the kind of eva-
sion or running away or shrinking up which takes place
is directly correlated with specific surrounding conditions. There is no one fear having diverse manifestations; there are as many qualitatively different fears as
there are objects responded to and different consequences sensed and observed.

Fear of the dark is different from fear of publicity,

fear of the dentist from fear of ghosts, fear of conspicuous success from fear of humiliation, fear of a
bat from fear of a bear.   Cowardice, embarrassment,
caution and reverence may all be regarded as forms of
fear.   They all have certain physical organic acts in
common—those of organic shrinkage, gestures of hesitation and retreat.   But each is qualitatively unique.
Each is what it is in virtue of its total interactions or
correlations with other acts and with the environing
medium, with consequences.   High explosives and the
aeroplane have brought into being something new in
conduct.   There is no error in calling it fear.   But
there is error, even from a limited clinical standpoint,
in permitting the classifying name to blot from view
the difference between fear of bombs dropped from the
sky and the fears which previously existed.   The new
fear is just as much and just as little original and
native as a child's fear of a stranger.

For any activity is original when it first occurs.   As
conditions are continually changing, new and *primitive*
activities are continually occurring.   The traditional
psychology of instincts obscures recognition of this
fact.   It sets up a hard-and-fast preordained class
under which specific acts are subsumed, so that their
own quality and originality are lost from view.   This is
why the novelist and dramatist are so much more illuminating as well as more interesting commentators on
conduct than the schematizing psychologist.   The
artist makes perceptible individual responses and thus
displays a new phase of human nature evoked in new

situations. In putting the case visibly and dramatically he reveals vital actualities. The scientific systematizer treats each act as merely another sample of some old principle, or as a mechanical combination of elements drawn from a ready-made inventory.

When we recognize the diversity of native activities and the varied ways in which they are modified through interactions with one another in response to different conditions, we are able to understand moral phenomena otherwise baffling. In the career of any impulse activity there are speaking generally three possibilities. It may find a surging, explosive discharge—blind, unintelligent. It may be sublimated—that is, become a factor coordinated intelligently with others in a continuing course of action. Thus a gust of anger may, because of its dynamic incorporation into disposition, be converted into an abiding conviction of social injustice to be remedied, and furnish the dynamic to carry the conviction into execution. Or an excitation of sexual attraction may reappear in art or in tranquil domestic attachments and services. Such an outcome represents the normal or desirable functioning of impulse; in which, to use our previous language, the impulse operates as a pivot, or reorganization of habit. Or again a released impulsive activity may be neither immediately expressed in isolated spasmodic action, nor indirectly employed in an enduring interest. It may be " suppressed."

Suppression is not annihilation. " Psychic " energy is no more capable of being abolished than the forms we recognize as physical. If it is neither exploded nor converted, it is turned inwards, to lead a surreptitious, subterranean life. An isolated or spasmodic manifestation is a sign of immaturity, crudity, savagery; a suppressed activity is the cause of all kinds of intellectual and moral pathology. One form of the resulting pathology constitutes " reaction " in the sense in which the historian speaks of reactions. A conventionally familiar instance is Stuart license after Puritan restraint. A striking modern instance is the orgy of extravagance following upon the enforced economies and hardships of war, the moral let-down after its highstrung exalted idealisms, the deliberate carelessness after an attention too intense and too narrow. Outward manifestation of many normal activities had been suppressed. But activities were not suppressed. They were merely dammed up awaiting their chance.

Now such " reactions " are simultaneous as well as successive. Resort to artificial stimulation, to alcoholic excess, sexual debauchery, opium and narcotics are examples. Impulses and interests that are not manifested in the regular course of serviceable activity or in recreation demand and secure a special manifestation. And it is interesting to note that there are two opposite forms. Some phenomena are characteristic of persons engaged in a routine monotonous life of toil attended with fatigue and hardship. And others are found in persons who are intellectual and executive, men whose activities are anything but monotonous, but are narrowed through over-specialization. Such men think too much, that is, too much along a *particular* line. They carry too heavy responsibilities; that is, their offices of service are not adequately shared with others. They seek relief by escape into a more sociable and easy-going world. The imperative demand for companionship not satisfied in ordinary activity is met by convivial indulgence. The other class has recourse to excess because its members have in ordinary occupations next to no opportunity for imagination. They make a foray into a more highly colored world as a substitute for a normal exercise of invention, planning and judgment. Having no regular responsibilities, they seek to recover an illusion of potency and of social recognition by an artificial exaltation of their submerged and humiliated selves.

Hence the love of pleasure against which moralists issue so many warnings. Not that love of pleasures is in itself in any way demoralizing. Love of the pleasures of cheerfulness, of companionship is one of the steadying influences in conduct. But pleasure has often become identified with special thrills, excitations, ticklings of sense, stirrings of appetite for the express purpose of enjoying the immediate stimulation irrespective of results. Such pleasures are signs of dissipation, dissoluteness, in the literal sense. An activity which is deprived of regular stimulation and normal function is piqued into isolated activity, and the result is division, disassociation. A life of routine and of over-specialization in non-routine lines seek occasions in which to arouse by abnormal means a *feeling* of sat-

isfaction without any accompanying objective fulfilment. Hence, as moralists have pointed out, the in-
satiable character of such appetites. Activities are not
really satisfied, that is fulfilled in objects. They continue to seek for gratification in more intensified stimulations. Orgies of pleasure-seeking, varying from
saturnalia to mild sprees, result.

It does not follow however that the sole alternative
is satisfaction by means of objectively serviceable action, that is by action which effects useful changes in
the environment. There is an optimistic theory of
nature according to which wherever there is natural
law there is also natural harmony. Since man as
well as the world is included in the scope of natural
law, it is inferred that there is natural harmony between human activities and surroundings, a harmony
which is disturbed only when man indulges in " artificial " departures from nature. According to this view,
all man has to do is to keep his occupations in balance
with the energies of the environment and he will be
both happy and efficient. Rest, recuperation, relief can
be found in a proper alternation of forms of useful
work. Do the things which surroundings indicate need
doing, and success, content, restoration of powers will
take care of themselves.

This benevolent view of nature falls in with a Puritanic devotion to work for its own sake and creates
distrust of amusement, play and recreation. They are
felt to be unnecessary, and worse, dangerous diversions
from the path of useful action which is also the path of

duty. Social conditions certainly impart to occupations as they are now carried on an undue element of fatigue, strain and drudgery. Consequently useful occupations which are so ordered socially as to engage thought, feed imagination and equalize the impact of stress would surely introduce a tranquillity and recreation which are now lacking. But there is good reason to think that even in the best conditions there is enough maladjustment between the necessities of the environment and the activities " natural " to man, so that constraint and fatigue would always accompany activity, and special forms of action be needed—forms that are significantly called re-creation.

Hence the immense moral importance of play and of fine, or make-believe, art—of activity, that is, which is make-believe from the standpoint of the useful arts enforced by the demands of the environment. When moralists have not regarded play and art with a censorious eye, they often have thought themselves carrying matters to the pitch of generosity by conceding that they may be morally indifferent or innocent. But in truth they are moral necessities. They are required to take care of the margin that exists between the total stock of impulses that demand outlet and the amount expended in regular action. They keep the balance which work cannot indefinitely maintain. They are required to introduce variety, flexibility and sensitiveness into disposition. Yet upon the whole the humanizing capabilities of sport in its varied forms, drama, fiction, music, poetry, newspapers have been neglected. They have been left in a kind of a moral no-man's territory. They have accomplished part of their function but they have not done what they are capable of doing. In many cases they have operated merely as reactions like those artificial and isolated stimulations already mentioned.

The suggestion that play and art have an indispensable moral function which should receive an attention now denied, calls out an immediate and vehement protest. We omit reference to that which proceeds from professional moralists to whom art, fun and sport are habitually under suspicion. For those interested in art, professional estheticians, will protest even more strenuously. They at once imagine that some kind of organized supervision if not censorship of play, drama and fiction is contemplated which will convert them into means of moral edification. If they do not think of Comstockian interference in the alleged interest of public morals, they at least think that what is intended is the elimination by persons of a Puritanic, unartistic temperament of everything not found sufficiently earnest and elevating, a fostering of art not for its own sake but as a means of doing good by something to somebody. There is a natural fear of injecting into art a spirit of earnest uplift, of surrendering art to the reformers.

But something quite other than this is meant. Relief from continuous moral activity—in the conventional sense of moral—is itself a moral necessity. The service of art and play is to engage and release impulses in ways quite different from those in which they are occupied and employed in ordinary activities. Their function is to forestall and remedy the usual exaggerations and deficits of activity, even of " moral " activity and to prevent a stereotyping of attention. To say that society is altogether too careless about the moral worth of art is not to say that carelessness about useful occupations is not a necessity for art. On the contrary, whatever deprives play and art of their own careless rapture thereby deprives them of their moral function. Art then becomes poorer as art as a matter of course, but it also becomes in the same measure less effectual in its pertinent moral office. It tries to do what other things can do better, and it fails to do what nothing but itself can do for human nature, softening rigidities, relaxing strains, allaying bitterness, dispelling moroseness, and breaking down the narrowness consequent upon specialized tasks.

Even if the matter be put in this negative way, the moral value of art cannot be depreciated. But there is a more positive function. Play and art add fresh and deeper meanings to the usual activities of life. In contrast with a Philistine relegation of the arts to a trivial by-play from serious concerns, it is truer to say that most of the significance now found in serious occupations originated in activities not immediately useful, and gradually found its way from them into objectively serviceable employments. For their spontaneity and liberation from external necessities permits to them an enhancement and vitality of meaning not possible in preoccupation with immediate needs. Later this meaning is transferred to useful activities and becomes a part of their ordinary working. In saying then that art and play have a moral office not adequately taken advantage of it is asserted that they are responsible to life, to the enriching and freeing of its meanings, not that they are responsible to a moral code, commandment or special task.

To a coarse view—and professed moral refinement is often given to taking coarse views—there is something vulgar not only in recourse to abnormal artificial exitents and stimulations but also in interest in useless games and arts. Negatively the two things have features which are alike. They both spring from failure of regular occupations to engage the full scope of impulses and instincts in an elastically balanced way. They both evince a surplusage of imagination over fact; a demand in imaginative activity for an outlet which is denied in overt activity. They both aim at reducing the domination of the prosaic; both are protests against the lowering of meanings attendant upon ordinary vocations. As a consequence no rule can be laid down for discriminating by direct inspection between unwholesome stimulations and invaluable excursions into appreciative enhancements of life. Their difference lies in the way they work, the careers to which they commit us.

Art releases energy and focuses and tranquilizes it. It releases energy in constructive forms. Castles in the air like art have their source in a turning of impulse away from useful production. Both are due to the failure in some part of man's constitution to secure fulfilment in ordinary ways. But in one case the conversion of direct energy into imagination is the starting point of an activity which *shapes* material; fancy is fed upon a stuff of life which assumes under its influence a rejuvenated, composed and enhanced form. In the other case, fancy remains an end in itself. It becomes an indulging in fantasies which bring about withdrawal from all realities, while wishes impotent in action build a world which yields temporary excitement. Any imagination is a sign that impulse is impeded and is groping for utterance. Sometimes the outcome is a refreshed useful habit; sometimes it is an articulation in creative art; and sometimes it is a futile romancing which for some natures does what self-pity does for others. The amount of potential energy of reconstruction that is dissipated in unexpressed fantasy supplies us with a fair measure of the extent to which the current organization of occupation balks and twists impulse, and, by the same sign, with a measure of the function of art which is not yet utilized.

The development of mental pathologies to the point where they need clinical attention has of late enforced a widespread consciousness of some of the evils of suppression of impulse. The studies of psychiatrists have made clear that impulses driven into pockets distil poison and produce festering sores. An organization of impulse into a working habit forms an interest. A surreptitious furtive organization which does not articulate in avowed expression forms a " complex." Current clinical psychology has undoubtedly overworked the influence of sexual impulse in this connection, refusing at the hands of some writers to recognize the operation of any other modes of disturbance. There are explanations of this onesidedness. The intensity of the sexual instinct and its organic ramifications produce many of the cases that are so noticeable as to demand the attention of physicians. And social taboos and the tradition of secrecy have put this impulse under greater strain than has been imposed upon others. If a society existed in which the existence of impulse toward food were socially disavowed until it was compelled to live an illicit, covert life, alienists would have plenty of cases of mental and moral disturbance to relate in connection with hunger.

The significant thing is that the pathology arising from the sex instinct affords a striking case of a universal principle. Every impulse is, as far as it goes, force, urgency. It must either be used in some function, direct or sublimated, or be driven into a concealed, hidden activity. It has long been asserted on empirical grounds that expression and enslavement result in corruption and perversion. We have at last discovered the reason for this fact. The wholesome and saving force of intellectual freedom, open confrontation, publicity, now has the stamp of scientific sanction. The evil of checking impulses is not that they are checked. Without inhibition there is no instigation of imagination, no redirection into more dis-

criminated and comprehensive activities. The evil resides in a refusal of direct attention which forces the
impulse into disguise and concealment, until it enacts
its own unavowed uneasy private life subject to no
inspection and no control.

A rebellious disposition is also a form of romanticism. At least rebels set out as romantics, or, in popular parlance, as idealists. There is no bitterness like
that of conscious impotency, the sense of suffocatingly
complete suppression. The world is hopeless to one
without hope. The rage of total despair is a vain effort at blind destructiveness. Partial suppression induces in some natures a picture of complete freedom,
while it arouses a destructive protest against existing
institutions as enemies that stand in the way of freedom. Rebellion has at least one advantage over recourse to artificial stimulation and to subconscious
nursings of festering sore spots. It engages in action
and thereby comes in contact with realities. It contains the possibility of learning something. Yet learning by this method is immensely expensive. The costs
are incalculable. As Napoleon said, every revolution
moves in a vicious circle. It begins and ends in excess.

To view institutions as enemies of freedom, and all
conventions as slaveries, is to deny the only means by
which positive freedom in action can be secured. A
general liberation of impulses may set things going
when they have been stagnant, but if the released forces
are on their way to anything they do not know the
way nor where they are going. Indeed, they are bound

to be mutually contradictory and hence destructive—destructive not only of the habits they wish to destroy but of themselves, of their own efficacy. Convention and custom are necessary to carrying forward impulse to any happy conclusion. A romantic return to nature and a freedom sought within the individual without regard to the existing environment finds its terminus in chaos. Every belief to the contrary combines pessimism regarding the actual with an even more optimistic faith in some natural harmony or other—a faith which is a survival of some of the traditional metaphysics and theologies which professedly are to be swept away. Not convention but stupid and rigid convention is the foe. And, as we have noted, a convention can be reorganized and made mobile only by using some other custom for giving leverage to an impulse.

Yet it is too easy to utter commonplaces about the superiority of constructive action to destructive. At all events the professed conservative and classicist of tradition seeks too cheap a victory over the rebel. For the rebel is not self-generated. In the beginning no one is a revolutionist simply for the fun of it, however it may be after the furor of destructive power gets under way. The rebel is the product of extreme fixation and unintelligent immobilities. Life is perpetuated only by renewal. If conditions do not permit renewal to take place continuously it will take place explosively. The cost of revolutions must be charged up to those who have taken for their aim arrest of custom instead of its readjustment. The only ones who have the right to criticize "radicals"—adopting for the moment that perversion of language which identifies the radical with the destructive rebel—are those who put as much effort into reconstruction as the rebels are putting into destruction. The primary accusation against the revolutionary must be directed against those who having power refuse to use it for ameliorations. They are the ones who accumulate the wrath that sweeps away customs and institutions in an undiscriminating avalanche. Too often the man who should be criticizing institutions expends his energy in criticizing those who would re-form them. What he really objects to is any disturbance of his own vested securities, comforts and privileged powers.

VII

We return to the original proposition. The position of impulse in conduct is intermediary. Morality is an endeavor to find for the manifestation of impulse in special situations an office of refreshment and renewal. The endeavor is not easy of accomplishment. It is easier to surrender the main and public channels of action and belief to the sluggishness of custom, and idealize tradition by emotional attachment to its ease, comforts and privileges instead of idealizing it in practice by making it more equably balanced with present needs. Again, impulses not used for the work of rejuvenation and vital recovery are sidetracked to find their own lawless barbarities or their own sentimental refinements. Or they are perverted to pathological careers—some of which have been mentioned.

In the course of time custom becomes intolerable because of what it suppresses and some accident of war or inner catastrophe releases impulses for unrestrained expression. At such times we have philosophies which identify progress with motion, blind spontaneity with freedom, and which under the name of the sacredness of individuality or a return to the norms of nature make impulse a law unto itself. The oscillation between impulse arrested and frozen in rigid custom and impulse isolated and undirected is seen most conspicuously when

169

epochs of conservatism and revolutionary ardor alternate. But the same phenomenon is repeated on a
smaller scale in individuals. And in society the two
tendencies and philosophies exist simultaneously; they
waste in controversial strife the energy that is needed
for specific criticism and specific reconstruction.

The release of some portion of the stock of impulses
is an opportunity, not an end. In its origin it is the
product of chance; but it affords imagination and invention *their* chance. The moral correlate of liberated
impulse is not immediate activity, but reflection upon
the way in which to use impulse to renew disposition
and reorganize habit. Escape from the clutch of custom gives an opportunity to do old things in new ways,
and thus to construct new ends and means. Breach
in the crust of the cake of custom releases impulses;
but it is the work of intelligence to find the ways of
using them. There is an alternative between anchoring
a boat in the harbor till it becomes a rotting hulk and
letting it loose to be the sport of every contrary gust.
To discover and define this alternative is the business
of mind, of observant, remembering, contriving disposition.

Habit as a vital art depends upon the animation of
habit by impulse; only this inspiriting stands between
habit and stagnation. But art, little as well as great,
anonymous as well as that distinguished by titles of
dignity, cannot be improvised. It is impossible without
spontaneity, but it is not spontaneity. Impulse is
needed to arouse thought, incite reflection and enliven

belief.   But only thought notes obstructions, invents tools, conceives aims, directs technique, and thus converts impulse into an art which lives in objects. Thought is born as the twin of impulse in every moment of impeded habit.   But unless it is nurtured, it speedily dies, and habit and instinct continue their civil warfare.   There is instinctive wisdom in the tendency of the young to ignore the limitations of the environment.   Only thus can they discover their own power and learn the differences in different kinds of environing limitations.   But this discovery when once made marks the birth of intelligence; and with its birth comes the responsibility of the mature to observe, to recall, to forecast.   Every moral life has its radicalism; but this radical factor does not find its full expression in direct action but in the courage of intelligence to go deeper than either tradition or immediate impulse goes.   To the study of intelligence in action we now turn our attention.

PART THREE

I

In discussing habit and impulse we have repeatedly met topics where reference to the work of thought was imperative. Explicit consideration of the place and office of intelligence in conduct can hardly begin otherwise than by gathering together these incidental references and reaffirming their significance. The stimulation of reflective imagination by impulse, its dependence upon established habits, and its effect in transforming habit and regulating impulse forms, accordingly, our first theme.

Habits are conditions of intellectual efficiency. They operate in two ways upon intellect. Obviously, they restrict its reach, they fix its boundaries. They are blinders that confine the eyes of mind to the road ahead. They prevent thought from straying away from its imminent occupation to a landscape more varied and picturesque but irrelevant to practice. Outside the scope of habits, thought works gropingly, fumbling in confused uncertainty; and yet habit made complete in routine shuts in thought so effectually that it is no longer needed or possible. The routineer's road is a ditch out of which he cannot get, whose sides enclose him, directing his course so thoroughly that he no longer thinks of his path or his destination. All habit-forming involves the beginning of an intellectual speccialization which if unchecked ends in thoughtless action.

Significantly enough this fullblown result is called absentmindedness. Stimulus and response are mechanically linked together in an unbroken chain. Each successive act facilely evoked by its predecessor pushes us automatically into the next act of a predetermined series. Only a signal flag of distress recalls consciousness to the task of carrying on. Fortunately nature which beckons us to this path of least resistance also puts obstacles in the way of our complete acceptance of its invitation. Success in achieving a ruthless and dull efficiency of action is thwarted by untoward circumstance. The most skilful aptitude bumps at times into the unexpected, and so gets into trouble from which only observation and invention extricate it. Efficiency in following a beaten path has then to be converted into breaking a new road through strange lands.

Nevertheless what in effect is love of ease has masqueraded morally as love of perfection. A goal of finished accomplishment has been set up which if it were attained would mean only mindless action. It has been called complete and free activity when in truth it is only a treadmill activity or marching in one place. The practical impossibility of reaching, in an all around way and all at once such a " perfection " has been recognized. But such a goal has nevertheless been conceived as the ideal, and progress has been defined as approximation to it. Under diverse intellectual skies the ideal has assumed diverse forms and colors. But all of them have involved the conception of a completed activity, a static perfection. Desire and need have been treated as signs of deficiency, and endeavor as proof not of power but of incompletion.

In Aristotle this conception of an end which exhausts all realization and excludes all potentiality appears as a definition of the highest excellence. It of necessity excludes all want and struggle and all dependencies. It is neither practical nor social. Nothing is left but a self-revolving, self-sufficing thought engaged in contemplating its own sufficiency. Some forms of Oriental morals have united this logic with a profounder psychology, and have seen that the final terminus on this road is Nirvana, an obliteration of all thought and desire. In medieval science, the ideal reappeared as a definition of heavenly bliss accessible only to a redeemed immortal soul. Herbert Spencer is far enough away from Aristotle, medieval Christianity and Buddhism; but the idea re-emerges in his conception of a goal of evolution in which adaptation of organism to environment is complete and final. In popular thought, the conception lives in the vague thought of a remote state of attainment in which we shall be beyond " temptation," and in which virtue by its own inertia will persist as a triumphant consummation. Even Kant who begins with a complete scorn

for happiness ends with an " ideal " of the eternal and
undisturbed union of virtue and joy, though in his
case nothing but a symbolic approximation is admitted
to be feasible.

The fallacy in these versions of the same idea is
perhaps the most pervasive of all fallacies in philosophy. So common is it that one questions whether it
might not be called *the* philosophical fallacy. It consists in the supposition that whatever is found true
under certain conditions may forthwith be asserted universally or without limits and conditions. Because a
thirsty man gets satisfaction in drinking water, bliss
consists in being drowned. Because the success of any
particular struggle is measured by reaching a point of
frictionless action, therefore there is such a thing as an
all-inclusive end of effortless smooth activity endlessly
maintained. It is forgotten that success is success *of*
a specific effort, and satisfaction the fulfilment *of* a
specific demand, so that success and satisfaction become meaningless when severed from the wants and
struggles whose consummations they are, or when
taken universally. The philosophy of Nirvana comes
the closest to admission of this fact, but even it holds
Nirvana to be desirable.

Habit is however more than a restriction of thought.
Habits become negative limits because they are first
positive agencies. The more numerous our habits the
wider the field of possible observation and foretelling.
The more flexible they are, the more refined is perception in its discrimination and the more delicate the pres-

entation evoked by imagination. The sailor is intellectually at home on the sea, the hunter in the forest,
the painter in his studio, the man of science in his laboratory. These commonplaces are universally recognized in the concrete; but their significance is obscured
and their truth denied in the current general theory
of mind. For they mean nothing more or less than
that habits formed in process of exercising biological
aptitudes are the sole agents of observation, recollection, foresight and judgment: a mind or consciousness
or soul in general which performs these operations is
a myth.

The doctrine of a single, simple and indissoluble soul
was the cause and the effect of failure to recognize that
concrete habits are the means of knowledge and
thought. Many who think themselves scientifically
emancipated and who freely advertise the soul for a
superstition, perpetuate a false notion of what knows,
that is, of a separate knower. Nowadays they usually
fix upon consciousness in general, as a stream or process
or entity; or else, more specifically upon sensations and
images as the tools of intellect. Or sometimes they
think they have scaled the last heights of realism by
adverting grandiosely to a formal knower in general
who serves as one term in the knowing relation;
by dismissing psychology as irrelevant to knowledge
and logic, they think to conceal the psychological mon-
ster they have conjured up.

Now it is dogmatically stated that no such conceptions of the seat, agent or vehicle will go psychologic-

ally at the present time. Concrete habits do all the perceiving, recognizing, imagining, recalling, judging, conceiving and reasoning that is done. " Consciousness," whether as a stream or as special sensations and images, expresses functions of habits, phenomena of their formation, operation, their interruption and reorganization.

Yet habit does not, of itself, know, for it does not of itself stop to think, observe or remember. Neither does impulse of itself engage in reflection or contemplation. It just lets go. Habits by themselves are too organized, too insistent and determinate to need to indulge in inquiry or imagination. And impulses are too chaotic, tumultuous and confused to be able to know even if they wanted to. Habit as such is too definitely adapted to an environment to survey or analyze it, and impulse is too indeterminately related to the environment to be capable of reporting anything about it. Habit incorporates, enacts or overrides objects, but it doesn't know them. Impulse scatters and obliterates them with its restless stir. A certain delicate combination of habit and impulse is requisite for observation, memory and judgment. Knowledge which is not projected against the black unknown lives in the muscles, not in consciousness.

We may, indeed, be said to *know how* by means of our habits. And a sensible intimation of the practical function of knowledge has led men to identify all acquired practical skill, or even the instinct of animals, with knowledge. We walk and read aloud, we get off and on street cars, we dress and undress, and do a thousand useful acts without thinking of them. We know something, namely, how to do them. Bergson's philosophy of intuition is hardly more than an elaborately documented commentary on the popular conception that by instinct a bird knows how to build a nest and a spider to weave a web. But after all, this practical work done by habit and instinct in securing prompt and exact adjustment to the environment is not knowledge, except by courtesy. Or, if we choose to call it knowledge— and no one has the right to issue an ukase to the contrary—then other things also called knowledge, knowledge *of* and *about* things, knowledge *that* things are thus and so, knowledge that involves reflection and conscious appreciation, remains of a different sort, unaccounted for and undescribed.

For it is a commonplace that the more suavely efficient a habit the more unconsciously it operates. Only a hitch in its workings occasions emotion and provokes thought. Carlyle and Rousseau, hostile in temperament and outlook, yet agree in looking at consciousness as a kind of disease, since we have no consciousness of bodily or mental organs as long as they work at ease in perfect health. The idea of disease is, however, aside from the point, unless we are pessimistic enough to regard every slip in total adjustment of a person to its surroundings as something abnormal—a point of view which once more would identify well-being with perfect automatism. The truth is that in every waking moment, the complete balance of the organism and its environment is constantly interfered with and as constantly restored. Hence the " stream of consciousness " in general, and in particular that phase of it celebrated by William James as alternation of flights and perchings. Life is interruptions and recoveries. Continuous interruption is not possible in the activities of an individual. Absence of perfect equilibrium is not equivalent to a complete crushing of organized activity. When the disturbance amounts to such a pitch as that, the self goes to pieces. It is like shell-shock. Normally, the environment remains sufficiently in harmony with the body of organized activities to sustain most of them in active function. But a novel factor in the surroundings releases some impulse which tends to initiate a different and incompatible activity, to bring about a redistribution of the elements of organized activity between those have been respectively central and subsidiary. Thus the hand guided by the eye moves toward a surface. Visual quality is the dominant element. The hand comes in contact with an object. The eye does not cease to operate but some unexpected quality of touch, a voluptuous smoothness or annoying heat, compels a readjustment in which the touching, handling activity strives to dominate the action. Now at these moments of a shifting in activity conscious feeling and thought arise and are accentuated. The disturbed adjustment of organism and environment is reflected in a temporary strife which concludes in a coming to terms of the old habit and the new impulse.

In this period of redistribution impulse determines the direction of movement. It furnishes the focus about which reorganization swirls. Our attention in short is always directed forward to bring to notice something which is imminent but which as yet escapes us. Impulse defines the peering, the search, the inquiry. It is, in logical language, the movement into the unknown, not into the immense inane of the unknown at large, but into that special unknown which when it is hit upon restores an ordered, unified action. During this search, old habit supplies content, filling, definite, recognizable, subject-matter. It begins as vague presentiment of what we are going towards. As organized habits are definitely deployed and focused, the confused situation takes on form, it is " cleared up "—the essential function of intelligence. Processes become objects. Without habit there is only irritation and confused hesitation. With habit alone there is a machine-like repetition, a duplicating recurrence of old acts. With conflict of habits and release of impulse there is conscious search.

II

We are going far afield from any direct moral issue. But the problem of the place of knowledge and judgment in conduct depends upon getting the fundamental psychology of thought straightened out. So the excursion must be continued. We compare life to a traveler faring forth. We may consider him first at a moment where his activity is confident, straightforward, organized. He marches on giving no direct attention to his path, nor thinking of his destination. Abruptly he is pulled up, arrested. Something is going wrong in his activity. From the standpoint of an onlooker, he has met an obstacle which must be overcome before his behavior can be unified into a successful ongoing. From his own standpoint, there is shock, confusion, perturbation, uncertainty. For the moment he doesn't know what hit him, as we say, nor where he is going. But a new impulse is stirred which becomes the starting point of an investigation, a looking into things, a trying to see them, to find out what is going on. Habits which were interfered with begin to get a new direction as they cluster about the impulse to look and see. The blocked habits of locomotion give him a sense of where he *was* going, of what he had set out to do, and of the ground already traversed. As he looks, he sees definite things which are not just things at large but which are related

to his course of action.   The momentum of the activity
entered upon persists as a sense of direction, of aim;
it is an anticipatory project.   In short, he recollects,
observes and plans.

The trinity of these forecasts, perceptions and re-
membrances form a subject-matter of discriminated
and identified objects.   These objects represent habits
turned inside out.   They exhibit both the onward tendency of habit and the objective conditions which have
been incorporated within it.   Sensations in immediate
consciousness are elements of action dislocated through
the shock of interruption.   They never, however, completely monopolize the scene; for there is a body of
residual undisturbed habits which is reflected in remem-
bered and perceived objects having a meaning.   Thus
out of shock and puzzlement there gradually emerges a
figured framework of objects, past, present, future.
These shade off variously into a vast penumbra of
vague, unfigured things, a setting which is taken for
granted and not at all explicitly presented.   The complexity of the figured scene in its scope and refinement
of contents depends wholly upon prior habits and their
organization.   The reason a baby can know little and
an experienced adult know much when confronting the
same things is not because the latter has a " mind "
which the former has not, but because one has already
formed habits which the other has still to acquire.   The
scientific man and the philosopher like the carpenter,
the physician and politician know with their habits not
with their " consciousness."   The latter is eventual, not

a source. Its occurrence marks a peculiarly delicate
connection between highly organized habits and unorganized impulses. Its contents or objects, observed,
recollected, projected and generalized into principles,
represent the incorporated material of habits coming
to the surface, because habits are disintegrating at the
touch of conflicting impulses. But they also gather
themselves together to comprehend impulse and make
it effective.

This account is more or less strange as psychology
but certain aspects of it are commonplaces in a static
logical formulation. It is, for example, almost a truism
that knowledge is both synthetic and analytic; a set of
discriminated elements connected by relations. This
combination of opposite factors of unity and difference,
elements and relations, has been a standing paradox and
mystery of the theory of knowledge. It will remain so
until we connect the theory of knowledge with an empirically verifiable theory of behavior. The steps of
this connection have been sketched and we may enumer-
ate them. We know at such times as habits are
impeded, when a conflict is set up in which impulse is
released. So far as this impulse sets up a definite forward tendency it constitutes the forward, prospective
character of knowledge. In this phase unity or synthesis is found. We are striving to unify our responses,
to achieve a consistent environment which will restore
unity of conduct. Unity, relations, are prospective;
they mark out lines converging to a focus. They are
" ideal." But *what* we know, the objects that present

themselves with definiteness and assurance, are retrospective; they are the conditions which have been mastered, incorporated in the past. They are elements, discriminated, analytic just because old habits so far as they are checked are also broken into objects which define the obstruction of ongoing activity. They are " real," not ideal. Unity is something sought; split, division is something given, at hand. Were we to carry the same psychology into detail we should come upon the explanation of perceived particulars and conceived universals, of the relation of discovery and proof, induction and deduction, the discrete and the continuous. Anything approaching an adequate discussion is too technical to be here in place. But the main point, however technical and abstract it may be in statement, is of far reaching importance for everything concerned with moral beliefs, conscience and judgments of right and wrong.

The most general, if vaguest issue, concerns the nature of the organ of moral knowledge. As long as knowledge in general is thought to be the work of a special agent, whether soul, consciousness, intellect or a knower in general, there is a logical propulsion towards postulating a special agent for knowledge of moral distinctions. Consciousness and conscience have more than a verbal connection. If the former is something in itself, a seat or power which antecedes intellectual functions, why should not the latter be also a unique faculty with its own separate jurisdiction? If reason in general is independent of empirically verifiable realities of human nature, such as instincts and organized habits, why should there not also exist a moral or practical reason independent of natural operations? On the other hand if it is recognized that knowing is carried on through the medium of natural factors, the assumption of special agencies for moral knowing becomes outlawed and incredible. Now the matter of the existence or non-existence of such special agencies is no technically remote matter. The belief in a separate organ involves belief in a separate and independent subject-matter. The question fundamentally at issue is nothing more or less than whether moral values, regulations, principles and objects form a separate and independent domain or whether they are part and parcel of a normal development of a life process.

These considerations explain why the denial of a separate organ of knowledge, of a separate instinct or impulse toward knowing, is not the wilful philistinism it is sometimes alleged to be. There is of course a sense in which there is a distinctive impulse, or rather habitual disposition, to know. But in the same sense there is an impulse to aviate, to run a typewriter or write stories for magazines. Some activities result in knowledge, as others result in these other things. The result may be so important as to induce distinctive attention to the activities in order to foster them. From an incident, almost a by-product, attainment of truth, physical, social, moral, may become the leading characteristic of some activities. Under such circumstances, they become transformed. Knowing is then a distinctive activity, with its own ends and its peculiarly adapted processes. All this is a matter of course. Having hit upon knowledge accidentally, as it were, and the product being liked and its importance noted, knowledge-getting becomes, upon occasion, a definite occupation. And education confirms the disposition, as it may confirm that of a musician or carpenter or tennis-player. But there is no more an original separate impulse or power in one case than in the other. Every habit is impulsive, that is projective, urgent, and the habit of knowing is no exception.

The reason for insisting on this fact is not failure to appreciate the distinctive value of knowledge when once it comes into existence. This value is so immense it may be called unique. The aim of the discussion is not to subordinate knowing to some hard, prosaic utilitarian end. The reason for insistence upon the derivative position of knowing in activity, roots in a sense for fact, and in a realization that the doctrine of a separate original power and impulse of knowledge cuts knowledge off from other phases of human nature, and results in its non-natural treatment. The isolation of intellectual disposition from concrete empirical facts of biological impulse and habit-formation entails a denial of the continuity of mind with nature. Aristotle asserted that the faculty of pure knowing enters a man from without as through a door. Many since his day have asserted that knowing and doing have no intrinsic connection with each other. Reason is asserted to have

no responsibility to experience; conscience is said to be
a sublime oracle independent of education and social influences. All of these views follow naturally from a
failure to recognize that all knowing, judgment, belief
represent an acquired result of the workings of natural
impulses in connection with environment.

Upon the ethical side, as has been intimated, the matter at issue concerns the nature of conscience. Conscience has been asserted by orthodox moralists to be
unique in origin and subject-matter. The same view is
embodied by implication in all those popular methods
of moral training which attempt to fix rigid authoritative notions of right and wrong by disconnecting moral
judgments from the aids and tests which are used in
other forms of knowledge. Thus it has been asserted
that conscience is an original faculty of illumination
which (if it has not been dimmed by indulgence in sin)
shines upon moral truths and objects and reveals them
without effort for precisely what they are. Those who
hold this view differ enormously among themselves as
to the nature of the objects of conscience. Some hold
them to be general principles, others individual acts,
others the order of worth among motives, others the
sense of duty in general, others the unqualified authority of right. Still others carry the implied logic of
authority to conclusion, and identify knowledge of
moral truths with a divine supernatural revelation of a
code of commandments.

But among these diversities there is agreement about
one fundamental. There must be a separate non-

natural faculty of moral knowledge because the things to be known, the matters of right and wrong, good and evil, obligation and responsibility, form a separate domain, separate that is from that of ordinary action in its usual human and social significance. The latter activities may be prudential, political, scientific, economic. But, from the standpoint of these theories, they have no moral meaning until they are brought under the purview of this separate unique department of our nature. It thus turns out that the so-called intuitional theories of moral knowledge concentrate in themselves all the ideas which are subject to criticism in these pages: Namely, the assertion that morality is distinct in origin, working and destiny from the natural structure and career of human nature. This fact is the excuse, if excuse be desired, for a seemingly technical excursion that links intellectual activity with the conjoint operation of habit and impulse.

III

So far the discussion has ignored the fact that there is an influential school of moralists (best represented in contemporary thought by the utilitarians) which also insists upon the natural, empirical character of moral judgments and beliefs. But unfortunately this school has followed a false psychology; and has tended, by calling out a reaction, actually to strengthen the hands of those who persist in assigning to morals a separate domain of action and in demanding a separate agent of moral knowledge. The essentials of this false psychology consist in two traits. The first, that knowledge originates from sensations (instead of from habits and impulses); and the second, that judgment about good and evil in action consists in calculation of agreeable and disagreeable consequences, of profit and loss. It is not surprising that this view seems to many to degrade morals, as well as to be false to facts. If the logical outcome of an empirical view of moral knowledge is that all morality is concerned with calculating what is expedient, politic, prudent, measured by consequences in the ways of pleasurable and painful sensations, then, say moralists of the orthodox school, we will have naught to do with such a sordid view: It is a reduction to the absurd of its premisses. We will have a separate department for morals and a separate organ of moral knowledge.

Our first problem is then to investigate the nature of ordinary judgments upon what it is best or wise to do, or, in ordinary language, the nature of deliberation. We begin with a summary assertion that deliberation is a dramatic rehearsal (in imagination) of various competing possible lines of action. It starts from the blocking of efficient overt action, due to that conflict of prior habit and newly released impulse to which reference has been made. Then each habit, each impulse, involved in the temporary suspense of overt action takes its turn in being tried out. Deliberation is an experiment in finding out what the various lines of possible action are really like. It is an experiment in making various combinations of selected elements of habits and impulses, to see what the resultant action would be like if it were entered upon. But the trial is in imagination, not in overt fact. The experiment is carried on by tentative rehearsals in thought which do not affect physical facts outside the body. Thought runs ahead and foresees outcomes, and thereby avoids having to await the instruction of actual failure and disaster. An act overtly tried out is irrevocable, its consequences cannot be blotted out. An act tried out in imagination is not final or fatal. It is retrievable.

Each conflicting habit and impulse takes its turn in projecting itself upon the screen of imagination. It unrolls a picture of its future history, of the career it would have if it were given head. Although overt exhibition is checked by the pressure of contrary propulsive tendencies, this very inhibition gives habit a chance at manifestation in thought. Deliberation means precisely that activity is disintegrated, and that its various elements hold one another up. While none has force enough to become the center of a re-directed activity, or to dominate a course of action, each has enough power to check others from exercising mastery. Activity does not cease in order to give way to reflection; activity is turned from execution into intra-organic channels, resulting in dramatic rehearsal.

If activity were directly exhibited it would result in certain experiences, contacts with the environment. It would succeed by making environing objects, things and persons, co-partners in its forward movement; or else it would run against obstacles and be troubled, possibly defeated. These experiences of contact with objects and their qualities give meaning, character, to an otherwise fluid, unconscious activity. We find out what seeing means by the objects which are seen. They constitute the significance of visual activity which would otherwise remain a blank. " Pure " activity is for consciousness pure emptiness. It acquires a content or filling of meanings only in static termini, what it comes to rest in, or in the obstacles which check its onward movement and deflect it. As has been remarked, the object is that which objects.

There is no difference in this respect between a visible course of conduct and one proposed in deliberation. We have no direct consciousness of what we purpose to do. We can judge its nature, assign its meaning, only by following it into the situations whither it leads, noting the objects against which it runs and seeing how they rebuff or unexpectedly encourage it. In imagination as in fact we know a road only by what we see as we travel on it. Moreover the objects which prick out the course of a proposed act until we can see its design also serve to direct eventual overt activity. Every object hit upon as the habit traverses its imaginary path has a direct effect upon existing activities. It reinforces, inhibits, redirects habits already working or stirs up others which had not previously actively entered in. In thought as well as in overt action, the objects experienced in following out a course of action attract, repel, satisfy, annoy, promote and retard. Thus deliberation proceeds. To say that at last it ceases is to say that choice, decision, takes place.

What then is choice? Simply hitting in imagination upon an object which furnishes an adequate stimulus to the recovery of overt action. Choice is made as soon as some habit, or some combination of elements of habits and impulse, finds a way fully open. Then energy is released. The mind is made up, composed, unified. As long as deliberation pictures shoals or rocks or troublesome gales as marking the route of a contemplated voyage, deliberation goes on. But when the various factors in action fit harmoniously together, when imagination finds no annoying hindrance, when there is a picture of open seas, filled sails and favoring winds, the voyage is definitely entered upon. This decisive direction of action constitutes choice. It is a great error to suppose that we have no preferences until there is a choice. We are always biased beings, tending in one direction rather than another. The occasion of deliberation is an *excess* of preferences, not natural apathy or an absence of likings. We want things that are incompatible with one another; therefore we have to make a choice of what we *really* want, of the course of action, that is, which most fully releases activities. Choice is not the emergence of preference out of indifference. It is the emergence of a unified preference out of competing preferences. Biases that had held one another in check now, temporarily at least, reinforce one another, and constitute a unified attitude. The moment arrives when imagination pictures an objective consequence of action which supplies an adequate stimulus and releases definitive action. All deliberation is a search for a *way* to act, not for a final terminus. Its office is to facilitate stimulation.

Hence there is reasonable and unreasonable choice. The object thought of may simply stimulate some impulse or habit to a pitch of intensity where it is temporarily irresistible. It then overrides all competitors and secures for itself the sole right of way. The object looms large in imagination; it swells to fill the field. It allows no room for alternatives; it absorbs us, enraptures us, carries us away, sweeps us off our feet by its own attractive force. Then choice is arbitrary, unreasonable. But the object thought of may be one which stimulates by unifying, harmonizing, different competing tendencies. It may release an activity in which all are fulfilled, not indeed, in their original form, but in a " sublimated " fashion, that is in a way which modifies the original direction of each by reducing it to a component along with others in an action of transformed quality. Nothing is more extraordinary than the delicacy, promptness and ingenuity with which deliberation is capable of making eliminations and recombinations in projecting the course of a possible activity. To every shade of imagined circumstance there is a vibrating response; and to every complex situation a sensitiveness as to its integrity, a feeling of whether it does justice to all facts, or overrides some to the advantage of others. Decision is reasonable when deliberation is so conducted. There may be error in the result, but it comes from lack of data not from ineptitude in handling them.

These facts give us the key to the old controversy as to the respective places of desire and reason in conduct. It is notorious that some moralists have deplored the influence of desire; they have found the heart of strife between good and evil in the conflict of desire with reason, in which the former has force on its side and the latter authority. But reasonableness is in fact a quality of an effective relationship among desires rather than a thing opposed to desire. It signifies the order, perspective, proportion which is achieved, during deliberation, out of a diversity of earlier incompatible preferences. Choice is reasonable when it induces us to act reasonably; that is, with regard to the claims of each of the competing habits and impulses. This implies, of course, the presence of a comprehensive object, one which coordinates, organizes and functions each factor of the situation which gave rise to conflict, suspense and deliberation. This is as true when some " bad " impulses and habits enter in as when approved ones require unification. We have already seen the effects of choking them off, of efforts at direct suppression. Bad habits can be subdued only by being utilized as elements in a new, more generous and comprehensive scheme of action, and good ones be preserved from rot only by similar use.

The nature of the strife of reason and passion is well stated by William James. The cue of passion, he says in effect, is to keep imagination dwelling upon those objects which are congenial to it, which feed it, and which by feeding it intensify its force, until it crowds out all thought of other objects. An impulse or habit which is strongly emotional magnifies all objects that are congruous with it and smothers those which are opposed whenever they present themselves. A passionate activity learns to work itself up artificially —as Oliver Cromwell indulged in fits of anger when he wanted to do things that his conscience would not justify. A presentiment is felt that if the thought of contrary objects is allowed to get a lodgment in imagination, these objects will work and work to chill and freeze out the ardent passion of the moment.

The conclusion is not that the emotional, passionate phase of action can be or should be eliminated in behalf of a bloodless reason. More "passions," not fewer, is the answer. To check the influence of hate there must be sympathy, while to rationalize sympathy there are needed emotions of curiosity, caution, respect for the freedom of others—dispositions which evoke objects which balance those called up by sympathy, and prevent its degeneration into maudlin sentiment and meddling interference. Rationality, once more, is not a force to evoke against impulse and habit. It is the attainment of a working harmony among diverse desires. "Reason" as a noun signifies the happy cooperation of a multitude of dispositions, such as sympathy, curiosity, exploration, experimentation, frankness, pursuit—to follow things through—circumspection, to look about at the context, etc., etc. The elaborate systems of science are born not of reason but of impulses at first slight and flickering; impulses to handle, move about, to hunt, to uncover, to mix things separated and divide things combined, to talk and to listen. Method is their effectual organization into continuous dispositions of inquiry, development and testing. It occurs after these acts and because of their consequences. Reason, the rational attitude, is the resulting disposition, not a ready-made antecedent which can be invoked at will and set into movement. The man who would intelligently cultivate intelligence will widen, not narrow, his life of strong impulses while aiming at their happy coincidence in operation.

The clew of impulse is, as we say, to start something. It is in a hurry. It rushes us off our feet. It leaves no time for examination, memory and foresight. But the clew of reason is, as the phrase also goes, to stop and think. Force, however, is required to stop the ongoing of a habit or impulse. This is supplied by another habit. The resulting period of delay, of suspended and postponed overt action, is the period in which activities that are refused direct outlet project imaginative counterparts. It signifies, in technical phrase, the mediation of impulse. For an isolated impulse *is* immediate, narrowing the world down to the directly present. Variety of competing tendencies enlarges the world. It brings a diversity of considerations before the mind, and enables action to take place finally in view of an object generously conceived and delicately refined, composed by a long process of selections and combinations. In popular phrase, to be deliberate is to be slow, unhurried. It takes time to put objects in order.

There are however vices of reflection as well as of impulse. We may not look far enough ahead because we are hurried into action by stress of impulse; but we may also become overinterested in the delights of reflection; we become afraid of assuming the responsibilities of decisive choice and action, and in general be sicklied over by a pale cast of thought. We may become so curious about remote and abstract matters that we give only a begrudged, impatient attention to the things right about us. We may fancy we are glorifying the love of truth for its own sake when we are only indulging a pet occupation and slighting demands of the immediate situation. Men who devote themselves to thinking are likely to be unusually unthinking in some respects, as for example in immediate personal relationships. A man to whom exact scholarship is an absorbing pursuit may be more than ordinarily vague in ordinary matters. Humility and impartiality may be shown in a specialized field, and pettiness and arrogance in dealing with other persons. " Reason " is not an antecedent force which serves as a panacea. It is a laborious achievement of habit needing to be continually worked over. A balanced arrangement of propulsive activities manifested in deliberation—namely, reason—depends upon a sensitive and proportionate emotional sensitiveness. Only a one-sided, over-specialized emotion leads to thinking of it as separate from emotion. The traditional association of justice and reason has good psychology back of it. Both imply a balanced distribution of thought and energy. Deliberation is irrational in the degree in which an end is so fixed, a passion or interest so absorbing, that the foresight of consequences is warped to include only what furthers execution of its predetermined bias. Deliberation is rational in the degree in which forethought flexibly remakes old aims and habits, institutes perception and love of new ends and acts.

IV

We now return to a consideration of the utilitarian theory according to which deliberation consists in calculation of courses of action on the basis of the profit and loss to which they lead. The contrast of this notion with fact is obvious. The office of deliberation is not to supply an inducement to act by figuring out where the most advantage is to be procured. It is to resolve entanglements in existing activity, restore continuity, recover harmony, utilize loose impulse and redirect habit. To this end observation of present conditions, recollection of previous situations are devoted. Deliberation has its beginning in troubled activity and its conclusion in choice of a course of action which straightens it out. It no more resembles the casting-up of accounts of profit and loss, pleasures and pains, than an actor engaged in drama resembles a clerk recording debit and credit items in his ledger.

The primary fact is that man is a being who responds in action to the stimuli of the environment. This fact is complicated in deliberation, but it certainly is not abolished. We continue to react to an object presented in imagination as we react to objects presented in observation. The baby does not move to the mother's breast because of calculation of the advantages of warmth and food over against the pains of effort. Nor does the miser seek gold, nor the architect strive to make plans, nor the physician to heal, because of reckonings of comparative advantage and disadvantage. Habit, occupation, furnishes the necessity of forward action in one case as instinct does in the other. We do not act *from* reasoning; but reasoning puts before us objects which are not directly or sensibly present, so that we then may react directly to these objects, with aversion, attraction, indifference or attachment, precisely as we would to the same objects if they were physically present. In the end it results in a case of direct stimulus and response. In one case the stimulus is presented at once through sense; in the other case, it is indirectly reached through memory and constructive imagination. But the matter of directness and indirectness concerns the way the stimulus is reached, not the way in which it operates.

Joy and suffering, pain and pleasure, the agreeable and disagreeable, play their considerable rôle in deliberation. Not, however, by way of a calculated estimate of future delights and miseries, but by way of experiencing present ones. The reaction of joy and sorrow, elation and depression, is as natural a response to objects presented in imagination as to those presented in sense. Complacency and annoyance follow hard at the heels of any object presented in image as they do upon its sensuous experience. Some objects when thought of are congruent to our existing state of activity. They fit in, they are welcome. They agree, or are agreeable, not as matter of calculation but as matter of experienced fact.   Other objects rasp; they cut across activity; they are tiresome, hateful, unwelcome.   They disagree with the existing trend of activity, that is, they are disagreeable, and in no other way than as a bore who prolongs his visit, a dun we can't pay, or a pestiferous mosquito who goes on buzzing.   We do not think of future losses and expansions. We think, through imagination, of objects into which in the future some course of action will run, and we are *now* delighted or depressed, pleased or pained at what is presented.   This running commentary of likes and dislikes, attractions and disdains, joys and sorrows, reveals to any man who is intelligent enough to note them and to study their occasions his own character.   It instructs him as to the composition and direction of the activities that make him what he is.   To know what jars an activity and what agrees with it is to know something important about that activity and about ourselves.

Some one may ask what practical difference it makes whether we are influenced by calculation of future joys and annoyances or by experience of present ones.   To such a question one can hardly reply except in the words " All the difference in the world."   In the first place, no difference can be more important than that which concerns the nature of the *subject-matter* of deliberation.   The calculative theory would have it that this subject-matter is future feelings, sensations, and that actions and thought are external means to get and avoid these sensations.   If such a theory has any practical influence, it is to advise a person to concentrate upon his own most subjective and private feelings. It gives him no choice except between a sickly introspection and an intricate calculus of remote, inaccessible and indeterminate results. In fact, deliberation, as a tentative trying-out of various courses of action, is outlooking. It flies toward and settles upon objective situations not upon feelings. No doubt we sometimes fall to deliberating upon the effect of action upon our future feelings, thinking of a situation mainly with reference to the comforts and discomforts it will excite in us. But these moments are precisely our sentimental moments of self-pity or self-glorification. They conduce to morbidity, sophistication, isolation from others; while facing our acts in terms of their objective consequences leads to enlightenment and to consideration of others. The first objection therefore to deliberation as a calculation of future feelings is that, if it is consistently adhered to, it makes an abnormal case the standard one.

If however an objective estimate is attempted, thought gets speedily lost in a task impossible of achievement. Future pleasures and pains are influenced by two factors which are independent of present choice and effort. They depend upon our own state at some future moment and upon the surrounding circumstances of that moment. Both of these are variables which change independently of present resolve and action. They are much more important determinants of future sensations than is anything which can now be calculated. Things sweet in anticipation are bitter in actual taste, things we now turn from in aversion are welcome at another moment in our career. Independently of deep changes in character, such as from mercifulness to callousness, from fretfulness to cheerfulness, there are unavoidable changes in the waxing and waning of activity. A child pictures a future of unlimited toys and unrestricted sweetmeats. An adult pictures an object as giving pleasure while he is empty while the thing arrives in a moment of repletion. A sympathetic person reckons upon the utilitarian basis the pains of others as a debit item in his calculations. But why not harden himself so that others' sufferings won't count? Why not foster an arrogant cruelty so that the suffering of others which will follow from one's own action will fall on the credit side of the reckoning, be pleasurable, all to the good?

Future pleasures and pains, even of one's own, are among the things most elusive of calculation. Of all things they lend themselves least readily to anything approaching a mathematical calculus. And the further into the future we extend our view, and the more the pleasures of others enter into the account, the more hopeless does the problem of estimating future consequences become. All of the elements become more and more indeterminate. Even if one could form a fairly accurate picture of the things that give pleasure to most people at the present moment—an exceedingly difficult task—he cannot foresee the detailed circumstances which will give a decisive turn to enjoyment at future times and remote places. Do pleasures due to defective education or unrefined disposition, to say nothing of the pleasures of sensuality and brutality, rank the same as those of cultivated persons having acute social sensitiveness? The only reason the impossibility of the hedonistic calculus is not self-evident is that theorists in considering it unconsciously substitute for calculation of future pleasures an appreciation of present ones, a present realization in imagination of future objective situations.

For, in truth, a man's judgment of future joys and sorrows is but a projection of what now satisfies and annoys him. A man of considerate disposition now feels hurt at the thought of an act bringing harm to others, and so he is on the lookout for consequences of that sort, ranking them as of high importance. He may even be so abnormally sensitive to such consequences that he is held back from needed vigorous action. He fears to do the things which are for the real welfare of others because he shrinks from the thought of the pain to be inflicted upon them by needed measures. A man of an executive type, engrossed in carrying through a scheme, will react in present emotion to everything concerned with its external success; the pain its execution brings to others will not occur to him, or if it does, his mind will easily glide over it. This sort of consequence will seem to him of slight importance in comparison with the commercial or political changes which bulk in his plans. What a man foresees and fails to foresee, what he appraises highly and at a low rate,

what he deems important and trivial, what he dwells
upon and what he slurs over, what he easily recalls and
what he naturally forgets—all of these things depend
upon his character. His estimate of future consequences of the agreeable and annoying is consequently
of much greater value as an index of what he now is
than as a prediction of future results.

One has only to read between the lines to see the
enormous difference that marks off modern utilitarianism from epicureanism, in spite of similarities in professed psychologies. Epicureanism is too worldly-wise
to indulge in attempts to base present action upon precarious estimates of future and universal pleasures and
pains. On the contrary it says let the future go, for
life is uncertain. Who knows when it will end, or what
fortune the morrow will bring? Foster, then, with jeal-
ous care every gift of pleasure now allotted to you,
dwell upon it with lingering love, prolong it as best you
may. Utilitarianism on the contrary was a part of a
philanthropic and reform movement of the nineteenth
century. Its commendation of an elaborate and impossible calculus was in reality part of a movement to
develop a type of character which should have a wide
social outlook, sympathy with the experiences of all
sentient creatures, one zealous about the social effects
of all proposed acts, especially those of collective legislation and administration. It was concerned not with
extracting the honey of the passing moment but with
breeding improved bees and constructing hives.

After all, the object of foresight of consequences is

not to predict the future. It is to ascertain the meaning of present activities and to secure, so far as possible, a present activity with a unified meaning. We are not the creators of heaven and earth; we have no responsibility for their operations save as their motions are altered by our movements. Our concern is with the significance of that slight fraction of total activity which starts from ourselves. The best laid plans of men as well of mice gang aglee; and for the same reason: inability to dominate the future. The power of man and mouse is infinitely constricted in comparison with the power of events. Men always build better or worse than they know, for their acts are taken up into the broad sweep of events.

Hence the problem of deliberation is not to calculate future happenings but to appraise present proposed actions. We judge present desires and habits by their tendency to produce certain consequences. It is our business to watch the course of our action so as to see what is the significance, the import of our habits and dispositions. The future outcome is not certain. But neither is it certain what the present fire will do in the future. It may be unexpectedly fed or extinguished. But its *tendency* is a knowable matter, what it will do under certain circumstances. And so we know what is the tendency of malice, charity, conceit, patience. We know by observing their consequences, by recollecting what we have observed, by using that recollection in constructive imaginative forecasts of the future, by using the thought of future consequence to tell the quality of the act now proposed.

Deliberation is not calculation of indeterminate future results. The present, not the future, is ours. No shrewdness, no store of information will make it ours. But by constant watchfulness concerning the tendency of acts, by noting disparities between former judgments and actual outcomes, and tracing that part of the disparity that was due to deficiency and excess in disposition, we come to know the meaning of present acts, and to guide them in the light of that meaning. The moral is to develop conscientiousness, ability to judge the significance of what we are doing and to use that judgment in directing what we do, not by means of direct cultivation of something called conscience, or reason, or a faculty of moral knowledge, but by fostering those impulses and habits which experience has shown to make us sensitive, generous, imaginative, impartial in perceiving the tendency of our inchoate dawning activities. Every attempt to forecast the future is subject in the end to the auditing of present concrete impulse and habit. Therefore the important thing is the fostering of those habits and impulses which lead to a broad, just, sympathetic survey of situations.

The occasion of deliberation, that is of the attempt to find a stimulus to complete overt action in thought of some future object, is confusion and uncertainty in present activities. A similar devision in activities and need of a like deliberative activity for the sake of recovery of unity is sure to recur, to recur again and again, no matter how wise the decision. Even the most comprehensive deliberation leading to the most momentous choice only fixes a disposition which has to be continuously applied in new and unforeseen conditions, re-adapted by future deliberations. Always our old habits and dispositions carry us into new fields. We have to be always learning and relearning the meaning of our active tendencies. Does not this reduce moral life to the futile toil of a Sisyphus who is forever rolling a stone uphill only to have it roll back so that he has to repeat his old task? Yes, judged from progress made in a control of conditions which shall stay put and which excludes the necessity of future deliberations and reconsiderations. No, because continual search and experimentation to discover the meaning of changing activity, keeps activity alive, growing in significance. The future situation involved in deliberation is of necessity marked by contingency. What it will be in fact remains dependent upon conditions that escape our foresight and power of regulation. But foresight which draws liberally upon the lessons of past experience reveals the tendency, the meaning, of present action; and, once more, it is this present meaning rather than the future outcome which counts. Imaginative forethought of the probable consequences of a proposed act keeps that act from sinking below consciousness into routine habit or whimsical brutality. It preserves the meaning of that act alive, and keeps it growing in depth and refinement of meaning. There is no limit to the amount of meaning which reflective and meditative habit is capable of importing into even simple acts, just as the most splendid successes of the skilful executive who manipulates events may be accompanied by an incredibly meager and superficial consciousness.

V

The reason for dividing conduct into two distinct regions, one of expediency and the other of morality, disappears when the psychology that identifies ordinary deliberation with calculation is disposed of. There is seen to be but one issue involved in all reflection upon conduct: The rectifying of present troubles, the harmonizing of present incompatibilities by projecting a course of action which gathers into itself the meaning of them all. The recognition of the true psychology also reveals to us the nature of good or satisfaction. Good consists in the meaning that is experienced to belong to an activity when conflict and entanglement of various incompatible impulses and habits terminate in a unified orderly release in action. This human good, being a fulfilment conditioned upon thought, differs from the pleasures which an animal nature—of course we also remain animals so far as we do not think—hits upon accidentally. Moreover there is a genuine difference between a false good, a spurious satisfaction, and a " true " good, and there is an empirical test for discovering the difference. The unification which ends thought in act may be only a superficial compromise, not a real decision but a postponement of the issue. Many of our so-called decisions are of this nature. Or it may present, as we have seen, a victory of a tem-

porarily intense impulse over its rivals, a unity by oppression and suppression, not by coordination. These
seeming unifications which are not unifications of fact
are revealed by the event, by subsequent occurrences.
It is one of the penalties of evil choice, perhaps the chief
penalty, that the wrong-doer becomes more and more incapable of detecting these objective revelations of
himself.

In quality, the good is never twice alike. It never
copies itself. It is new every morning, fresh every
evening. It is unique in its every presentation For it
marks the resolution of a distinctive complication of
competing habits and impulses which can never repeat
itself. Only with a habit rigid to the point of immo-
bility could exactly the same good recur twice. And
with such rigid routines the same good does not after
all recur, for it does not even occur. There is no consciousness at all, either of good or bad. Rigid habits
sink below the level of any meaning at all. And since
we live in a moving world, they plunge us finally against
conditions to which they are not adapted and so terminate in disaster.

To utilitarianism with all its defects belongs the distinction of enforcing in an unforgettable way the fact
that moral good, like every good, consists in a satisfaction of the forces of human nature, in welfare, happiness. To Bentham remains, in spite of all crudities
and eccentricities, the imperishable renown of forcing
home to the popular consciousness that " conscience,"
intelligence applied to in moral matters, is too often

not intelligence but is veiled caprice, dogmatic *ipse dixitism*, vested class interest. It is truly conscience only as it contributes to relief of misery and promotion of happiness. An examination of utilitarianism brings out however the catastrophe involved in thinking of the good to which intelligence is pertinent as consisting in future pleasures and pains, and moral reflection as their algebraic calculus. It emphasizes the contrast between such conceptions of good and of intelligence, and the facts of human nature according to which good, happiness, is found in the present meaning of activity, depending upon the proportion, order and freedom introduced into it by thought as it discovers objects which release and unify otherwise contending elements.

An adequate discussion of why utilitarianism with its just insight into the central place of good, and its ardent devotion to rendering morals more intelligent and more equitably human took its onesided course (and thereby provoked an intensified reaction to transcendental and dogmatic morals) would take us far afield into social conditions and the antecedent history of thought. We can deal with only factor, the domination of intellectual interest by economic considerations. The industrial revolution was bound in any case to give a new direction to thought. It enforced liberation from other-worldly concerns by fixing attention upon the possibility of the betterment of this world through control and utilization of natural forces; it opened up marvelous possibilities in industry and commerce, and new social conditions conducive to invention, ingenuity, enterprise, constructive energy and an impersonal habit of mind dealing with mechanisms rather than appearances. But new movements do not start in a new and clear field. The context of old institutions and corresponding habits of thought persisted. The new movement was perverted in theory because prior established conditions deflected it in practice. Thus the new industrialism was largely the old feudalism, living in a bank instead of a castle and brandishing the check of credit instead of the sword.

An old theological doctrine of total depravity was continued and carried over in the idea of an inherent laziness of human nature which rendered it averse to useful work, unless bribed by expectations of pleasure, or driven by fears of pains. This being the " incentive " to action, it followed that the office of reason is only to enlighten the search for good or gain by instituting a more exact calculus of profit and loss. Happiness was thus identified with a maximum net gain of pleasures on the basis of analogy with business conducted for pecuniary profit, and directed by means of a science of accounting dealing with quantities of receipts and expenses expressed in definite monetary units.* For business was conducted as matter of fact with primary reference to procuring gain and averting loss. Gain and loss were reckoned in terms of units of

---

* I owe the suggestion of this mode of interpreting the hedonistic calculus of utilitarianism to Dr. Wesley Mitchell. See his articles in *Journal of Political Economy*, vol. 18. Compare also his article in *Political Science Quarterly*, vol. 33.

money, assumed to be fixed and equal, exactly compar
able whether loss or gain occurred, while business foresight reduced future prospects to definitely measured
forms, to dollars and cents. A dollar is a dollar, past,
present or future; and every business transaction, every
expenditure and consumption of time, energy, goods,
is, in theory, capable of exact statement in terms of
dollars. Generalize this point of view into the notion
that gain is the object of *all* action; that gain takes the
form of pleasure; that there are definite, commensu-
rable units of pleasure, which are exactly offset by units
of pain (loss), and the working psychology of the
Benthamite school is at hand.

Now admitting that the device of money accounting
makes possible more exact estimates of the consequences
of many acts than is otherwise possible, and that accordingly the use of money and accounting may work a
triumph for the application of intelligence in daily affairs, yet there exists a difference in kind between business calculation of profit and loss and deliberation upon
what purposes to form. Some of these differences are
inherent and insuperable. Others of them are due to
the nature of present business conducted for pecuniary
profit, and would disappear if business were conducted
primarily for service of needs. But it is important to
see *how* in the latter case the assimilation of business
accounting and normal deliberation would occur. For
it would not consist in making deliberation identical
with calculation of loss and gain; it would proceed in
the opposite direction. It would make accounting and

auditing a subordinate factor in discovering the meaning of present activity. Calculation would be a means of stating future results more exactly and objectively and thus of making action more humane. Its function would be that of statistics in all social science.

But first as to the inherent difference between deliberation regarding business profit and loss and deliberation about ordinary conduct. The distinction between wide and narrow use of reason has already been noted. The latter holds a fixed end in view and deliberates only upon means of reaching it. The former regards the end-in-view in deliberation as tentative and permits, nay encourages the coming into view of consequences which will transform it and create a new purpose and plan. Now business calculation is obviously of the kind where the end is taken for granted and does not enter into deliberation. It resembles the case in which a man has already made his final decision, say to take a walk, and deliberates only upon what walk to take. His end-in-view already exists; it is not questioned. The question is as to comparative advantages of this tramp or that. Deliberation is not free but occurs within the limits of a decision reached by some prior deliberation or else fixed by unthinking routine. Suppose, however, that a man's question is not which path to walk upon, but whether to walk or to stay with a friend whom continued confinement has rendered peevish and uninteresting as a companion. The utilitarian theory demands that in the latter case the two alternatives still be of the same kind, alike in quality, that their only difference be a quantitative one, of plus or minus in pleasure. This assumption that all desires and dispositions, all habits and impulses, are the same in quality is equivalent to the assertion that no real or significant conflict among them is possible; and hence there is no need of discovering an object and an activity which will bring them into unity. It asserts by implication that there is no genuine doubt or suspense as to the meaning of any impulse or habit. Their meaning is ready-made, fixed: pleasure. The only " problem " or doubt is as to the *amount* of pleasure (or pain) that is involved.

This assumption does violence to fact. The poignancy of situations that evoke reflection lies in the fact that we really do not know the meaning of the tendencies that are pressing for action. We have to search, to experiment. Deliberation is a work of discovery. Conflict is acute; one impulse carries us one way into one situation, and another impulse takes us another way to a radically different objective result. Deliberation is not an attempt to do away with this opposition of quality by reducing it to one of amount. It is an attempt to *uncover* the conflict in its full scope and bearing. What we want to find out is what difference each impulse and habit imports, to reveal qualitative incompatibilities by detecting the different courses to which they commit us, the different dispositions they form and foster, the different situations into which they plunge us.

In short, the thing actually at stake in any serious

deliberation is not a difference of quantity, but what kind of person one is to become, what sort of self is in the making, what kind of a world is making. This is plain enough in those crucial decisions where the course of life is thrown into widely different channels, where the pattern of life is rendered different and diversely dyed according as this alternative or that is chosen. Deliberation as to whether to be a merchant or a school teacher, a physician or a politician is not a choice of quantities. It is just what it appears to be, a choice of careers which are incompatible with one another, within each of which definitive inclusions and rejections are involved. With the difference in career belongs a difference in the constitution of the self, of habits of thought and feeling as well as of outward action. With it comes profound differences in all future objective relationships. Our minor decisions differ in acuteness and range, but not in principle. Our world does not so obviously hang upon any one of them; but put together they make the world what it is in meaning for each one of us. Crucial decisions can hardly be more than a disclosure of the cumulative force of trivial choices.

A radical distinction thus exists between deliberation where the only question is whether to invest money in this bond or that stock, and deliberation where the primary decision is as to the *kind* of activity which is to be engaged in. Definite quantitative calculation is possible in the former case because a decision as to kind or direction of action does not have to be made. It has been decided already, whether by persistence of habit, or prior deliberation, that the man is to be an investor. The significant thing in decisions proper, the course of action, the kind of a self simply, doesn't enter in; it isn't in question. To reduce all cases of judgment of action to this simplified and comparatively unimportant case of calculation of quantities, is to miss the whole point of deliberation.*

It is another way of saying the same thing to note that business calculations about pecuniary gain never concern direct use in experience. They are, as such, not deliberations about good or satisfaction at all. The man who decides to put business activity before all other claims whatsoever, before that of family or country or art or science, does make a choice about satisfaction or good. But he makes it as a man, not as a business man. On the other hand, what is to be *done* with business profit when it accrues (except to invest it in similar undertakings) does not enter at all into a strictly business deliberation. Its use, in which alone good or satisfaction is found, is left indeterminate, contingent upon further deliberation, or else is left matter of routine habit. We do not eat money, or wear it, or marry it, or listen for musical strains to issue from it. If by any chance a man prefers a less amount of money to a greater amount, it is not for economic reasons. Pecuniary profit in itself, in other words, is always strictly

---

* So far as I am aware Dr. H. W. Stuart was the first to point out this difference between economic and moral valuations in his essay in *Studies in Logical Theory.*

instrumental, and it is of the nature of this instrument to be effective in proportion to size. In choosing with respect to it, we are not making a significant choice, a choice of ends.

We have already seen, however, there is something abnormal and in the strict sense impossible in mere means, in, that is, instruments totally dissevered from ends. We may view economic activity in abstraction, but it does not *exist* by itself. Business takes for granted non-business uses to which its results are to be put. The stimuli for economic activity (in the sense in which business means activity subject to monetary reckoning) are found in non-pecuniary, non-economic activities. Taken by itself then economic action throws no light upon the nature of satisfaction and the relation of intelligence to it, because the whole question of satisfaction is either taken for granted or else is ignored by it. Only when money-making is itself taken as a good does it exhibit anything pertinent to the question. And when it is so taken, then the question is not one of future gain but of present activity and its meaning. Business then becomes an activity carried on for its own sake. It is then a career, a continuous occupation in which are developed daring, adventure, power, rivalry, overcoming of competitors, conspicuous achievement which attracts admiration, play of imagination, technical knowledge, skill in foresight and making combinations, management of men and goods and so on. In this case, it exemplifies what has been said about good or happiness as incorporating in itself at *present* the foreseen future consequences that result from intelligent action. The problem concerns the quality of such a good.

In short the attempt to assimilate other activities to the model of economic activity (defined as a calculated pursuit of gain) reverses the state of the facts. The " economic man " defined as a creature devoted to an enlightened or calculating pursuit of gain is morally objectionable because the conception of such a being empirically falsifies empirical facts. Love of pecuniary gain is an undoubted and powerful fact. But it and its importance are affairs of social not of psychological nature. It is not a primary fact which can be used to account for other phenomena. It depends upon other impulses and habits. It expresses and organizes the use to which they are put. It cannot be used to define the nature of desire, effort and satisfaction, because it embodies a socially selected type of desire and satisfaction. It affords, like steeple-chasing, or collecting postage stamps, seeking political office, astronomical observation of the heavens, a special case of desire, effort, and happiness. And like them it is subject to examination, criticism and valuation in the light of the place it occupies in the system of developing activities.

The reason that it is so easy and for specific purposes so useful to select economic activities and subject them to separate scientific treatment is because the men who engage in it are men who are also more than business men, whose usual habits may be more or less safely

guessed at. As human beings they have desires and occupations which are affected by social custom, expectation and admiration. The uses to which gains will be
put, that is the current scheme of activities into which
they enter as factors, are passed over only because they
are so inevitably present. Support of family, of church,
philanthropic benefactions, political influence, automo-
biling, command of luxuries, freedom of movement, respect from others, are in general terms some of the
obvious activities into which economic activity fits.
This context of activities enters into the real make-up
and meaning of economic activity. Calculated pursuit
of gain is in fact never what it is made out to be when
economic action is separated from the rest of life, for
in fact it is what it is because of a complex social environment involving scientific, legal, political and domestic conditions.

A certain tragic fate seems to attend all intellectual
movements. That of utilitarianism is suggested in the
not infrequent criticism that it exaggerated the rôle of
rational thought in human conduct, that it assumed
that everybody is moved by conscious considerations
and that all that is really necessary is to make the process of consideration sufficiently enlightened. Then it
is objected that a better psychology reveals that men
are not moved by thought but rather by instinct and
habit. Thus a partially sound criticism is employed to
conceal the one factor in utilitarianism from which we
ought to learn something; is used to foster an obscuran-
tist doctrine of trusting to impulse, instinct or intui-

tion. Neither the utilitarians nor any one else can exaggerate the proper office of reflection, of intelligence,
in conduct. The mistake lay not here but in a false
conception of what constitutes reflection, deliberation.
The truth that men are not moved by consideration of
self-interest, that men are not good judges of where
their interests lie and are not moved to act by these
judgments, cannot properly be converted into the belief
that consideration of consequences is a negligible factor
in conduct. So far as it is negligible in fact it evinces
the rudimentary character of civilization. We may
indeed safely start from the assumption that impulse
and habit, not thought, are the primary determinants
of conduct. But the conclusion to be drawn from these
facts is that the need is therefore the greater for cultivation of thought. The error of utilitarianism is not
at this point. It is found in its wrong conception of
what thought, deliberation, is and does.

VI

Our problem now concerns the nature of ends, that is ends-in-view or aims. The essential elements in the problem have already been stated. It has been pointed out that the ends, objectives, of conduct are those foreseen consequences which influence present deliberation and which finally bring it to rest by furnishing an adequate stimulus to overt action. Consequently ends arise and function within action. They are not, as current theories too often imply, things lying beyond activity at which the latter is directed. They are not strictly speaking ends or termini of action at all. They are terminals of deliberation, and so turning points *in* activity. Many opposed moral theories agree however in placing ends beyond action, although they differ in their notions of what the ends are. The utilitarian sets up pleasure as such an outside-and-beyond, as something necessary to induce action and in which it terminates. Many harsh critics of utilitarianism have however agreed that there is some end in which action terminates, a final goal. They have denied that pleasure is such an outside aim, and put perfection or self-realization in its place. The entire popular notion of " ideals " is infected with this conception of some fixed end beyond activity at which we should aim. According to this view ends-in-themselves come before aims.

We have a moral aim only as our purpose coincides with some end-in-itself. We *ought* to aim at the latter whether we actually do or not.

When men believed that fixed ends existed for all normal changes in nature, the conception of similar ends for men was but a special case of a general belief. If the changes in a tree from acorn to full-grown oak were regulated by an end which was somehow immanent or potential in all the less perfect forms, and if change was simply the effort to realize a perfect or complete form, then the acceptance of a like view for human conduct was consonant with the rest of what passed for science. Such a view, consistent and systematic, was foisted by Aristotle upon western culture and endured for two thousand years. When the notion was expelled from natural science by the intellectual revolution of the seventeenth century, logically it should also have disappeared from the theory of human action. But man is not logical and his intellectual history is a record of mental reserves and compromises. He hangs on to what he can in his old beliefs even when he is compelled to surrender their logical basis. So the doctrine of fixed ends-in-themselves at which human acts are—or should be—directed and by which they are regulated if they are regulated at all persisted in morals, and was made the cornerstone of orthodox moral theory. The immediate effect was to dislocate moral from natural science, to divide man's world as it never had been divided in prior culture. One point of view, one method and spirit animated inquiry into natural occurrences;

a radically opposite set of ideas prevailed about man's affairs. Completion of the scientific change begun in the seventeenth century thus depends upon a revision of the current notion of ends of action as fixed limits and conclusions.

In fact, ends are ends-in-view or aims. They arise out of natural effects or consequences which in the beginning are hit upon, stumbled upon so far as any purpose is concerned. Men *like* some of the consequences and *dislike* others. Henceforth (or till attraction and repulsion alter) attaining or averting similar consequences are aims or ends. These consequences constitute the meaning and value of an activity as it comes under deliberation. Meantime of course imagination is busy. Old consequences are enhanced, recombined, modified in imagination. Invention operates. Actual consequences, that is effects which have happened in the past, become possible future consequences of acts still to be performed. This operation of imaginative thought complicates the relation of ends to activity, but it does not alter the substantial fact: Ends are foreseen consequences which arise in the course of activity and which are employed to give activity added meaning and to direct its further course. They are in no sense ends *of* action. In being ends of *deliberation* they are redirecting pivots *in* action.

Men shoot and throw. At first this is done as an " instinctive " or natural reaction to some situation. The result when it is observed gives a new meaning to the activity. Henceforth men in throwing and shooting think of it in terms of its outcome; they act intelligently or have an end. Liking the activity in its acquired meaning, they not only " take aim " when they throw instead of throwing at random, but they find or make targets at which to aim. This is the origin and nature of " goals " of action. They are ways of defining and deepening the meaning of activity. Having an end or aim is thus a characteristic of *present* activity. It is the means by which an activity becomes adapted when otherwise it would be blind and disorderly, or by which it gets meaning when otherwise it would be mechanical. In a strict sense an end-in-view is a *means* in present action; present action is not a means to a remote end. Men do not shoot because targets exist, but they set up targets in order that throwing and shooting may be more effective and significant.

A mariner does not sail towards the stars, but by noting the stars he is aided in conducting his present activity of sailing. A port or harbor is his objective, but only in the sense of *reaching* it not of taking possession of it. The harbor stands in his thought as a significant point at which his activity will need re-direction. Activity will not cease when the port is attained, but merely the *present direction* of activity. The port is as truly the beginning of another mode of activity as it is the termination of the present one. The only reason we ignore this fact is because it is empirically taken for granted. We know without thinking that our " ends " are perforce beginnings. But theories of ends and ideals have converted a theoretical ignoring which is equivalent to practical acknowledgment into an intellectual denial, and have thereby confused and perverted the nature of ends.

Even the most important among all the consequences of an act is not necessarily its aim. Results which are objectively most important may not even be thought of at all; ordinarily a man does not think in connection with exercise of his profession that it will sustain him and his family in existence. The end-thought-of is uniquely important, but it is indispensable to state the respect in which it is important. It gives the decisive clew to the act to be performed under the existing circumstances. It is that particular foreseen object that will stimulate the act which relieves existing troubles, straightens out existing entanglements. In a temporary annoyance, even if only that caused by the singing of a mosquito, the thought of that which gives relief may engross the mind in spite of consequences much more important, objectively speaking. Moralists have deplored such facts as evidence of levity. But the remedy, if a remedy be needed, is not found in insisting upon the importance of ends in general. It is found in a change of the dispositions which make things either immediately troublesome or tolerable or agreeable.

When ends are regarded as literally ends to action rather than as directive stimuli to present choice they are frozen and isolated. It makes no difference whether the " end " is " natural " good like health or a " moral " good like honesty. Set up as complete and exclusive, as demanding and justifying action as a means to itself, it leads to narrowness; in extreme cases fanaticism, inconsiderateness, arrogance and hypocrisy. Joshua's reputed success in getting the sun to stand still to serve his desire is recognized to have involved a miracle. But moral theorists constantly assume that the continuous course of events can be arrested at the point of a particular object; that men can plunge with their own desires into the unceasing flow of changes, and seize upon some object as their end irrespective of everything else. The use of intelligence to discover the object that will best operate as a releasing and unifying stimulus in the existing situation is discounted. One reminds one's self that one's end is justice or charity or professional achievement or putting over a deal for a needed public improvement, and further questionings and qualms are stilled.

It is customary to suppose that such methods merely ignore the question of the morality of the means which are used to secure the end desired. Common sense revolts against the maxim, conveniently laid off upon Jesuits or other far-away people, that the end justifies the means. There is no incorrectness in saying that the question of means employed is overlooked in such cases. But analysis would go further if it were also pointed out that overlooking means is only a device for failing to note those ends, or consequences, which, if they were noted would be seen to be so evil that action would be estopped. Certainly nothing can justify or condemn means except ends, results. But we have to include consequences impartially. Even admitting that lying will save a man's soul, whatever that may mean, it would still be true that lying will have other consequences, namely, the usual consequences that follow from tampering with good faith and that lead lying to be condemned. It is wilful folly to fasten upon some single end or consequence which is liked, and permit the view of that to blot from perception all other undesired and undesirable consequences. It is like supposing that when a finger held close to the eye covers up a distant mountain the finger is really larger than the mountain. Not *the* end—in the singular—justifies the means; for there is no such thing as the single all-important end. To suppose that there is such an end is like working over again, in behalf of our private wishes, the miracle of Joshua in arresting the course of nature. It is not possible adequately to characterize the presumption, the falsity and the deliberate perversion of intelligence involved in refusal to note the plural effects that flow from any act, a refusal adopted in order that we may justify an act by picking out that one consequence which will enable us to do what we wish to do and for which we feel the need of justification.

Yet this assumption is continually made. It is made by implication in the current view of purposes or ends-in-view as objects in themselves, instead of means to unification and liberation of present conflicting, confused habits and impulses. There is something almost sinister in the desire to label the doctrine that the end justifies the means with the name of some one obnoxious school. Politicians, especially if they have to do with

the foreign affairs of a nation and are called states-
men, almost uniformly act upon the doctrine that the
welfare of their own country justifies any measure irrespective of all the demoralization it works. Captains
of industry, great executives in all lines, usually work
upon this plan. But they are not the original offenders
by any means. Every man works upon it so far as he
permits himself to become so absorbed in one aspect of
what he is doing that he loses a view of its varied consequences, hypnotizing his attention by consideration
of just those consequences which in the abstract are
desirable and slurring over other consequences equally
real. Every man works upon this principle who becomes over-interested in any cause or project, and who
uses its desirability in the abstract to justify himself
in employing any means that will assist him in arriving,
ignoring all the collateral " ends " of his behavior. It
is frequently pointed out that there is a type of execu-
tive-man whose conduct seems to be as non-moral as
the action of the forces of nature. We all tend to
relapse into this non-moral condition whenever we want
any one thing intensely. In general, the identification
of the end prominent in conscious desire and effort with
the end is part of the technique of avoiding a reasonable survey of consequences. The survey is avoided
because of a subconscious recognition that it would reveal desire in its true worth and thus preclude action to
satisfy it—or at all events give us an uneasy conscience
in striving to realize it. Thus the doctrine of the isolated, complete or fixed end limits intelligent examina-

tion, encourages insincerity, and puts a pseudo-stamp of moral justification upon success at any price.

Moralistic persons are given to escaping this evil by falling into another pit. They deny that consequences have anything at all to do with the morality of acts. Not ends but motives they say justify or condemn acts. The thing to do, accordingly, is to cultivate certain motives or dispositions, benevolence, purity, love of perfection, loyalty. The denial of consequences thus turns out formal, verbal. In reality a consequence is set up at which to aim, only it is a subjective consequence. " Meaning well " is selected as *the* consequence or end to be cultivated at all hazards, an end which is all-justifying and to which everything else is offered up in sacrifice. The result is a sentimental futile complacency rather than the brutal efficiency of the executive. But the root of both evils is the same. One man selects some external consequence, the other man a state of internal feeling, to serve as the end. The doctrine of meaning well as *the* end is if anything the more contemptible of the two, for it shrinks from accepting any responsibility for actual results. It is negative, self-protective and sloppy. It lends itself to complete self-deception.

Why have men become so attached to fixed, external ends? Why is it not universally recognized that an end is a device of intelligence in guiding action, instrumental to freeing and harmonizing troubled and divided tendencies? The answer is virtually contained in what was earlier said about rigid habits and their effect upon intelligence. Ends are, in fact, literally endless, forever coming into existence as new activities occasion new consequences. "Endless ends" is a way of saying that there are no ends—that is no fixed self-enclosed finalities. While however we cannot actually prevent change from occurring we can and do regard it as evil. We strive to retain action in ditches already dug. We regard novelties as dangerous, experiments as illicit and deviations as forbidden. Fixed and separate ends reflect a projection of our own fixed and non-interacting compartmental habits. We see only consequences which correspond to our habitual courses. As we have said, men did not begin to shoot because there were ready-made targets to aim at. They made things into targets by shooting at them, and then made special targets to make shooting more significantly interesting. But if generation after generation were shown targets they had had no part in constructing, if bows and arrows were thrust into their hands, and pressure were brought to bear upon them to keep them shooting in season and out, some wearied soul would soon propound to willing listeners the theory that shooting was unnatural, that man was naturally wholly at rest, and that targets existed in order that men might be forced to be active; that the duty of shooting and the virtue of hitting are externally imposed and fostered, and that otherwise there would be no such thing as a shooting-activity—that is, morality.

The doctrine of fixed ends not only diverts attention from examination of consequences and the intelligent creation of purpose, but, since means and ends are two ways of regarding the same actuality, it also renders men careless in their inspection of existing conditions. An aim not framed on the basis of a survey of those present conditions which are to be employed as means of its realization simply throws us back upon past habits. We then do not do what we intended to do but what we have got used to doing, or else we thrash about in a blind ineffectual way. The result is failure. Discouragement follows, assuaged perhaps by the thought that in any case the end is too ideal, too noble and remote, to be capable of realization. We fall back on the consoling thought that our moral ideals are too good for this world and that we must accustom ourselves to a gap between aim and execution. Actual life is then thought of as a compromise with the best, an enforced second or third best, a dreary exile from our true home in the ideal, or a temporary period of troubled probation to be followed by a period of unending attainment and peace. At the same time, as has been repeatedly pointed out, persons of a more practical turn of mind accept the world " as it is," that is as past customs have made it to be, and consider what advantages for themselves may be extracted from it. They form aims on the basis of existing habits of life which may be turned to their own private account. They employ intelligence in framing ends and selecting and arranging means. But intelligence is confined to manipulation; it does not extend to construction. It is the intelligence of the politician, administrator and professional executive—the kind of intelligence which has given a bad meaning to a word that ought to have a fine meaning, opportunism. For the highest task of intelligence is to grasp and realize genuine opportunity, possibility.

Roughly speaking, the course of forming aims is as follows. The beginning is with a wish, an emotional reaction against the present state of things and a hope for something different. Action fails to connect satisfactorily with surrounding conditions. Thrown back upon itself, it projects itself in an imagination of a scene which if it were present would afford satisfaction. This picture is often called an aim, more often an ideal. But in itself it is a fancy which may be only a phantasy, a dream, a castle in the air. In itself it is a romantic embellishment of the present; at its best it is material for poetry or the novel. Its natural home is not in the future but in the dim past or in some distant and supposedly better part of the present world. Every such idealized object is suggested by something actually experienced, as the flight of birds suggests the liberation of human beings from the restrictions of slow locomotion on dull earth. It becomes an aim or end only when it is worked out in terms of concrete conditions available for its realization, that is in terms of " means."

This transformation depends upon study of the conditions which generate or make possible the fact observed to exist already. The fancy of the delight of moving at will through the air became an actuality

only after men carefully studied the way in which a bird
although heavier than air actually sustains itself in
air. A fancy becomes an aim, in short, when some past
sequence of known cause-and-effect is projected into the
future, and when by assembling its causal conditions
we strive to generate a like result. We have to fall back
upon what has already happened naturally without design, and study it to see *how* it happened, which is what
is meant by causation. This knowledge joined to wish
creates a purpose. Many men have doubtless dreamed
of ability to have light in darkness without the trouble
of oil, lamps and friction. Glow-worms, lightning, the
sparks of cut electric conductors suggest such a possibility. But the picture remained a dream until an
Edison studied all that could be found out about such
casual phenomena of light, and then set to work to
search out and gather together the means for reproduc-
ing their operation. The great trouble with what
passes for moral ends and ideals is that they do not
get beyond the stage of fancy of something agreeable
and desirable based upon an emotional wish; very often,
at that, not even an original wish, but the wish of some
leader which has been conventionalized and transmitted
through channels of authority. Every gain in natural
science makes possible new aims. That is, the discovery
of how things *do* occur makes it possible to conceive
of their happening at will, and gives us a start on selecting and combining the conditions, the means, to
command their happening. In technical matters, this
lesson has been fairly well learned. But in moral mat-

ters, men still largely neglect the need of studying the
way in which results similar to those which we desire
actually happen. Mechanism is despised as of importance only in low material things. The consequent
divorce of moral ends from scientific study of natural
events renders the former impotent wishes, compensatory dreams in consciousness. In *fact* ends or
consequences are still determined by fixed habit and
the force of circumstance. The evils of idle dream-
ing and of routine are experienced in conjunction.
" Idealism " must indeed come first—the imagination of
some better state generated by desire. But unless ideals
are to be dreams and idealism a synonym for romanticism and phantasy-building, there must be a most
realistic study of actual conditions and of the mode or
law of natural events, in order to give the imagined or
ideal object definite form and solid substance—to give
it, in short, practicality and constitute it a working
end.

The acceptance of fixed ends in themselves is an
aspect of man's devotion to an ideal of certainty. This
affection was inevitably cherished as long as men believed that the highest things in physical nature are at
rest, and that science is possible only by grasping immutable forms and species: in other words, for much
the greater part of the intellectual history of mankind.
Only reckless sceptics would have dared entertain any
idea of ends except as fixed in themselves as long
as the whole structure of science was erected upon the
immobile. Behind however the conception of fixity

whether in science or morals lay adherence to certainty of " truth," a clinging to something fixed, born of fear of the new and of attachment to possessions. When the classicist condemns concession to impulse and holds up to admiration the patterns tested in tradition, he little suspects how much he is himself affected by un-avowed impulses—timidity which makes him cling to authority, conceit which moves him to be himself the authority who speaks in the name of authority, possessive impulse which fears to risk acquisition in new adventures. Love of certainty is a demand for guarantees in advance of action. Ignoring the fact that truth can be bought only by the adventure of experiment, dogmatism turns truth into an insurance company. Fixed ends upon one side and fixed " prin-ciples "—that is authoritative rules—on the other, are props for a feeling of safety, the refuge of the timid and the means by which the bold prey upon the timid.

VII

Intelligence is concerned with foreseeing the future so that action may have order and direction. It is also concerned with principles and criteria of judgment. The diffused or wide applicability of habits is reflected in the *general* character of principles: a principle is intellectually what a habit is for direct action. As habits set in grooves dominate activity and swerve it from conditions instead of increasing its adaptability, so principles treated as fixed rules instead of as helpful methods take men away from experience. The more complicated the situation, and the less we really know about it, the more insistent is the orthodox type of moral theory upon the prior existence of some fixed and universal principle or law which is to be directly applied and followed. Ready-made rules available at a moment's notice for settling any kind of moral difficulty and resolving every species of moral doubt have been the chief object of the ambition of moralists. In the much less complicated and less changing matters of bodily health such pretensions are known as quackery. But in morals a hankering for certainty, born of timidity and nourished by love of authoritative prestige, has led to the idea that absence of immutably fixed and universally applicable ready-made principles is equivalent to moral chaos.

In fact, situations into which change and the unexpected enter are a challenge to intelligence to create new principles. Morals must be a growing science if it is to be a science at all, not merely because all truth has not yet been appropriated by the mind of man, but because life is a moving affair in which old moral truth ceases to apply. Principles are methods of inquiry and forecast which require verification by the event; and the time honored effort to assimilate morals to mathematics is only a way of bolstering up an old dogmatic authority, or putting a new one upon the throne of the old. But the experimental character of moral judgments does not mean complete uncertainty and fluidity. Principles exist as hypotheses with which to experiment. Human history is long. There is a long record of past experimentation in conduct, and there are cumulative verifications which give many principles a well earned prestige. Lightly to disregard them is the height of foolishness. But social situations alter; and it is also foolish not to observe how old principles actually work under new conditions, and not to modify them so that they will be more effectual instruments in judging new cases. Many men are now aware of the harm done in legal matters by assuming the antecedent existence of fixed principles under which every new case may be brought. They recognize that this assumption merely puts an artificial premium on ideas developed under bygone conditions, and that their perpetuation in the present works inequity. Yet the choice is not between throwing away rules previously developed and sticking obstinately by them. The intelligent alternative is to revise, adapt, expand and alter them. The problem is one of continuous, vital readaptation.

The popular objection to casuistry is similar to the popular objection to the maxim that the end justifies the means. It is creditable to practical moral sense, but not to popular logical consistency. For recourse to casuistry is the only conclusion which can be drawn from belief in fixed universal principles, just as the Jesuit maxim is the only conclusion proper to be drawn from belief in fixed ends. Every act, every deed is individual. What is the sense in having fixed general rules, commandments, laws, unless they are such as to confer upon individual cases of action (where alone instruction is finally needed) something of their own infallible certainty? Casuistry, so-called, is simply the systematic effort to secure for particular instances of conduct the advantage of general rules which are asserted and believed in. By those who accept the notion of immutable regulating principles, casuistry ought to be lauded for sincerity and helpfulness, not dispraised as it usually is. Or else men ought to carry back their aversion to manipulation of particular cases, until they will fit into the procrustean beds of fixed rules, to the point where it is clear that all principles are empirical generalizations from the ways in which previous judgments of conduct have practically worked out. When this fact is apparent, these generalizations will be seen to be not fixed rules for deciding doubtful cases, but instrumentalities for their investigation, methods by which the net value of past experience is rendered available for present scrutiny of new perplexities. Then it will also follow that they are hypotheses to be tested and revised by their further working.*

Every such statement meets with prompt objection. We are told that in deliberation rival goods present themselves. We are faced by competing desires and ends which are incompatible with one another. They are all attractive, seductive. How then shall we choose among them? We can choose rationally among values, the argument continues, only if we have some fixed measure of values, just as we decide the respective lengths of physical things by recourse to the fixed foot-rule. One might reply that after all there is no fixed foot-rule, no fixed foot " in itself " and that the standard length or weight of measure is only another special portion of matter, subject to change from heat, moisture and gravitational position, defined only by conditions, relations. One might reply that the foot-rule is a tool which has been worked out in actual prior comparisons of concrete things for use in facilitating further comparisons. But we content ourselves with remarking that we find in this conception of a fixed antecedent standard another manifestation of the desire to escape the strain of the actual moral situation, its genuine uncertainty of possibilities and consequences.

---

*Among contemporary moralists, Mr. G. E. Moore may be cited as almost alone in having the courage of the convictions shared by many. He insists that it is the true business of moral theory to enable men to arrive at precise and sure judgments in concrete cases of moral perplexity.

We are confronted with another case of the all too
human love of certainty, a case of the wish for an intellectual patent issued by authority. The issue after all
is one of fact. The critic is not entitled to enforce
against the facts his private wish for a ready-made
standard which will relieve him from the burden of examination, observation and continuing generalization
and test.

The worth of this private wish is moreover open to
question in the light of the history of the development
of natural science. There was a time when in astronomy, chemistry and biology men claimed that judgment
of individual phenomena was possible only because the
mind was already in possession of fixed truths, universal principles, pre-ordained axioms. Only by their
means could contingent, varying particular events be
truly known. There was, it was argued, no way to
judge the truth of any particular statement about a
particular plant, heavenly body, or case of combustion
unless there was a general truth already in hand with
which to compare a particular empirical occurrence.
The contention was successful, that is for a long time
it maintained its hold upon men's minds. But its effect was merely to encourage intellectual laziness, reliance upon authority and blind acceptance of conceptions that had somehow become traditional. The actual advance of science did not begin till men broke
away from this method. When men insisted upon judging astronomical phenomena by bringing them directly
under established truths, those of geometry, they had

no astronomy, but only a private esthetic construction. Astronomy began when men trusted themselves to embarking upon the uncertain sea of events and were willing to be instructed by changes in the concrete. Then antecedent principles were tentatively employed as methods for conducting observations and experiments, and for organizing special facts: as hypotheses.

In morals now, as in physical science then, the work of intelligence in reaching such relative certainty, or tested probability, as is open to man is retarded by the false notion of fixed antecedent truths. Prejudice is confirmed. Rules formed accidentally or under the pressure of conditions long past, are protected from criticism and thus perpetuated. Every group and person vested with authority strengthens possessed power by harping upon the sacredness of immutable principle. Moral facts, that is the concrete careers of special courses of action, are not studied. There is no counterpart to clinical medicine. Rigid classifications forced upon facts are relied upon. And all is done, as it used to be done in natural science, in praise of Reason and in fear of the variety and fluctuation of actual happenings.

The hypothesis that each moral situation is unique and that consequently general moral principles are instrumental to developing the individualized meaning of situations is declared to be anarchic. It is said to be ethical atomism, pulverizing the order and dignity of morals. The question, again is not what our inherited habits lead us to prefer, but where the facts take us.

But in this instance the facts do not take us into atomism and anarchy. These things are specters seen by the critic when he is suddenly confused by the loss of customary spectacles. He takes his own confusion due to loss of artificial aids for an objective situation. *Because* situations in which deliberation is evoked are new, and therefore unique, general principles are needed. Only an uncritical vagueness will assume that the sole alternative to fixed generality is absence of continuity. Rigid habits insist upon duplication, repetition, recurrence; in their case there is accordingly fixed principles. Only there is no *principle* at all, that is, no conscious intellectual rule, for thought is not needed. But all habit has *continuity*, and while a flexible habit does not secure in its operation bare recurrence nor absolute assurance neither does it plunge us into the hopeless confusion of the absolutely different. To insist upon change and the new is to insist upon alteration *of* the old. In denying that the meaning of any genuine case of deliberation can be exhausted by treating it as a mere case of an established classification the value of classification is not denied. It is shown where its value lies, namely, in directing attention to resemblances and differences in the new case, in economizing effort in foresight. To call a generalization a tool is not to say it is useless; the contrary is patently the case. A tool is something to use. Hence it is also something to be improved by noting how it works. The need of such noting and improving is indispensable if, as is the case with moral principles, the tool has to be used in unwonted circumstances. Continuity of growth not atomism is thus the alternative to fixity of principles and aims. This is no Bergsonian plea for dividing the universe into two portions, one all of fixed, recurrent habits, and the other all spontaneity of flux. Only in such a universe would reason in morals have to take its choice between absolute fixity and absolute looseness.

Nothing is more instructive about the genuine value of generalization in conduct than the errors of Kant. He took the doctrine that the essence of reason is complete universality (and hence necessity and immutability), with the seriousness becoming the professor of logic. Applying the doctrine to morality he saw that this conception severed morals from connection with experience. Other moralists had gone that far before his day. But none of them had done what Kant proceeded to do: carry this separation of moral principles and ideals from experience to its logical conclusion. He saw that to exclude from principles all connection with empirical details meant to exclude all reference of any kind to consequences. He then saw with a clearness which does his logic credit that with such exclusion, reason becomes entirely empty: nothing is left except the universality of the universal. He was then confronted by the seemingly insoluble problem of getting moral instruction regarding special cases out of a principle that having forsworn intercourse with experience was barren and empty. His ingenious method was as follows. Formal universality means at least logical identity; it means self-consistency or absence of contradiction. Hence follows the method by which a would-be truly moral agent will proceed in judging the rightness of any proposed act. He will ask: Can its motive be made universal for all cases? How would one like it if by one's act one's motive in that act were to be erected into a universal law of actual nature? Would one then be willing to make the same choice?

Surely a man would hesitate to steal if by his choice to make stealing the motive of his act he were also to erect it into such a fixed law of nature that henceforth he and everybody else would always steal whenever property was in question. No stealing without property, and with universal stealing also no property; a clear self-contradiction. Looked at in the light of reason every mean, insincere, inconsiderate motive of action shrivels into a private exception which a person wants to take advantage of in his own favor, and which he would be horrified to have others act upon. It violates the great principle of logic that A is A. Kindly, decent acts, on the contrary, extend and multiply themselves in a continuing harmony.

This treatment by Kant evinces deep insight into the office of intelligence and principle in conduct. But it involves flat contradiction of Kant's own original intention to exclude consideration of concrete consequences. It turns out to be a method of recommending a broad impartial view of consequences. Our forecast of consequences is always subject, as we have noted, to the bias of impulse and habit. We see what we want to see, we obscure what is unfavorable to a cherished, probably unavowed, wish. We dwell upon favoring circumstances till they become weighted with reinforcing considerations. We don't give opposing consequences half a chance to develop in thought. Deliberation needs every possible help it can get against the twisting, exaggerating and slighting tendency of passion and habit. To form the habit of asking how we should be willing to be treated in a similar case—which is what Kant's maxim amounts to—is to gain an ally for impartial and sincere deliberation and judgment. It is a safeguard against our tendency to regard our own case as exceptional in comparison with the case of others. " Just this once," a plea for isolation; secrecy—a plea for non-inspection, are forces which operate in every passionate desire. Demand for consistency, for " universality," far from implying a rejection of all consequences, is a demand to survey consequences broadly, to link effect to effect in a chain of continuity. Whatever force works to this end *is* reason. For reason, let it be repeated is an outcome, a function, not a primitive force. What we need are those habits, dispositions which lead to impartial and consistent foresight of consequences. Then our judgments are reasonable; we are then reasonable creatures.

VIII

Certain critics in sympathy with at least the negative contention, the critical side, of such a theory as has been advanced, regard it as placing too much emphasis upon intelligence. They find it intellectualistic, cold-blooded. They say we must change desire, love, aspiration, admiration, and then action will be transformed. A new affection, a changed appreciation, brings with it a revaluation of life and insists upon its realization. A refinement of intellect at most only figures out better ways of reaching old and accustomed ends. In fact we are lucky if intellect does not freeze the ardor of generous desire and paralyze creative endeavor. Intellect is critical, unproductive while desire is generative. In its dispassionateness intellect is aloof from humanity and its needs. It fosters detachment where sympathy is needed. It cultivates contemplation when salvation lies in liberating desire. Intellect is analytic, taking things to pieces; its devices are the scalpel and test-tube. Affection is synthetic, unifying. This argument affords an opportunity for making more explicit those respective offices of wish and thought in forming ends which have already been touched upon.

First we must undertake an independent analysis of desire. It is customary to describe desires in terms of their objects, meaning by objects the things which figure as in imagination their goals. As the object is noble or base, so, it is thought, is desire. In any case, emotions rise and cluster about the object. This stands out so conspicuously in immediate experience that it monopolizes the central position in the traditional psychological theory of desire. Barring gross self-deception or the frustration of external circumstance, the outcome, or end-result, of desire is regarded by this theory as similar to the end-in-view or object consciously desired. Such, however, is not the case, as readily appears from the analysis of deliberation. In saying that the actual outcome of desire is different in kind from the object upon which desire consciously fastens, I do not mean to repeat the old complaint about the fallibility and feebleness of mortals in virtue of which man's hopes are frustrated and twisted in realization. The difference is one of diverse dimensions, not of degree or amount.

The object desired and the attainment of desire are no more alike than a signboard on the road is like the garage to which it points and which it recommends to the traveler. Desire is the forward urge of living creatures. When the push and drive of life meets no obstacle, there is nothing which we call desire. There is just life-activity. But obstructions present themselves, and activity is dispersed and divided. Desire is the outcome. It is activity surging forward to break through what dams it up. The " object " which then presents itself in thought as the goal of desire is the object of the environment *which, if it were present*, would secure

a re-unification of activity and the restoration of its
ongoing unity. The end-in-view of desire is that object
which were it present would link into an organized
whole activities which are now partial and competing.
It is no more like the actual end of desire, or the
resulting state attained, than the coupling of cars
which have been separated is like an ongoing single
train. Yet the train cannot go on without the coupling.

Such statements may seem contrary to common sense.
The pertinency of the illustration used will be denied.
No man desires the signboard which he sees, he desires
the garage, the objective, the ulterior thing. But does
he? Or is the garage simply a means by which a divided
body of activities is redintegrated or coordinated?
Is it desired in any sense for itself, or only because it is
the means of effective adjustment of a whole set of underlying habits? While common sense responds to the
ordinary statement of the end of desire, it also responds to a statement that no one desires the object
for its own sake, but only for what can be got out of it.
Here is just the point at which the theory that pleasure
is the real objective of desire makes its appeal. It
points out that not the physical object nor even its
possession is really wanted; that they are only means
to something personal and experiential. And hence it
is argued that they are means to pleasure. The present hypothesis offers an alternative: it says that they
are means of removal of obstructions to an ongoing,
unified system of activities. It is easy to see why an
objective looms so large and why emotional surge

and stress gather about it and lift it high above the floor of consciousness. The objective is (or is taken to be) the key to the situation. If we can attain it, lay hold of it, the trick is turned. It is like the piece of paper which carries the reprieve a condemned man waits for. Issues of life hang upon it. The desired object is in no sense the end or goal of desire, but it is the *sine qua non* of that end. A practical man will fix his attention upon it, and not dream about eventualities which are only dreams if the objective is not attained, but which will follow in their own natural course if it is reached. For then it becomes a factor in the system of activities. Hence the truth in the various so-called paradoxes of desire. If pleasure or perfection were the true end of desire, it would still be true that the way to attainment is not to think of them. For object thought of and object achieved exist in different dimensions.

In addition to the popular notions that either the object in view or else pleasure is the end of desire, there is a less popular theory that quiescence is the actual outcome or true terminal of desire. The theory finds its most complete practical statement in Buddhism. It is nearer the psychological truth than either of the other notions. But it views the attained outcome simply in its negative aspect. The end reached quiets the clash and removes the discomfort attendant upon divided and obstructed activity. The uneasiness, unrest, characteristic of desire is put to sleep. For this reason, some persons resort to intoxicants and anodynes. If

quiescence were the end and it could be perpetuated,
this way of removing disagreeable uneasiness would be
as satisfactory a way out as the way of objective effort.
But in fact desire satisfied does not bring quiescence
unqualifiedly, but that *kind* of quiescence which marks
the recovery of unified activity: the absence of internal
strife among habits and instincts. Equilibration of activities rather than quiescence is the actual result of
satisfied desire. This names the outcome positively,
rather than comparatively and negatively.

This disparity of dimensions in desire between the
object thought of and the outcome reached is the explanation of those self-deceptions which psycho-analysis has brought home to us so forcibly, but of which it
gives elaborately cumbrous accounts. The object
thought of and the outcome *never* agree. There is no
self-deceit in this fact. What, then, really happens
when the actual outcome of satisfied revenge figures in
thought as virtuous eagerness for justice? Or when
the tickled vanity of social admiration is masked as
pure love of learning? The trouble lies in the refusal
of a person to note the quality of the outcome, not in
the unavoidable disparity of desire's object and the outcome. The honest or integral mind attends to the result, and sees what it really is. For no terminal condition is exclusively terminal. Since it exists in time it
has consequences as well as antecedents. In being a
consummation it is also a force having causal potentialities. It is initial as well as terminal.

Self-deception originates in looking at an outcome in

one direction only—as a satisfaction of what has gone
before, ignoring the fact that what is attained is a state
of habits which will continue in action and which will
determine future results. Outcomes of desire are also
beginnings of new acts and hence are portentous. Satisfied revenge may *feel* like justice vindicated; the
prestige of learning may *feel* like an enlargement and
rectification of an objective outlook. But since different instincts and habits have entered into them, they
are actually, that is dynamically, unlike. The function
of moral judgment is to detect this unlikeness. Here,
again, the belief that we can know ourselves immediately
is as disastrous to moral science as the corresponding
idea regarding knowledge of nature was to physical
science. Obnoxious " subjectivity " of moral judgment
is due to the fact that the immediate or esthetic quality
swells and swells and displaces the thought of the active
potency which gives activity its moral quality.

We are all natural Jack Horners. If the plum comes
when we put in and pull out our thumb we attribute
the satisfactory result to personal virtue. The plum
is obtained, and it is not easy to distinguish obtaining
from attaining, acquisition from achieving. Jack Hor-
ner, Esq., put forth *some* effort; and results and efforts
are always more or less incommensurate. For the
result is always dependent to some extent upon the
favor or disfavor of circumstance. Why then should
not the satisfactory plum shed its halo retrospectively
upon what precedes and be taken as a sign of virtue?
In this way heroes and leaders are constructed. Such

is the worship of success. And the evil of success-worship is precisely the evil with which we have been dealing. " Success " is never merely final or terminal. Something else succeeds it, and its successors are influenced by its nature, that is by the persisting habits and impulses that enter into it. The world does not stop when the successful person pulls out his plum; nor does he stop, and the kind of success he obtains, and his attitude toward it, is a factor in what comes afterwards. By a strange turn of the wheel, the success of the ultra-practical man is psychologically like the refined enjoyment of the ultra-esthetic person. Both ignore the eventualities with which every state of experience is charged. There is no reason for not enjoying the present, but there is every reason for examination of the objective factors of *what* is enjoyed before we translate enjoyment into a belief in excellence. There is every reason in other words for cultivating another enjoyment, that of the habit of examining the productive potentialities of the objects enjoyed.

Analysis of desire thus reveals the falsity of theories which magnify it at the expense of intelligence. Impulse is primary and intelligence is secondary and in some sense derivative. There should be no blinking of this fact. But recognition of it as a fact exalts intelligence. For thought is not the slave of impulse to do its bidding. Impulse does not know what it is after; it cannot give orders, not even if it wants to. It rushes blindly into any opening it chances to find. Anything that expends it, satisfies it. One outlet is like another

to it. It is indiscriminate. Its vagaries and excesses
are the stock theme of classical moralists; and while
they point the wrong moral in urging the abdication
of impulse in favor of reason, their characterization of
impulse is not wholly wrong. What intelligence has to
do in the service of impulse is to act not as its obedient
servant but as its clarifier and liberator. And this can
be accomplished only by a study of the conditions and
causes, the workings and consequences of the greatest
possible variety of desires and combinations of desire.
Intelligence converts desire into plans, systematic plans
based on assembling facts, reporting events as they happen, keeping tab on them and analyzing them.

Nothing is so easy to fool as impulse and no one is
deceived so readily as a person under strong emotion.
Hence the idealism of man is easily brought to naught.
Generous impulses are aroused; there is a vague anticipation, a burning hope, of a marvelous future. Old
things are to pass speedily away and a new heavens
and earth are to come into existence. But impulse burns
itself up. Emotion cannot be kept at its full tide. Obstacles are encountered upon which action dashes itself
into ineffectual spray. Or if it achieves, by luck, a
transitory success, it is intoxicated, and plumes itself
on victory while it is on the road to sudden defeat.
Meantime, other men, not carried away by impulse, use
established habits and a shrewd cold intellect that manipulates them. The outcome is the victory of baser
desire directed by insight and cunning over generous
desire which does not know its way.

The realistic man of the world has evolved a regular technique for dealing with idealistic outbursts that threaten his supremacy. His aims are low, but he knows the means by which they are to be executed. His knowledge of conditions is narrow but it is effective within its confines. His foresight is limited to results that concern personal success, but is sharp, clearcut. He has no great difficulty in drafting the idealistic desire of others with its vague enthusiasms and its cloudy perceptions into canals where it will serve his own purposes. The energies excited by emotional idealism run into the materialistic reservoirs provided by the contriving thought of those who have not surrendered their minds to their sentiment.

The glorification of affection and aspiration at the expense of thought is a survival of romantic optimism. It assumes a pre-established harmony between natural impulse and natural objects. Only such a harmony justifies the belief that generous feeling will find its way illuminated by the sheer nobility of its own quality. Persons of a literary turn of mind are as subject to this fallacy as intellectual specialists are apt to the contrary fallacy that theorizing apart from force of impulse and habit will get affairs forward. They tend to fancy that things are as pliant to imagination as are words, that an emotion can compose affairs as if they were materials for a lyric poem. But if the objects of the environment were only as plastic as the materials of poetic art, men would never have been obliged to have recourse to creation in the medium of words. We idealize in fancy because our idealizations in fact are balked. And while the latter must start with imaginative idealizations instigated by release of generous impulse, they can be carried through only when the hard labor of observation, memory and foresight weds the vision of imagination to the organized efficiencies of habit.

Sometimes desire means not bare impulse but impulse which has sense of an objective. In this case desire and thought cannot be opposed, for desire includes thought within itself. The question is now how far the work of thought has been done, how adequate is its perception of its directing object. For the moving force may be a shadowy presentiment constructed by wishful hope rather than by study of conditions; it may be an emotional indulgence rather than a solid plan built upon the rocks of actuality discovered by accurate inquiries. There is no thought without the impeding of impulse. But the obstruction may merely intensify its blind surge forward; or it may divert the force of forward impulse into observation of existing conditions and forecast of their future consequences. This long way around is the short way home for desire.

No issue of morals is more far-reaching than the one herewith sketched. Historically speaking, there is point in the attacks of those who speak slightingly of science and intellect, and who would limit their moral significance to supplying incidental help to execution of purposes born of affection. Thought too often is specialized in a remote and separate pursuit, or em-

ployed in a hard way to contrive the instrumentalities
of "success." Intellect is too often made a tool for a
systematized apology for things as "they are," that
is for customs that benefit the class in power, or else
a road to an interesting occupation which accumulates
facts and ideas as other men gather dollars, while
priding itself on its ideal quality. No wonder that at
times catastrophes that affect men in common are welcomed. For the moment they turn science away from
its abstract technicalities into a servant of some human
aspiration; the hard, chilly calculations of intellect are
swept away by floods of sympathy and common
loyalties.

But, alas, emotion without thought is unstable. It
rises like the tide and subsides like the tide irrespective
of what it has accomplished. It is easily diverted into
any side channel dug by old habits or provided by cool
cunning, or it disperses itself aimlessly. Then comes
the reaction of disillusionment, and men turn all the
more fiercely to the pursuit of narrow ends where they
are habituated to use observation and planning and
where they have acquired some control of conditions.
The separation of warm emotion and cool intelligence
is the great moral tragedy. This division is perpetuated by those who deprecate science and foresight in
behalf of affection as it is by those who in the name of
an idol labeled reason would quench passion. The intellect is always inspired by some impulse. Even the
most case-hardened scientific specialist, the most abstract philosopher, is moved by some passion. But

an actuating impulse easily hardens into isolated habit. It is unavowed and disconnected. The remedy is not lapse of thought, but its quickening and extension to contemplate the continuities of existence, and restore the connection of the isolated desire to the companionship of its fellows. The glorification of " will " apart from thought turns out either a commitment to blind action which serves the purpose of those who guide their deeds by narrow plans, or else a sentimental, romantic faith in the harmonies of nature leading straight to disaster.

In words at least, the association of idealism with emotion and impulse has been repeatedly implied in the foregoing. The connection is more than verbal. Every end that man holds up, every project he entertains is ideal. It marks something wanted, rather than something existing. It is wanted because existence as it *now* is does not furnish it. It carries with itself, then, a sense of contrast to the achieved, to the existent. It outruns the seen and touched. It is the work of faith and hope even when it is the plan of the most hard-headed " practical " man. But though ideal in this sense it is not *an* ideal. Common sense revolts at calling every project, every design, every contrivance of cunning, ideal, because common sense includes above all in its conception of the ideal the *quality* of the plan proposed.

Idealistic revolt is blind and like every blind reaction sweeps us away. The quality of the ideal is exalted till it is something beyond all possibility of definite plan and execution. Its sublimity renders it inaccessibly remote. An ideal becomes a synonym for whatever is inspiring —and impossible. Then, since intelligence cannot be wholly suppressed, the ideal is hardened by thought into some high, far-away object. It is so elevated and so distant that it does not belong to this world or to experience. It is in technical language, transcendental; in common speech, supernatural, of heaven not of earth. The ideal is then a goal of final exhaustive, comprehensive perfection which can be defined only by complete contrast with the actual. Although impossible of realization and of conception, it is still regarded as the source of all generous discontent with actualities and of all inspiration to progress.

This notion of the nature and office of ideals combines in one contradictory whole all that is vicious in the separation of desire and thought. It strives while retaining the vagueness of emotion to simulate the objective definiteness of thought. It follows the natural course of intelligence in demanding an object which will unify and fulfil desire, and then cancels the work of thought by treating the object as ineffable and unrelated to present action and experience. It converts the surge of present impulse into a future end only to swamp the endeavor to clarify this end in a gush of unconsidered feeling. It is supposed that the thought of the ideal is necessary to arouse dissatisfaction with the present and to arouse effort to change it. But in reality the ideal is itself the product of discontent with conditions. Instead however of serving to organize and direct effort, it operates as a compensatory dream. It becomes another ready-made world. Instead of promoting effort at concrete transformations of what exists, it constitutes another kind of existence already somewhere in being. It is a refuge, an asylum from effort. Thus the energy that might be spent in transforming present ills goes into oscillating flights into a far away perfect world and the tedium of enforced returns into the necessities of the present evil world.

We can recover the genuine import of ideals and idealism only by disentangling this unreal mixture of thought and emotion. The action of deliberation, as we have seen, consists in selecting some foreseen consequence to serve as a stimulus to present action. It brings future possibilities into the present scene and thereby frees and expands present tendencies. But the selected consequence is set in an indefinite context of other consequences just as real as it is, and many of them much more certain in fact. The " ends " that are foreseen and utilized mark out a little island in an infinite sea. This limitation would be fatal were the proper function of ends anything else than to liberate and guide present action out of its perplexities and confusions. But this service constitutes the sole meaning of aims and purposes. Hence their slight extent in comparison with ignored and unforeseen consequences is of no import in itself. The " ideal " as it stands in popular thought, the notion of a complete and exhaustive realization, is remote from the true functions of ends, and would only embarrass us if it could be embraced in thought instead of being, as it is, a comment by the emotions.

For the sense of an indefinite context of consequences from among which the aim is selected enters into the *present* meaning of activity. The " end " is the figured pattern at the center of the field through which runs the axis of conduct. About this central figuration extends infinitely a supporting background in a vague whole, undefined and undiscriminated. At most intelligence but throws a spotlight on that little part of the whole which marks out the axis of movement. Even if the light is flickering and the illuminated portion stands forth only dimly from the shadowy background, it suffices if we are shown the way to move. To the rest of the consequences, collateral and remote, corresponds a background of feeling, of diffused emotion. This forms the stuff of the ideal.

From the standpoint of its *definite* aim any act is petty in comparison with the totality of natural events. What is accomplished directly as the outcome of a turn which our action gives the course of events is infinitesimal in comparison with their total sweep. Only an illusion of conceit persuades us that cosmic difference hangs upon even our wisest and most strenuous effort. Yet discontent with this limitation is as unreasonble as relying upon an illusion of external importance to keep ourselves going. In a genuine sense every act is already possessed of infinite import. The little part of the scheme of affairs which is modifiable by our efforts is continuous with the rest of the world. The boundaries of our garden plot join it to the world of our neighbors and our neighbors' neighbors. That small effort which we can put forth is in turn connected with an infinity of events that sustain and support it. The consciousness of this encompassing infinity of connections is ideal. When a sense of the infinite reach of an act physically occurring in a small point of space and occupying a petty instant of times comes home to us, the *meaning* of a present act is seen to be vast, immeasurable, unthinkable. This ideal is not a goal to be attained. It is a significance to be felt, appreciated. Though consciousness of it cannot become intellectualized (identified in objects of a distinct character) yet emotional appreciation of it is won only by those willing to think.

It is the office of art and religion to evoke such appreciations and intimations; to enhance and steady them till they are wrought into the texture of our lives. Some philosophers define religious consciousness as beginning where moral and intellectual consciousness leave off. In the sense that definite purposes and methods shade off of necessity into a vast whole which is incapable of objective presentation this view is correct. But they have falsified the conception by treating the religious consciousness as something that comes *after* an experience in which striving, resolution and foresight are found. To them morality and science are a striving; when striving ceases a moral holiday begins, an excursion beyond the utmost flight of legitimate thought and endeavor. But there is a point in *every* intelligent activity where effort ceases; where thought and doing fall back upon a course of events which effort and reflection cannot touch. There is a point *in* deliberate action where definite thought fades into the ineffable and undefinable— into emotion. If the sense of this effortless and unfathomable whole comes only in alternation with the sense of strain in action and labor in thought, then we spend our lives in oscillating between what is cramped and enforced and a brief transitory escape. The function of religion is then caricatured rather than realized. Morals, like war, is thought of as hell, and religion, like peace, as a respite. The religious experience is a reality in so far as in the midst of effort to foresee and regulate future objects we are sustained and expanded in feebleness and failure by the sense of an enveloping whole. Peace in action not after it is the contribution of the ideal to conduct.

IX

Over and over again, one point has recurred for criticism;—the subordination of activity to a result outside itself. Whether that goal be thought of as pleasure, as virtue, as perfection, as final enjoyment of salvation, is secondary to the fact that the moralists who have asserted fixed ends have in all their differences from one another agreed in the basic idea that present activity is but a means. We have insisted that happiness, reasonableness, virtue, perfecting, are on the contrary parts of the present significance of present action. Memory of the past, observation of the present, foresight of the future are indispensable. But they are indispensable *to* a present liberation, an enriching growth of action. Happiness is fundamental in morals only because happiness is not something to be sought for, but is something now attained, even in the midst of pain and trouble, whenever recognition of our ties with nature and with fellow-men releases and informs our action. Reasonableness is a necessity because it is the perception of the continuities that take action out of its immediateness and isolation into connection with the past and future.

Perhaps the criticism and insistence have been too incessant. They may have provoked the reader to reaction. He may readily concede that orthodox theo-

ries have been onesided in sacrificing the present to
future good, making of the present but an onerous
obligation or a sacrifice endured for future gain. But
why, he may protest, go to an opposite extreme and
make the future but a means to the significance of the
present? Why should the power of foresight and effort
to shape the future, to regulate what is to happen, be
slighted? Is not the effect of such a doctrine to weaken
putting forth of endeavor in order to make the future
better than the present? Control of the future may be
limited in extent, but it is correspondingly precious;
we should jealously cherish whatever encourages and
sustains effort to that end. To make little of this possibility, in effect, it will be argued, is to decrease the
care and endeavor upon which progress depends.

Control of the future is indeed precious in exact
proportion to its difficulty, its moderate degree of at-
tainability. Anything that actually tends to make that
control less than it now is would be a movement backward into sloth and triviality. But there is a difference between future improvement as a result and as a
direct aim. To make it an aim is to throw away the
surest means of attaining it, namely attention to the
full use of present resources in the present situation.
Forecast of future conditions, scientific study of past
and present in order that the forecast may be intelligent, are indeed necessities. Concentration of intellectual concern upon the future, solicitude for scope and
precision of estimate characteristic of any well conducted affair, naturally give the impression that their

animating purpose is control of the future. But thought about future happenings is the only way we can judge the present; it is the only way to appraise its significance. Without such projection, there can be no projects, no plans for administering present energies, overcoming present obstacles. Deliberately to subordinate the present to the future is to subject the comparatively secure to the precarious, exchange resources for liabilities, surrender what is under control to what is, relatively, incapable of control.

The *amount* of control which will come into existence in the future is not within control. But such an amount as turns out to be practicable accrues only in consequence of the best possible management of present means and obstacles. Dominating *intellectual* pre-occupation with the future is the way by which efficiency in dealing with the present is attained. It is a way, not a goal. And, upon the very most hopeful outlook, study and planning are more important in the meaning, the enrichment of content, which they add to present activity than is the increase of external control they effect. Nor is this doctrine passivistic in tendency. What sense is there in increased external control except to increase the intrinsic significance of living? The future that is foreseen is a future that is sometime to be a present. Is the value of *that* present also to be postponed to a future date, and so on indefinitely? Or, if the good we are struggling to attain in the future is one to be actually realized when that future becomes present, why should not the good of *this* present be equally precious? And is there, again, any intelligent way of modifying the future except to attend to the full possibilities of the present? Scamping the present in behalf of the future leads only to rendering the future less manageable. It increases the probability of molestation by future events.

Remarks cast in this form probably seem too much like a logical manipulation of the concepts of present and future to be convincing. Building a house is a typical instance of an intelligent activity. It is an activity directed by a plan, a design. The plan is itself based upon a foresight of future uses. This foresight is in turn dependent upon an organized survey of past experiences and of present conditions, a recollection of former experiences of living in houses and an acquaintance with present materials, prices, resources, etc. Now if a legitimate case of subordination of present to regulation of the future may anywhere be found, it is in such a case as this. For a man usually builds a house for the sake of the comfort and security, the "control," thereby afforded to future living rather than just for the fun—or the trouble—of building. If in such a case inspection shows that, after all, intellectual concern with the past and future is for the sake of directing present activity and giving it meaning, the conclusion may be accepted for other cases.

Note that the present activity is the only one really under control. The man may die before the house is built, or his financial conditions may change, or he may need to remove to another place. If he attempts to provide for all contingencies, he will never do anything; if he allows his attention to be much distracted by them, he won't do well his present planning and execution. The more he considers the future uses to which the house will probably be put the better he will do his present job which is the activity of building. Control of future living, such as it may turn out to be, is wholly dependent upon taking his present activity, seriously and devotedly, as an end, not a means. And a man has his hands full in doing well what now needs to be done. Until men have formed the habit of using intelligence fully as a guide to present action they will never find out how much control of future contingencies is possible. As things are, men so habitually scamp present action in behalf of future " ends " that the facts for estimating the extent of the possibility of reduction of future contingencies have not been disclosed. What a man *is* doing limits both his direct control and his responsibility. We must not confuse the act of building with the house when built. The latter *is* a means, not a fulfilment. But it is such only because it enters into a new activity which is present not future. Life is continuous. The act of building in time gives way to the acts connected with a domicile. But everywhere the good, the fulfilment, the meaning of activity, resides in a present made possible by judging existing conditions in their connections.

If we seek for an illustration on a larger scale, education furnishes us with a poignant example. As traditionally conducted, it strikingly exhibits a subordination of the living present to a remote and precarious future. To prepare, to get ready, is its key-note. The actual outcome is lack of adequate preparation, of intelligent adaptation. The professed exaltation of the future turns out in practice a blind following of tradition, a rule of thumb muddling along from day to day; or, as in some of the projects called industrial education, a determined effort on the part of one class of the community to secure *its* future at the expense of another class. If education were conducted as a process of fullest utilization of present resources, liberating and guiding capacities that are now urgent, it goes without saying that the lives of the young would be much richer in meaning than they are now. It also follows that intelligence would be kept busy in studying all indications of power, all obstacles and perversions, all products of the past that throw light upon present capacity, and in forecasting the future career of impulse and habit now active—not for the sake of subordinating the latter but in order to treat them intelligently. As a consequence whatever fortification and expansion of the future that is possible will be achieved—as it is now dismally unattained.

A more complicated instance is found in the dominant quality of our industrial activity. It may be dogmatically declared that the roots of its evils are found in the separation of production from consumption—that is, actual consummation, fulfilment. A normal case of their relationship is found in the taking of food. Food is consumed and vigor is produced. The difference between the two is one of directions or dimensions distinguished by intellect. In reality there is simply conversion of energy from one form to another wherein it is more available—of greater significance. The activity of the artist, the sportsman, the scientific inquirer exemplifies the same balance. Activity should be productive. This is to say it should have a bearing on the future, should effect control of it. But so far as a productive action is intrinsically creative, it has its own intrinsic value. Reference to future products and future enjoyments is but a way of enhancing perception of an immanent meaning. A skilled artisan who enjoys his work is aware that what he is making is made for future use. Externally his action is one technically labeled " production." It seems to illustrate the subjection of present activity to remote ends. But actually, morally, psychologically, the sense of the utility of the article produced is a factor in the present significance of action due to the present utilization of abilities, giving play to taste and skill, accomplishing something now. The moment production is severed from immediate satisfaction, it becomes " labor," drudgery, a task reluctantly performed.

Yet the whole tendency of modern economic life has been to assume that consumption will take care of itself provided only production is grossly and intensely attended to. Making things is frantically accelerated; and every mechanical device used to swell the senseless bulk. As a result most workers find no replenishment, no renewal and growth of mind, no fulfilment in work.

They labor to get mere means of later satisfaction. This when procured is isolated in turn from production and is reduced to a barren physical affair or a sensuous compensation for normal goods denied. Meantime the fatuity of severing production from consumption, from present enriching of life, is made evident by economic crises, by periods of unemployment alternating with periods of exercise, work or " over-production." Production apart from fulfilment becomes purely a matter of quantity; for distinction, quality, is a matter of present meaning. Esthetic elements being excluded, the mechanical reign. Production lacks criteria; one thing is better than another if it can be made faster or in greater mass. Leisure is not the nourishment of mind in work, nor a recreation; it is a feverish hurry for diversion, excitement, display, otherwise there is no leisure except a sodden torpor. Fatigue due for some to monotony and for others to overstrain in maintaining the pace is inevitable. Socially, the separation of production and consumption, means and ends, is the root of the most profound division of classes. Those who fix the " ends " for production are in control, those who engage in isolated productive activity are the subject-class. But if the latter are oppressed the former are not truly free. Their consumptions are accidental ostentation and extravagance, not a normal consummation or fulfilment of activity. The remainder of their lives is spent in enslavement to keeping the machinery going at an increasingly rapid rate.

Meantime class struggle grows between those whose

productive labor is enforced by necessity and those who are privileged consumers. And the exaggeration of production due to its isolation from ignored consumption so hypnotizes attention that even would-be reformers, like Marxian socialists, assert that the entire social problem focuses at the point of production. Since this separation of means from ends signifies an erection of means into ends, it is no wonder that a "materialistic conception of history" emerges. It is not an invention of Marx; it is a record of fact so far as the separation in question obtains. For practicable idealism is found only in a fulfilment, a consumption which is a replenishing, growth, renewal of mind and body. Harmony of social interests is found in the wide-spread sharing of activities significant in themselves, that is to say, at the point of *consumption.** But the forcing of production apart from consumption leads to the monstrous belief that class-struggle civil war is a means of social progress, instead of a register of the barriers to its attainment. Yet here too the Marxian reads aright the character of most current economic activity.

The history of economic activity thus exemplifies the moral consequences of the separation of present activity and future "ends" from each other. It also embodies the difficulty of the problem—the tax placed by it upon thought and good will. For the professed idealist and the hard-headed materialist or "practical" man, have conspired together to sustain this situation.

* Acknowledgment is due "The Social Interpretation of History" by Maurice Williams.

The " idealist " sets up as the ideal not fullness of meaning of the present but a remote goal. Hence the present is evacuated of meaning. It is reduced to being a mere external instrument, an evil necessity due to the distance between us and significant valid satisfaction. Appreciation, joy, peace in present activity are suspect. They are regarded as diversions, temptations, unworthy relaxations. Then since human nature *must* have present realization, a sentimental, romantic enjoyment of the ideal becomes a substitute for intelligent and rewarding activity. The utopia cannot be realized in fact but it may be appropriated in fantasy and serve as an anodyne to blunt the sense of a misery which after all endures. Some private key to a present entering upon remote and superior bliss is sought, just as the evangelical enjoys a complacent and superior sense of a salvation unobtained by fellow mortals. Thus the normal demand for realization, for satisfaction in the present, is abnormally met.

Meantime the practical man wants something definite, tangible and presumably obtainable for which to work. He is looking after " a good thing " as the average man is looking after a " good time," that natural caricature of an intrinsically significant activity. Yet his activity is impractical. He is looking for satisfaction somewhere else than where it can be found. In his utopian search for a future good he neglects the only place where good can be found. He empties present activity of meaning by making it a mere instrumentality. When the future arrives it is only after all another

despised present. By habit as well as by definition it
is still a means to something which has yet to come.
Again human nature must have its claims satisfied, and
sensuality is the inevitable recourse. Usually a compromise is worked out, by which a man for his working-
hours accepts the philosophy of activity for some future result, while at odd leisure times he enters by conventionally recognized channels upon an enjoyment of
" spiritual " blessings and " ideal " refinements. The
problem of serving God and Mammon is thus solved.
The situation exemplifies the concrete meaning of the
separation of means from ends which is the intellectual
reflex of the divorce of theory and practice, intelligence
and habit, foresight and present impulse. Moralists
have spent time and energy in showing what happens
when appetite, impulse, is indulged without reference to
consequences and reason. But they have mostly ignored
the counterpart evils of an intelligence that conceives
ideals and goods which do not enter into present impulse
and habit. The life of reason has been specialized,
romanticized, or made a heavy burden. This situation
embodies the import of the problem of actualizing the
place of intelligence in conduct.

Our whole account of the place of intelligence in conduct is exposed however to the charge of being itself
romantic, a compensatory idealization. The history of
mind is a record of intellect which registers, with more
or less inaccuracy, what has happened after it has happened. The crisis in which the intervention of foreseeing and directing mind is needed passes unnoted,

with attention directed toward incidentals and irrele-
vancies. The work of intellect is *post mortem*. The
rise of social science, it will be pointed out, has increased the amount of registering that occurs. Social
post mortems occur much more frequently than they
used to. But one of the things which the unbiased mind
will register is the impotency of discussion, analysis
and reporting in modifying the course of events. The
latter goes its way unheeding. The reply that this
condition of matters shows not the impotency of intelligence but that what passes for science is not science
is too easy a retort to be satisfactory. We must have
recourse to some concrete facts or surrender our doctrine just at the moment when we have formulated it.

Technical affairs give evidence that the work of inquiry, reporting an analysis is not always ineffectual.
The development of a chain of " nation-wide " tobacco
shops, of a well managed national telephone system, of
the extension of the service of an electric-light plant
testify to the fact that study, reflection and the formation of plans do in some instances determine a course
of events. The effect is seen in both engineering management and in national commercial expansion. Such
potency however, it must be admitted, is limited to just
those matters that are called technical in contrast with
the larger affairs of humanity. But if we seek, as we
should, for a definition of " technical," we can hardly
find any save one that goes in a circle: Affairs are technical in which observation, analysis and intellectual organization are determining factors. Is the conclusion

to be drawn a conviction that our wider social interests are so different from those in which intelligence is a directing factor that in the former science must always remain a belated visitor coming upon the scene after matters are settled? No, the logical conclusion is that as yet we have no technique in important economic, political and international affairs. Complexity of conditions render the difficulties in the way of the development of a technique enormous. It is imaginable they will never be overcome. But our choice is between the development of a technique by which intelligence will become an intervening partner and a continuation of a regime of accident, waste and distress.

PART FOUR

Conduct when distributed under heads like habit, impulse and intelligence gets artificially shredded. In discussing each of these topics we have run into the others. We conclude, then, with an attempt to gather together some outstanding considerations about conduct as a whole.

I

The foremost conclusion is that morals has to do with all activity into which alternative possibilities enter. For wherever they enter a difference between better and worse arises. Reflection upon action means uncertainty and consequent need of decision as to which course is better. The better is the good; the best is not better than the good but is simply the discovered good. Comparative and superlative degrees are only paths to the positive degree of action. The worse or evil is a rejected good. In deliberation and before choice no evil presents itself as evil. Until it is rejected, it is a competing good. After rejection, it figures not as a lesser good, but as the bad of that situation.

Actually then only deliberate action, conduct into which reflective choice enters, is distinctively moral, for only then does there enter the question of better and worse. Yet it is a perilous error to draw a hard and fast line between action into which deliberation and choice enter and activity due to impulse and matter-of-fact habit. One of the consequences of action is to involve us in predicaments where we have to reflect upon things formerly done as matter of course. One of the chief problems of our dealings with others is to induce them to reflect upon affairs which they usually perform from unreflective habit. On the other hand, every reflective choice tends to relegate some conscious issue into a deed or habit henceforth taken for granted and not thought upon. Potentially therefore every and any act is within the scope of morals, being a candidate for possible judgment with respect to its better-or-worse quality. It thus becomes one of the most perplexing problems of reflection to discover just how far to carry it, what to bring under examination and what to leave to unscrutinized habit. Because there is no final recipe by which to decide this question all moral judgment is experimental and subject to revision by its issue.

The recognition that conduct covers every act that is judged with reference to better and worse and that the need of this judgment is potentially coextensive with all portions of conduct, saves us from the mistake which makes morality a separate department of life. Potentially conduct is one hundred per cent of our acts.

Hence we must decline to admit theories which identify morals with the purification of motives, edifying character, pursuing remote and elusive perfection, obeying supernatural command, acknowledging the authority of duty. Such notions have a dual bad effect. First they get in the way of observation of conditions and consequences. They divert thought into side issues. Secondly, while they confer a morbid exaggerated quality upon things which are viewed under the aspect of morality, they release the larger part of the acts of life from serious, that is moral, survey. Anxious solicitude for the few acts which are deemed moral is accompanied by edicts of exemption and baths of immunity for most acts. A moral moratorium prevails for everyday affairs.

When we observe that morals is at home wherever considerations of the worse and better are involved, we are committed to noting that morality is a continuing process not a fixed achievement. Morals means growth of conduct in meaning; at least it means that kind of expansion in meaning which is consequent upon observations of the conditions and outcome of conduct. It is all one with growing. Growing and growth are the same fact expanded in actuality or telescoped in thought. In the largest sense of the word, morals is education. It is learning the meaning of what we are about and employing that meaning in action. The good, satisfaction, " end," of growth of present action in shades and scope of meaning is the only good within our control, and the only one, accordingly, for which responsibility exists. The rest is luck, fortune. And the tragedy of the moral notions most insisted upon by the morally self-conscious is the relegation of the only good which can fully engage thought, namely present meaning of action, to the rank of an incident of a remote good, whether that future good be defined as pleasure, or perfection, or salvation, or attainment of virtuous character.

"Present" activity is not a sharp narrow knife-blade in time. The present is complex, containing within itself a multitude of habits and impulses. It is enduring, a course of action, a process including memory, observation and foresight, a pressure forward, a glance backward and a look outward. It is of *moral* moment because it marks a transition in the direction of breadth and clarity of action or in that of triviality and confusion. Progress is present reconstruction adding fullness and distinctness of meaning, and retrogression is a present slipping away of significance, determinations, grasp. Those who hold that progress can be perceived and measured only by reference to a remote goal, first confuse meaning with space, and then treat spatial position as absolute, as limiting movement instead of being bounded in and by movement. There are plenty of negative elements, due to conflict, entanglement and obscurity, in most of the situations of life, and we do not require a revelation of some supreme perfection to inform us whether or no we are making headway in present rectification. We move on from the worse and into, not just towards, the better, which is authenticated not by comparison with the foreign but in what is indigenous. Unless progress is a present reconstructing, it is nothing; if it cannot be told by qualities belonging to the movement of transition it can never be judged.

Men have constructed a strange dream-world when they have supposed that without a fixed ideal of a remote good to inspire them, they have no inducement to get relief from present troubles, no desires for liberation from what oppresses and for clearing-up what confuses present action. The world in which we could get enlightenment and instruction about the direction in which we are moving only from a vague conception of an unattainable perfection would be totally unlike our present world. Sufficient unto the day is the evil thereof. Sufficient it is to stimulate us to remedial action, to endeavor in order to convert strife into harmony, monotony into a variegated scene, and limitation into expansion. The converting is progress, the only progress conceivable or attainable by man. Hence every situation has its own measure and quality of progress, and the need for progress is recurrent, constant. If it is better to travel than to arrive, it is because traveling is a constant arriving, while arrival that precludes further traveling is most easily attained by going to sleep or dying. We find our clews to direction in the projected recollections of definite experienced goods not in vague anticipations, even when we label the vagueness perfection, the Ideal, and proceed to manipulate its definition with dry dialectic logic.

Progress means increase of present meaning, which involves multiplication of sensed distinctions as well as
harmony, unification. This statement may, perhaps, be
made generally, in application to the experience of
humanity. If history shows progress it can hardly be
found elsewhere than in this complication and extension
of the significance found within experience. It is clear
that such progress brings no surcease, no immunity
from perplexity and trouble. If we wished to transmute this generalization into a categorical imperative
we should say: " So act as to increase the meaning of
present experience." But even then in order to get instruction about the concrete quality of such increased
meaning we should have to run away from the law and
study the needs and alternative possibilities lying within a unique and localized situation. The imperative,
like everything absolute, is sterile. Till men give up
the search for a general formula of progress they will
not know where to look to find it.

A business man proceeds by comparing today's liabilities and assets with yesterday's, and projects plans
for tomorrow by a study of the movement thus indicated in conjunction with study of the conditions of
the environment now existing. It is not otherwise with
the business of living. The future is a projection of the
subject-matter of the present, a projection which is not
arbitrary in the extent in which it divines the movement
of the moving present. The physician is lost who would
guide his activities of healing by building up a picture
of perfect health, the same for all and in its nature

complete and self-enclosed once for all. He employs
what he has discovered about actual cases of good
health and ill health and their causes to investigate the
present ailing individual, so as to further his recovering; recovering, an intrinsic and living process rather
than recovery, which is comparative and static. Moral
theories, which however have not remained mere theories
but which have found their way into the opinions of
the common man, have reversed the situation and made
the present subservient to a rigid yet abstract future.

The ethical import of the doctrine of evolution is
enormous. But its import has been misconstrued because the doctrine has been appropriated by the very
traditional notions which in truth it subverts. It has
been thought that the doctrine of evolution means the
complete subordination of present change to a future
goal. It has been constrained to teach a futile dogma
of approximation, instead of a gospel of present
growth. The usufruct of the new science has been
seized upon by the old tradition of fixed and external
ends. In fact evolution means continuity of change;
and the fact that change may take the form of present growth of complexity and interaction. Significant
stages in change are found not in access of fixity of
attainment but in those crises in which a seeming fixity
of habits gives way to a release of capacities that have
not previously functioned: in times that is of readjustment and redirection.

No matter what the present success in straightening
out difficulties and harmonizing conflicts, it is certain

that problems will recur in the future in a new form
or on a different plane. Indeed every genuine accomplishment instead of winding up an affair and enclos-
ing it as a jewel in a casket for future contemplation,
complicates the practical situation. It effects a new
distribution of energies which have henceforth to be
employed in ways for which past experience gives no
exact instruction. Every important satisfaction of an
old want creates a new one; and this new one has to
enter upon an experimental adventure to find its satisfaction. From the side of what has gone before
achievement settles something. From the side of what
comes after, it complicates, introducing new problems,
unsettling factors. There is something pitifully juven-
ile in the idea that " evolution," progress, means a
definite sum of accomplishment which will forever stay
done, and which by an exact amount lessens the amount
still to be done, disposing once and for all of just so
many perplexities and advancing us just so far on our
road to a final stable and unperplexed goal. Yet the
typical nineteenth century, mid-victorian conception of
evolution was precisely a formulation of such a consum-
mate juvenilism.

If the true ideal is that of a stable condition free
from conflict and disturbance, then there are a number
of theories whose claims are superior to those of the
popular doctrine of evolution. Logic points rather in
the direction of Rousseau and Tolstoi who would recur
to some primitive simplicity, who would return from
complicated and troubled civilization to a state of na-

ture. For certainly progress in civilization has not only
meant increase in the scope and intricacy of problems
to be dealt with, but it entails increasing instability.
For in multiplying wants, instruments and possibilities,
it increases the variety of forces which enter into relations with one another and which have to be intelligently directed. Or again, Stoic indifference or Bud-
dhist calm have greater claims. For, it may be argued,
since all objective achievement only complicates the situation, the victory of a final stability can be secured
only by renunciation of desire. Since every satisfaction of desire increases force, and this in turn creates
new desires, withdrawal into an inner passionless state,
indifference to action and attainment, is the sole road
to possession of the eternal, stable and final reality.

Again, from the standpoint of definite approximation
to an ultimate goal, the balance falls heavily on the side
of pessimism. The more striving the more attainments,
perhaps; but also assuredly the more needs and the
more disappointments. The more we do and the more
we accomplish, the more the end is vanity and vexation. From the standpoint of attainment of good that
stays put, that constitutes a definite sum performed
which lessens the amount of effort required in order to
reach the ultimate goal of final good, progress *is* an
illusion. But we are looking for it in the wrong place.
The world war is a bitter commentary on the nineteenth
century misconception of moral achievement—a misconception however which it only inherited from the
traditional theory of fixed ends, attempting to bolster

up that doctrine with aid from the "scientific" theory
of evolution. The doctrine of progress is not yet bank-
rupt. The bankruptcy of the notion of fixed goods to
be attained and stably possessed may possibly be the
means of turning the mind of man to a tenable theory
of progress—to attention to present troubles and possibilities.

Adherents of the idea that betterment, growth in
goodness, consists in approximation to an exhaustive,
stable, immutable end or good, have been compelled to
recognize the truth that in fact we envisage the good
in specific terms that are relative to existing needs, and
that the attainment of every specific good merges insensibly into a new condition of maladjustment with its
need of a new end and a renewed effort. But they
have elaborated an ingenious dialectical theory to account for the facts while maintaining their theory in-
tact. The goal, the ideal, is infinite; man is finite, subject to conditions imposed by space and time. The
specific character of the ends which man entertains
and of the satisfaction he achieves is due therefore
precisely to his empirical and finite nature in its contrast with the infinite and complete character of the
true reality, the end. Consequently when man reaches
what he had taken to be the destination of his journey
he finds that he has only gone a piece on the road. Infinite vistas still stretch before him. Again he sets his
mark a little way further ahead, and again when he
reaches the station set, he finds the road opening before
him in unexpected ways, and sees new distant objects

beckoning him forward. Such is the popular doctrine.

By some strange perversion this theory passes for moral idealism. An office of inspiration and guidance is attributed to the thought of the goal of ultimate completeness or perfection. As matter of fact, the idea sincerely held brings discouragement and despair not inspiration or hopefulness. There is something either ludicrous or tragic in the notion that inspiration to continued progress is had in telling man that no matter what he does or what he achieves, the outcome is negligible in comparison with what he set out to achieve, that every endeavor he makes is bound to turn out a failure compared with what should be done, that every attained satisfaction is only forever bound to be only a disappointment. The honest conclusion is pessimism. All is vexation, and the greater the effort the greater the vexation. But the fact is that it is not the negative aspect of an outcome, its failure to reach infinity, which renews courage and hope. Positive attainment, actual enrichment of meaning and powers opens new vistas and sets new tasks, creates new aims and stimulates new efforts. The facts are not such as to yield unthinking optimism and consolation; for they render it impossible to rest upon attained goods. New struggles and failures are inevitable. The total scene of action remains as before, only for us more complex, and more subtly unstable. But this very situation is a consequence of expansion, not of failures of power, and when grasped and admitted it is a challenge to intelligence. Instruction in what to do next can never come from an infinite goal, which for us is bound to be empty. It can be derived only from study of the deficiencies, irregularities and possibilities of the actual situation.

In any case, however, arguments about pessimism and optimism based upon considerations regarding fixed attainment of good and evil are mainly literary in quality. Man continues to live because he is a living creature not because reason convinces him of the certainty or probability of future satisfactions and achievements. He is instinct with activities that carry him on. Individuals here and there cave in, and most individuals sag, withdraw and seek refuge at this and that point. But man as man still has the dumb pluck of the animal. He has endurance, hope, curiosity, eagerness, love of action. These traits belong to him by structure, not by taking thought. Memory of past and foresight of future convert dumbness to some degree of articulateness. They illumine curiosity and steady courage. Then when the future arrives with its inevitable disappointments as well as fulfilments, and with new sources of trouble, failure loses something of its fatality, and suffering yields fruit of instruction not of bitterness. Humility is more demanded at our moments of triumph than at those of failure. For humility is not a caddish self-depreciation. It is the sense of our slight inability even with our best intelligence and effort to command events; a sense of our dependence upon forces that go their way without our wish and plan. Its purport is not to relax effort but to make us prize every opportunity of present growth. In morals, the infinitive and the imperative develop from the participle, present tense. Perfection means perfecting, fulfilment, fulfilling, and the good is now or never.

Idealistic philosophies, those of Plato, Aristotle, Spinoza, like the hypothesis now offered, have found the good in meanings belonging to a conscious life, a life of reason, not in external achievement. Like it, they have exalted the place of intelligence in securing fulfilment of conscious life. These theories have at least not subordinated conscious life to external obedience, not thought of virtue as something different from excellence of life. But they set up a transcendental meaning and reason, remote from present experience and opposed to it; or they insist upon a special form of meaning and consciousness to be attained by peculiar modes of knowledge inaccessible to the common man, involving not continuous reconstruction of ordinary experience, but its wholesale reversal. They have treated regeneration, change of heart, as wholesale and self-enclosed, not as continuous.

The utilitarians also made good and evil, right and wrong, matters of conscious experience. In addition they brought them down to earth, to everyday experience. They strove to humanize other-worldly goods. But they retained the notion that the good is future, and hence outside the meaning of present activity. In so far it is sporadic, exceptional, subject to accident, passive, an enjoyment not a joy, something hit upon, not a fulfilling. The future end is for them not *so*

remote from present action as the Platonic realm of
ideals, or as the Aristotelian rational thought, or the
Christian heaven, or Spinoza's conception of the universal whole.   But still it is separate in principle and
in fact from present activity.   The next step is to identify the sought for good with the meaning of our
impulses and our habits, and the specific *moral* good
or virtue with *learning* this meaning, a learning that
takes us back not into an isolated self but out into the
open-air world of objects and social ties, terminating
in an increment of present significance.

Doubtless there are those who will think that we
thus escape from remote and external ends only to fall
into an Epicureanism which teaches us to subordinate
everything else to present satisfactions.   The hypothesis preferred may seem to some to advise a subjective,
self-centered life of intensified consciousness, an esthet-
ically dilettante type of egoism.   For is not its lesson
that we should concentrate attention, each upon the
consciousness accompanying his action so as to refine
and develop it?   Is not this, like all subjective morals,
an anti-social doctrine, instructing us to subordinate
the objective consequences of our acts, those which promote the welfare of others, to an enrichment of our
private conscious lives?

It can hardly be denied that as compared with the
dogmas against which it reacted there is an element of
truth in Epicureanism.   It strove to center attention
upon what is actually within control and to find the
good in the present instead of in a contingent uncer-

tain future. The trouble with it lies in its account of present good. It failed to connect this good with the full reach of activities. It contemplated good of withdrawal rather than of active participation. That is to say, the objection to Epicureanism lies in its conception of what constitutes present good, not in its emphasis upon satisfaction as at present. The same remark may be made about every theory which recognizes the individual self. If any such theory is objectionable, the objection is against the character or quality assigned to the self. Of course an individual is the bearer or carrier of experience. What of that? Everything depends upon the kind of experience that centers in him. Not the residence of experience counts, but its contents, what's in the house. The center is not in the abstract amenable to our control, but what gathers about it is our affair. We can't help being individual selves, each one of us. If selfhood as such is a bad thing, the blame lies not with the self but with the universe, with providence. But in fact the distinction between a selfishness with which we find fault and an unselfishness which we esteem is found in the quality of the activities which proceed from and enter into the self, according as they are contractive, exclusive, or expansive, outreaching. Meaning exists for some self, but this truistic fact doesn't fix the quality of any particular meaning. It may be such as to make the self small, or such as to exalt and dignify the self. It is as impertinent to decry the worth of experience because it is connected with a self as it is fantastic to idealize personality just as personality aside from the question what sort of a person one is.

Other persons are selves too. If one's own present experience is to be depreciated in its meaning because it centers in a self, why act for the welfare of others? Selfishness for selfishness, one is as good as another; our own is worth as much as another's. But the recognition that good is always found in a present growth of significance in activity protects us from thinking that welfare can consist in a soup-kitchen happiness, in pleasures we can confer upon others from without. It shows that good is the same in quality wherever it is found, whether in some other self or in one's own. An activity has meaning in the degree in which it establishes and acknowledges variety and intimacy of connections. As long as any social impulse endures, so long an activity that shuts itself off will bring inward dissatisfaction and entail a struggle for compensatory goods, no matter what pleasures or external successes acclaim its course.

To say that the welfare of others, like our own, consists in a widening and deepening of the perceptions that give activity its meaning, in an educative growth, is to set forth a proposition of political import. To "make others happy" except through liberating their powers and engaging them in activities that enlarge the meaning of life is to harm them and to indulge ourselves under cover of exercising a special virtue. Our moral measure for estimating any existing arrangement or any proposed reform is its effect upon impulse and habits. Does it liberate or suppress, ossify or render flexible, divide or unify interest? Is perception quickened or dulled? Is memory made apt and extensive or narrow and diffusely irrelevant? Is imagination diverted to fantasy and compensatory dreams, or does it add fertility to life? Is thought creative or pushed one side into pedantic specialisms? There is a sense in which to set up social welfare as an end of action only promotes an offensive condescension, a harsh interference, or an oleaginous display of complacent kindliness. It always tends in this direction when it is aimed at giving happiness to others directly, that is, as we can hand a physical thing to another. To foster conditions that widen the horizon of others and give them command of their own powers, so that they can find their own happiness in their own fashion, is the way of " social " action. Otherwise the prayer of a freeman would be to be left alone, and to be delivered, above all, from " reformers " and " kind " people.

II

Since morals is concerned with conduct, it grows out of specific empirical facts. Almost all influential moral theories, with the exception of the utilitarian, have refused to admit this idea. For Christendom as a whole, morality has been connected with supernatural commands, rewards and penalties. Those who have escaped this superstition have contented themselves with converting the difference between this world and the next into a distinction between the actual and the ideal, what is and what should be. The actual world has not been surrendered to the devil in name, but it is treated as a display of physical forces incapable of generating moral values. Consequently, moral considerations must be introduced from above. Human nature may not be officially declared to be infected because of some aboriginal sin, but it is said to be sensuous, impulsive, subjected to necessity, while natural intelligence is such that it cannot rise above a reckoning of private expediency.

But in fact morals is the most humane of all subjects. It is that which is closest to human nature; it is ineradicably empirical, not theological nor metaphysical nor mathematical. Since it directly concerns human nature, everything that can be known of the human mind and body in physiology, medicine, anthropology, and psychology is pertinent to moral inquiry. Human nature exists and operates in an environment. And it is not " in " that environment as coins are in a box, but as a plant is in the sunlight and soil. It is of them, continuous with their energies, dependent upon their support, capable of increase only as it utilizes them, and as it gradually rebuilds from their crude indifference an environment genially civilized. Hence physics, chemistry, history, statistics, engineering science, are a part of disciplined moral knowledge so far as they enable us to understand the conditions and agencies through which man lives, and on account of which he forms and executes his plans. Moral science is not something with a separate province. It is physical, biological and historic knowledge placed in a human context where it will illuminate and guide the activities of men.

The path of truth is narrow and straitened. It is only too easy to wander beyond the course from this side to that. In a reaction from that error which has made morals fanatic or fantastic, sentimental or authoritative by severing them from actual facts and forces, theorists have gone to the other extreme. They have insisted that natural laws are themselves moral laws, so that it remains, after noting them, only to conform to them. This doctrine of accord with nature has usually marked a transition period. When mythology is dying in its open forms, and when social life is so disturbed that custom and tradition fail to supply their wonted control, men resort to Nature as a norm.

They apply to Nature all the eulogistic predicates previously associated with divine law; or natural law is conceived of as the only true divine law. This happened in one form in Stoicism. It happened in another form in the deism of the eighteenth century with its notion of a benevolent, harmonious, wholly rational order of Nature.

In our time this notion has been perpetuated in connection with a laissez-faire social philosophy and the theory of evolution. Human intelligence is thought to mark an artificial interference if it does more than register fixed natural laws as rules of human action. The process of natural evolution is conceived as the exact model of human endeavor. The two ideas met in Spencer. To the " enlightened " of a former generation, Spencer's evolutionary philosophy seemed to afford a scientific sanction for the necessity of moral progress, while it also proved, up to the hilt, the futility of deliberate " interference " with the benevolent operations of nature. The idea of justice was identified with the law of cause and effect. Transgression of natural law wrought in the struggle for existence its own penalty of elimination, and conformity with it brought the reward of increased vitality and happiness. By this process egoistic desire is gradually coming into harmony with the necessity of the environment, till at last the individual automatically finds happiness in doing what the natural and social environment demands, and serves himself in serving others. From this point of view, earlier " scientific " philosophers made a mistake, but only the mistake of anticipating the date of complete natural harmony. All that reason can do is to acknowledge the evolutionary forces, and thereby refrain from retarding the arrival of the happy day of perfect harmony. Meantime justice demands that the weak and ignorant suffer the effect of violation of natural law, while the wise and able reap the rewards of their superiority.

The fundamental defect of such views is that they fail to see the difference made in conditions and energies by perception of them. It is the first business of mind to be " realistic," to see things " as they are." If, for example, biology can give us knowledge of the causes of competency and incompetency, strength and weakness, that knowledge is all to the good. A non-sentimental morals will seek for all the instruction natural science can give concerning the biological conditions and consequences of inferiority and superiority. But knowledge of facts does not entail conformity and acquiescence. The contrary is the case. Perception of things as they are is but a stage in the process of making them different. They have already begun to be different in being known, for by that fact they enter into a different context, a context of foresight and judgment of better and worse. A false psychology of a separate realm of consciousness is the only reason this fact is not generally acknowledged. Morality resides not in perception of fact, but in the *use* made of its perception. It is a monstrous assumption that its sole use is to utter benedictions upon fact and its offspring. It is the part of intelligence to tell when to use the fact to conform and perpetuate, and when to use it to vary conditions and consequences.

It is absurd to suppose that knowledge about the connection between inferiority and its consequences prescribes adherence to that connection. It is like supposing that knowledge of the connection between malaria and mosquitoes enjoins breeding mosquitoes. The fact when it is known enters into a new environment. Without ceasing to belong to the physical environment it enters also into a medium of human activities, of desires and aversions, habits and instincts. It thereby gains new potencies, new capacities. Gunpowder in water does not act the same as gunpowder next a flame. A fact known does not operate the same as a fact unperceived. When it is known it comes into contact with the flame of desire and the cold bath of antipathy. Knowledge of the conditions that breed incapacity may fit into some desire to maintain others in that state while averting it for one's self. Or it may fall in with a character which finds itself blocked by such facts, and therefore strives to use knowledge of causes to make a change in effects. Morality begins at this point of use of knowledge of natural law, a use varying with the active system of dispositions and desires. Intelligent action is not concerned with the bare consequences of the thing known, but with consequences *to be* brought into existence by action conditioned on the knowledge. Men may use their knowledge to induce conformity or exaggeration, or to effect change and abolition of conditions.   The quality of these consequences determines the question of better or worse.

The exaggeration of the harmony attributed to Nature aroused men to note its disharmonies.   An optimistic view of natural benevolence was followed by a more honest, less romantic view of struggle and conflict in nature.   After Helvetius and Bentham came Malthus and Darwin.   The problem of morals is the problem of desire and intelligence.   What is to be done with these facts of disharmony and conflict?   After we have discovered the place and consequences of conflict in nature, we have still to discover its place and working in human need and thought.   What is its office, its function, its *possibility*, or use?   In general, the answer is simple. Conflict is the gadfly of thought.   It stirs us to observation and memory.   It instigates to invention.   It shocks us out of sheep-like passivity, and sets us at noting and contriving.   Not that it always effects this result; but that conflict is a *sine qua non* of reflection and ingenuity.   When this possibility of making use of conflict has once been noted, it is possible to utilize it systematically to substitute the arbitration of mind for that of brutal attack and brute collapse.   But the tendency to take natural law for a norm of action which the supposedly scientific have inherited from eighteenth century rationalism leads to an idealization of the principle of conflict itself.   Its office in promoting progress through arousing intelligence is overlooked, and it is erected into the generator of progress.   Karl Marx borrowed from the dialectic of Hegel the idea of the

necessity of a negative element, of opposition, for advance. He projected it into social affairs and reached
the conclusion that all social development comes from
conflict between classes, and that therefore class-war-
fare is to be cultivated. Hence a supposedly scientific
form of the doctrine of social evolution preaches social
hostility as the road to social harmony. It would be
difficult to find a more striking instance of what happens
when natural events are given a social and practical
sanctification. Darwinism has been similarly used
to justify war and the brutalities of competition for
wealth and power.

The excuse, the provocation, though not the justification for such a doctrine is found in the actions of those
who say peace, peace, when there is no peace, who refuse
to recognize facts as they are, who proclaim a natural
harmony of wealth and merit, of capital and labor, and
the natural justice, in the main, of existing conditions.
There is something horrible, something that makes one
fear for civilization, in denunciations of class-differ-
ences and class struggles which proceed from a class in
power, one that is seizing every means, even to a monopoly of moral ideals, to carry on its struggle for
class-power. This class adds hypocrisy to conflict and
brings all idealism into disrepute. It does everything
which ingenuity and prestige can do to give color to
the assertions of those who say that all moral considerations are irrelevant, and that the issue is one of
brute trial of forces between this side and that. The
alternative, here as elsewhere, is not between denying

facts in behalf of something termed moral ideals and accepting facts as final.   There remains the possibility of recognizing facts and using them as a challenge to intelligence to modify the environment and change habits.

III

The place of natural fact and law in morals brings us
to the problem of freedom. We are told that seriously
to import empirical facts into morals is equivalent to
an abrogation of freedom. Facts and laws mean necessity we are told. The way to freedom is to turn our
back upon them and take flight to a separate ideal
realm. Even if the flight could be successfully accomplished, the efficacy of the prescription may be
doubted. For we need freedom in and among
actual events, not apart from them. It is to
be hoped therefore that there remains an alternative; that the road to freedom may be found in that
knowledge of facts which enables us to employ them in
connection with desires and aims. A physician or engineer is free in his thought and his action in the degree
in which he knows what he deals with. Possibly we find
here the key to any freedom.

What men have esteemed and fought for in the name
of liberty is varied and complex—but certainly it has
never been a metaphysical freedom of will. It seems
to contain three elements of importance, though on
their face not all of them are directly compatible with
one another. (i) It includes efficiency in action, ability to carry out plans, the absence of cramping and
thwarting obstacles. (ii) It also includes capacity to

vary plans, to change the course of action, to experience novelties. And again (iii) it signifies the power of desire and choice to be factors in events.

Few men would purchase even a high amount of efficient action along definite lines at the price of monotony, or if success in action were bought by all abandonment of personal preference. They would probably feel that a more precious freedom was possessed in a life of ill-assured objective achievement that contained undertaking of risks, adventuring in new fields, a pitting of personal choice against the odds of events, and a mixture of success and failures, provided choice had a career. The slave is a man who executes the wish of others, one doomed to act along lines predetermined to regularity. Those who have defined freedom as ability to act have unconsciously assumed that this ability is exercised in accord with desire, and that its operation introduces the agent into fields previously unexplored. Hence the conception of freedom as involving three factors.

Yet efficiency in execution cannot be ignored. To say that a man is free to choose to walk while the only walk he can take will lead him over a precipice is to strain words as well as facts. Intelligence is the key to freedom in act. We are likely to be able to go ahead prosperously in the degree in which we have consulted conditions and formed a plan which enlists their consenting cooperation. The gratuitous help of unforeseen circumstance we cannot afford to despise. Luck, bad if not good, will always be with us. But it has a way

of favoring the intelligent and showing its back to the
stupid. And the gifts of fortune when they come are
fleeting except when they are made taut by intelligent
adaptation of conditions. In neutral and adverse circumstances, study and foresight are the only roads to
unimpeded action. Insistence upon a metaphysical
freedom of will is generally at its most strident pitch
with those who despise knowledge of matters-of-fact.
They pay for their contempt by halting and confined
action. Glorification of freedom in general at the expense of positive abilities in particular has often characterized the official creed of historic liberalism. Its
outward sign is the separation of politics and law from
economics. Much of what is called the " individualism " of the early nineteenth century has in truth little
to do with the nature of individuals. It goes back to a
metaphysics which held that harmony between man and
nature can be taken for granted, if once certain artificial restrictions upon man are removed. Hence it
neglected the necessity of studying and regulating industrial conditions so that a nominal freedom can
be made an actuality. Find a man who believes that all
men need is freedom *from* oppressive legal and political
measures, and you have found a man who, unless he is
merely obstinately maintaining his own private privileges, carries at the back of his head some heritage of
the metaphysical doctrine of free-will, plus an optimistic confidence in natural harmony. He needs a philosophy that recognizes the objective character of freedom and its dependence upon a congruity of environ-

ment with human wants, an agreement which can be obtained only by profound thought and unremitting application. For freedom as a fact depends upon conditions of work which are socially and scientifically buttressed. Since industry covers the most pervasive relations of man with his environment, freedom is unreal which does not have as its basis an economic command of environment.

I have no desire to add another to the cheap and easy solutions which exist of the seeming conflict between freedom and organization. It is reasonably obvious that organization may become a hindrance to freedom; it does not take us far to say that the trouble lies not in organization but in over-organization. At the same time, it must be admitted that there is no effective or objective freedom without organization. It is easy to criticize the contract theory of the state which states that individuals surrender some at least of their natural liberties in order to make secure as civil liberties what they retain. Nevertheless there is some truth in the idea of surrender and exchange. A certain natural freedom is possessed by man. That is to say, in some respects harmony exists between a man's energies and his surroundings such that the latter support and execute his purposes. In so far he is free; without such a basic natural support, conscious contrivances of legislation, administration and deliberate human institution of social arrangements cannot take place. In this sense natural freedom is prior to political freedom and is its condition. But we cannot trust wholly to a free-

dom thus procured. It is at the mercy of accident.
Conscious agreements among men must supplement and
in some degree supplant freedom of action which is the
gift of nature. In order to arrive at these agreements,
individuals have to make concessions. They must con-
sent to curtailment of some natural liberties in order
that any of them may be rendered secure and enduring.
They must, in short, enter into an organization with
other human beings so that the activities of others may
be permanently counted upon to assure regularity of
action and far-reaching scope of plans and courses of
action. The procedure is not, in so far, unlike surrendering a portion of one's income in order to buy insurance against future contingencies, and thus to render
the future course of life more equably secure. It would
be folly to maintain that there is no sacrifice; we can
however contend that the sacrifice is a reasonable one,
justified by results.

Viewed in this light, the relation of individual freedom to organization is seen to be an experimental affair. It is not capable of being settled by abstract
theory. Take the question of labor unions and the
closed or open shop. It is folly to fancy that no restrictions and surrenders of prior freedoms and possibilities of future freedoms are involved in the extension of this particular form of organization. But to
condemn such organization on the theoretical ground
that a restriction of liberty is entailed is to adopt a
position which would have been fatal to every advance
step in civilization, and to every net gain in effective

freedom. Every such question is to be judged not on the basis of antecedent theory but on the basis of concrete consequences. The question is to the balance of freedom and security achieved, as compared with practicable alternatives. Even the question of the point where membership in an organization ceases to be a voluntary matter and becomes coercive or required, is also an experimental matter, a thing to be decided by scientifically conducted study of consequences, of pros and cons. It is definitely an affair of specific detail, not of wholesale theory. It is equally amusing to see one man denouncing on grounds of pure theory the coercion of workers by a labor union while he avails himself of the increased power due to corporate action in business and praises the coercion of the political state; and to see another man denouncing the latter as pure tyranny, while lauding the power of industrial labor organizations. The position of one or the other may be justified in particular cases, but justification is due to results in practice not to general theory.

Organization tends, however, to become rigid and to limit freedom. In addition to security and energy in action, novelty, risk, change are ingredients of the freedom which men desire. Variety is more than the spice of life; it is largely of its essence, making a difference between the free and the enslaved. Invariant virtue appears to be as mechanical as uninterrupted vice, for true excellence changes with conditions. Unless character rises to overcome some new difficulty or conquer some temptation from an unexpected quarter

we suspect its grain is only a veneer. Choice is an element in freedom and there can be no choice without
unrealized and precarious possibilities. It is this demand for genuine contingency which is caricatured in
the orthodox doctrine of a freedom of indifference, a
power to choose this way or that apart from any habit
or impulse, without even a desire on the part of will to
show off. Such an indetermination of choice is not
desired by the lover of either reason or excitement.
The theory of arbitrary free choice represents indeterminateness of conditions grasped in a vague and lazy
fashion and hardened into a desirable attribute of will.
Under the title of freedom men prize such uncertainty
of conditions as give deliberation and choice an opportunity. But uncertainty of volition which is more than
a reflection of uncertainty of conditions is the mark of
a person who has acquired imbecility of character
through permanent weakening of his springs of action.

Whether or not indeterminateness, uncertainty,
actually exists in the world is a difficult question. It is
easier to think of the world as fixed, settled once for
all, and man as accumulating all the uncertainty there
is in his will and all the doubt there is in his intellect.
The rise of natural science has facilitated this dualistic
partitioning, making nature wholly fixed and mind
wholly open and empty. Fortunately for us we do not
have to settle the question. A hypothetical answer is
enough. *If* the world is already done and done for, if
its character is entirely achieved so that its behavior
is like that of a man lost in routine, then the only free-

dom for which man can hope is one of efficiency in overt
action. But *if* change is genuine, if accounts are still
in process of making, and if objective uncertainty is the
stimulus to reflection, then variation in action, novelty
and experiment, have a true meaning. In any case the
question is an objective one. It concerns not man in
isolation from the world but man in his connection with
it. A world that is at points and times indeterminate
enough to call out deliberation and to give play to
choice to shape its future is a world in which will is
free, not because it is inherently vacillating and unstable, but because deliberation and choice are determining and stabilizing factors.

Upon an empirical view, uncertainty, doubt, hesitation, contingency and novelty, genuine change which is
not mere disguised repetition, are facts. Only deduc-
tive reasoning from certain fixed premisses creates a
bias in favor of complete determination and finality.
To say that these things exist only in human experience
not in the world, and exist there only because of our
" finitude " is dangerously like paying ourselves with
words. Empirically the life of man seems in these respects as in others to express a culmination of facts in
nature. To admit ignorance and uncertainty in man
while denying them to nature involves a curious dualism. Variability, initiative, innovation, departure from
routine, experimentation are empirically the manifestation of a genuine nisus in things. At all events it is
these things that are precious to us under the name
of freedom. It is their elimination from the life of a

slave which makes his life servile, intolerable to the freeman who has once been on his own, no matter what his animal comfort and security. A free man would rather take his chance in an open world than be guaranteed in a closed world.

These considerations give point to the third factor in love of freedom: the desire to have desire count as a factor, a force. Even if will chooses unaccountably, even if it be a capricious impulse, it does not follow that there are real alternatives, genuine possibilities, open in the future. What we want is possibilities open in the *world* not in the will, except as will or deliberate activity reflects the world. To foresee future objective alternatives and to be able by deliberation to choose one of them and thereby weight its chances in the struggle for future existence, measures our freedom. It is assumed sometimes that if it can be shown that deliberation determines choice and deliberation is determined by character and conditions, there is no freedom. This is like saying that because a flower comes from root and stem it cannot bear fruit. The question is not what are the antecedents of deliberation and choice, but what are their consequences. What do they do that is distinctive? The answer is that they give us all the control of future possibilities which is open to us. And this control is the crux of our freedom. Without it, we are pushed from behind. With it we walk in the light.

The doctrine that knowledge, intelligence rather than will, constitutes freedom is not new. It has been preached by moralists of many a school. All rationalists have identified freedom with action emancipated by insight into truth. But insight into necessity has by them been substituted for foresight of possibilities. Tolstoi for example expressed the idea of Spinoza and Hegel when he said that the ox is a slave as long as he refuses to recognize the yoke and chafes under it, while if he identifies himself with its necessity and draws willingly instead of rebelliously, he is free. But as long as the yoke is a yoke it is impossible that voluntary identification with it should occur. Conscious submission is then either fatalistic submissiveness or cowardice. The ox accepts in fact not the yoke but the stall and the hay to which the yoke is a necessary incident. But if the ox foresees the consequences of the use of the yoke, if he anticipates the possibility of harvest, and identifies himself not with the yoke but with the realization of its possibilities, he acts freely, voluntarily. He hasn't accepted a necessity as unavoidable; he has welcomed a possibility as a desirability.

Perception of necessary law plays, indeed, a part. But no amount of insight into necessity brings with it, as such, anything but a consciousness of necessity. Freedom is the " truth of necessity " only when we use one " necessity " to alter another. When we use the law to foresee consequences and to consider how they may be averted or secured, then freedom begins. Employing knowledge of law to enforce desire in execution gives power to the engineer. Employing knowledge of law in order to submit to it without further action constitutes fatalism, no matter how it be dressed up. Thus we recur to our main contention. Morality depends upon events, not upon commands and ideals alien to nature. But intelligence treats events as moving, as fraught with possibilities, not as ended, final. In forecasting their possibilities, the distinction between better and worse arises. Human desire and ability cooperates with this or that natural force according as this or that eventuality is judged better. We do not use the present to control the future. We use the foresight of the future to refine and expand present activity. In this use of desire, deliberation and choice, freedom is actualized.

IV

Intelligence becomes ours in the degree in which we use it and accept responsibility for consequences. It is not ours originally or by production. " It thinks " is a truer psychological statement than " I think." Thoughts sprout and vegetate; ideas proliferate. They come from deep unconscious sources. " I think " is a statement about voluntary action. Some suggestion surges from the unknown. Our active body of habits appropriates it. The suggestion then becomes an assertion. It no longer merely comes to us. It is accepted and uttered by us. We act upon it and thereby assume, by implication, its consequences. The stuff of belief and proposition is not originated by us. It comes to us from others, by education, tradition and the suggestion of the environment. Our intelligence is bound up, so far as its materials are concerned, with the community life of which we are a part. We know what it communicates to us, and know according to the habits it forms in us. Science is an affair of civilization not of individual intellect.

So with conscience. When a child acts, those about him re-act. They shower encouragement upon him, visit him with approval, or they bestow frowns and rebuke. What others do to us when we act is as natural a consequence of our action as what the fire does to us when we plunge our hands in it. The social environment may be as artificial as you please. But its action in response to ours is natural not artificial. In language and imagination we rehearse the responses of others just as we dramatically enact other consequences. We foreknow how others will act, and the foreknowledge is the beginning of judgment passed on action. We know *with* them; there is conscience. An assembly is formed within our breast which discusses and appraises proposed and performed acts. The community without becomes a forum and tribunal within, a judgment-seat of charges, assessments and exculpations. Our thoughts of our own actions are saturated with the ideas that others entertain about them, ideas which have been expressed not only in explicit instruction but still more effectively in reaction to our acts.

Liability is the beginning of responsibility. We are held accountable by others for the consequences of our acts. They visit their like and dislike of these consequences upon us. In vain do we claim that these are not ours; that they are products of ignorance not design, or are incidents in the execution of a most laudable scheme. Their authorship is imputed to us. We are disapproved, and disapproval is not an inner state of mind but a most definite act. Others say to us by their deeds we do not care a fig whether you did this deliberately or not. We intend that you *shall* deliberate before you do it again, and that if possible your deliberation shall prevent a repetition of this act we object to. The reference in blame and every unfavor-

able judgment is prospective, not retrospective. Theories about responsibility may become confused, but in
practice no one is stupid enough to try to change the
past. Approbation and disapprobation are ways of
influencing the formation of habits and aims; that is,
of influencing future acts. The individual is *held* accountable for what he *has* done in order that he may be
responsive in what he is *going* to do. Gradually persons learn by dramatic imitation to hold themselves
accountable, and liability becomes a voluntary deliberate acknowledgment that deeds are our own, that
their consequences come from us.

These two facts, that moral judgment and moral
responsibility are the work wrought in us by the social
environment, signify that all morality is social; not
because we *ought* to take into account the effect of our
acts upon the welfare of others, but because of facts.
Others *do* take account of what we do, and they respond accordingly to our acts. Their responses actually *do* affect the meaning of what we do. The significance thus contributed is as inevitable as is the effect
of interaction with the physical environment. In fact
as civilization advances the physical environment gets
itself more and more humanized, for the meaning of
physical energies and events becomes involved with the
part they play in human activities. Our conduct *is*
socially conditioned whether we perceive the fact or
not.

The effect of custom on habit, and of habit upon
thought is enough to prove this statement. When we

begin to forecast consequences, the consequences that most stand out are those which will proceed from other people. The resistance and the cooperation of others is the central fact in the furtherance or failure of our schemes. Connections with our fellows furnish both the opportunities for action and the instrumentalities by which we take advantage of opportunity. All of the actions of an individual bear the stamp of his community as assuredly as does the language he speaks. Difficulty in reading the stamp is due to variety of impressions in consequence of membership in many groups. This social saturation is, I repeat, a matter of fact, not of what should be, not of what is desirable or undesirable. It does not guarantee the rightness of goodness of an act; there is no excuse for thinking of evil action as individualistic and right action as social. Deliberate unscrupulous pursuit of self-interest is as much conditioned upon social opportunities, training and assistance as is the course of action prompted by a beaming benevolence. The difference lies in the quality and degree of the perception of ties and interdependencies; in the use to which they are put. Consider the form commonly assumed today by self-seeking; namely command of money and economic power. Money is a social institution; property is a legal custom; economic opportunities are dependent upon the state of society; the objects aimed at, the rewards sought for, are what they are because of social admiration, prestige, competition and power. If money-making is morally obnoxious it is because of the way these social facts are handled, not because a money-making man has withdrawn from society into an isolated selfhood or turned his back upon society. His "individualism" is not found in his original nature but in his habits acquired under social influences. It is found in his concrete aims, and these are reflexes of social conditions. Well-grounded moral objection to a mode of conduct rests upon the kind of social connections that figure, not upon lack of social aim. A man may attempt to utilize social relationships for his own advantage in an inequitable way; he may intentionally or unconsciously try to make them feed one of his own appetites. Then he is denounced as egoistic. But both his course of action and the disapproval he is subject to are facts *within* society. They are social phenomena. He pursues his unjust advantage as a social asset.

Explicit recognition of this fact is a prerequisite of improvement in moral education and of an intelligent understanding of the chief ideas or "categories" of morals. Morals is as much a matter of interaction of a person with his social environment as walking is an interaction of legs with a physical environment. The character of walking depends upon the strength and competency of legs. But it also depends upon whether a man is walking in a bog or on a paved street, upon whether there is a safeguarded path set aside or whether he has to walk amid dangerous vehicles. If the standard of morals is low it is because the education given by the interaction of the individual with his social en-

vironment is defective. Of what avail is it to preach
unassuming simplicity and contentment of life when
communal admiration goes to the man who " succeeds "
—who makes himself conspicuous and envied because of
command of money and other forms of power? If a
child gets on by peevishness or intrigue, then others
are his accomplices who assist in the habits which are
built up. The notion that an abstract ready-made
conscience exists in individuals and that it is only necessary to make an occasional appeal to it and to indulge
in occasional crude rebukes and punishments, is associated with the causes of lack of definitive and orderly
moral advance. For it is associated with lack of attention to social forces.

There is a peculiar inconsistency in the current idea
that morals *ought* to be social. The introduction of
the moral " ought " into the idea contains an implicit
assertion that morals depend upon something apart
from social relations. Morals *are* social. The question of ought, should be, is a question of better and
worse *in* social affairs. The extent to which the weight
of theories has been thrown against the perception of
the place of social ties and connections in moral activity is a fair measure of the extent to which social forces
work blindly and develop an accidental morality. The
chief obstacle for example to recognizing the truth of
a proposition frequently set forth in these pages to the
effect that all conduct is potential, if not actual, matter of moral judgment is the habit of identifying moral
judgment with praise and blame. So great is the in-

fluence of this habit that it is safe to say that every professed moralist when he leaves the pages of theory and faces some actual item of his own or others' behavior, first or "instinctively" thinks of acts as moral or non-moral in the degree in which they are exposed to condemnation or approval. Now this kind of judgment is certainly not one which could profitably be dispensed with. Its influence is much needed. But the tendency to equate it with all moral judgment is largely responsible for the current idea that there is a sharp line between moral conduct and a larger region of non-moral conduct which is a matter of expediency, shrewdness, success or manners.

Moreover this tendency is a chief reason why the social forces effective in shaping actual morality work blindly and unsatisfactorily. Judgment in which the emphasis falls upon blame and approbation has more heat than light. It is more emotional than intellectual. It is guided by custom, personal convenience and resentment rather than by insight into causes and consequences. It makes toward reducing moral instruction, the educative influence of social opinion, to an immediate personal matter, that is to say, to an adjustment of personal likes and dislikes. Fault-finding creates resentment in the one blamed, and approval, complacency, rather than a habit of scrutinizing conduct objectively. It puts those who are sensitive to the judgments of others in a standing defensive attitude, creating an apologetic, self-accusing and self-exculpating habit of mind when what is needed is an impersonal impartial habit of observation. "Moral" persons get so occupied with defending their conduct from real and imagined criticism that they have little time left to see what their acts really amount to, and the habit of self-blame inevitably extends to include others since it is a habit.

Now it is a wholesome thing for any one to be made aware that thoughtless, self-centered action on his part exposes him to the indignation and dislike of others. There is no one who can be safely trusted to be exempt from immediate reactions of criticism, and there are few who do not need to be braced by occasional expressions of approval. But these influences are immensely overdone in comparison with the assistance that might be given by the influence of social judgments which operate without accompaniments of praise and blame; which enable an individual to see for himself what he is doing, and which put him in command of a method of analyzing the obscure and usually unavowed forces which move him to act. We need a permeation of judgments on conduct by the method and materials of a science of human nature. Without such enlightenment even the best-intentioned attempts at the moral guidance and improvement of others often eventuate in tragedies of misunderstanding and division, as is so often seen in the relations of parents and children.

The development therefore of a more adequate science of human nature is a matter of first-rate importance. The present revolt against the notion that psy-

chology is a science of consciousness may well turn out
in the future to be the beginning of a definitive turn
in thought and action.   Historically there are good
reasons for the isolation and exaggeration of the conscious phase of human action, an isolation which for-
got that " conscious " is an adjective of some acts and
which erected the resulting abstraction, " consciousness," into a noun, an existence separate and complete.
These reasons are interesting not only to the student
of technical philosophy but also to the student of the
history of culture and even of politics.   They have to
do with the attempt to drag realities out of occult es-
sences and hidden forces and get them into the light of
day.   They were part of the general movement called
phenomenalism, and of the growing importance of individual life and private voluntary concerns.   But the
effect was to isolate the individual from his connections
both with his fellows and with nature, and thus to create an artificial human nature, one not capable of being
understood and effectively directed on the basis of
analytic understanding.   It shut out from view, not to
say from scientific examination, the forces which really
move human nature.   It took a few surface phenomena
for the whole story of significant human motive-forces
and acts.

As a consequence physical science and its technological applications were highly developed while the science of man, moral science, is backward.   I believe
that it is not possible to estimate how much of the difficulties of the present world situation are due to the

disproportion and unbalance thus introduced into affairs. It would have seemed absurd to say in the seventeenth century that in the end the alteration in methods of physical investigation which was then beginning would prove more important than the religious wars of that century. Yet the wars marked the end of one era; the dawn of physical science the beginning of a new one. And a trained imagination may discover that the nationalistic and economic wars which are the chief outward mark of the present are in the end to be less significant than the development of a science of human nature now inchoate.

It sounds academic to say that substantial bettering of social relations waits upon the growth of a scientific social psychology. For the term suggests something specialized and remote. But the formation of habits of belief, desire and judgment is going on at every instant under the influence of the conditions set by men's contact, intercourse and associations with one another. This is the fundamental fact in social life and in personal character. It is the fact about which traditional human science gives no enlightenment—a fact which this traditional science blurs and virtually denies. The enormous rôle played in popular morals by appeal to the supernatural and quasi-magical is in effect a desperate admission of the futility of our science. Consequently the whole matter of the formation of the predispositions which effectively control human relationships is left to accident, to custom and immediate personal likings, resentments and ambitions. It is a commonplace that modern industry and commerce are conditioned upon a control of physical energies due to proper methods of physical inquiry and analysis. We have no social arts which are comparable because we have so nearly nothing in the way of psychological science. Yet through the development of physical science, and especially of chemistry, biology, physiology, medicine and anthropology we now have the basis for the development of such a science of man. Signs of its coming into existence are present in the movements in clinical, behavioristic and social (in its narrower sense) psychology.

At present we not only have no assured means of forming character except crude devices of blame, praise, exhortation and punishment, but the very meaning of the general notions of moral inquiry is matter of doubt and dispute. The reason is that these notions are discussed in isolation from the concrete facts of the interactions of human beings with one another—an abstraction as fatal as was the old discussion of phlogiston, gravity and vital force apart from concrete correlations of changing events with one another. Take for example such a basic conception as that of Right involving the nature of authority in conduct. There is no need here to rehearse the multitude of contending views which give evidence that discussion of this matter is still in the realm of opinion. We content ourselves with pointing out that this notion is the last resort of the anti-empirical school in morals and that it proves the effect of neglect of social conditions.

In effect its adherents argue as follows: "Let us concede that concrete ideas about right and wrong and particular notions of what is obligatory have grown up within experience. But we cannot admit this about the idea of Right, of Obligation itself. Why does moral authority exist at all? Why is the claim of the Right recognized in conscience even by those who violate it in deed? Our opponents say that such and such a course is wise, expedient, better. But *why* act for the wise, or good, or better? Why not follow our own immediate devices if we are so inclined? There is only one answer: We have a moral nature, a conscience, call it what you will. And this nature responds directly in acknowledgment of the supreme authority of the Right over all claims of inclination and habit. We may not act in accordance with this acknowledgment, but we still know that the authority of the moral law, although not its power, is unquestionable. Men may differ indefinitely according to what their experience has been as to just *what* is Right, what its contents are. But they all spontaneously agree in recognizing the supremacy of the claims of whatever is thought of as Right. Otherwise there would be no such thing as morality, but merely calculations of how to satisfy desire.

Grant the foregoing argument, and all the apparatus of abstract moralism follows in its wake. A remote goal of perfection, ideals that are contrary in a wholesale way to what is actual, a free will of arbitrary choice; all of these conceptions band themselves together with that of a non-empirical authority of Right and a non-empirical conscience which acknowledges it. They constitute its ceremonial or formal train.

Why, indeed, acknowledge the authority of Right? That many persons do not acknowledge it in fact, in action, and that all persons ignore it at times, is assumed by the argument. Just what is the significance of an alleged recognition of a supremacy which is continually denied in fact? How much would be lost if it were dropped out, and we were left face to face with actual facts? If a man lived alone in the world there might be some sense in the question " Why be moral? " were it not for one thing: No such question would then arise. As it is, we live in a world where other persons live too. Our acts affect them. They perceive these effects, and react upon us in consequence. Because they are living beings they make demands upon us for certain things from us. They approve and condemn—not in abstract theory but in what they do to us. The answer to the question " Why not put your hand in the fire? " is the answer of fact. If you do your hand will be burnt. The answer to the question why acknowledge the right is of the same sort. For Right is only an abstract name for the multitude of concrete demands in action which others impress upon us, and of which we are obliged, if we would live, to take some account. Its authority is the exigency of their demands, the efficacy of their insistencies. There may be good ground for the contention that in theory the idea of the right is subordinate to that of the good, being a statement of the course proper to attain good. But in fact it

signifies the totality of social pressures exercised upon
us to induce us to think and desire in certain ways.
Hence the right can in fact become the road to the good
only as the elements that compose this unremitting
pressure are enlightened, only as social relationships
become themselves reasonable.

It will be retorted that all pressure is a non-moral
affair partaking of force, not of right; that right must
be ideal. Thus we are invited to enter again the circle
in which the ideal has no force and social actualities no
ideal quality. We refuse the invitation because social
pressure is involved in our own lives, as much so as the
air we breathe and the ground we walk upon. If we
had desires, judgments, plans, in short a mind, apart
from social connections, then the latter would be external and their action might be regarded as that of a non-
moral force. But we live mentally as physically only
in and *because* of our environment. Social pressure is
but a name for the interactions which are always going
on and in which we participate, living so far as we par-
take and dying so far as we do not. The pressure is
not ideal but empirical, yet empirical here means only
actual. It calls attention to the fact that considerations of right are claims originating not outside of life,
but within it. They are " ideal " in precisely the degree in which we intelligently recognize and act upon
them, just as colors and canvas become ideal when
used in ways that give an added meaning to life.

Accordingly failure to recognize the authority of
right means defect in effective apprehension of the real-

ities of human association, not an arbitrary exercise of
free will. This deficiency and perversion in apprehension indicates a defect in education—that is to say, in
the operation of actual conditions, in the consequences
upon desire and thought of existing interactions and
interdependencies. It is false that every person has a
consciousness of the supreme authority of right and
then misconceives it or ignores it in action. One has
such a sense of the claims of social relationships as
those relationships enforce in one's desires and observations. The belief in a separate, ideal or transcendental, practically ineffectual Right is a reflex of the
inadequacy with which existing institutions perform
their educative office—their office in generating observation of social continuities. It is an endeavor to
" rationalize " this defect. Like all rationalizations, it
operates to divert attention from the real state of
affairs. Thus it helps maintain the conditions which
created it, standing in the way of effort to make our
institutions more humane and equitable. A theoretical
acknowledgment of the supreme authority of Right, of
moral law, gets twisted into an effectual substitute for
acts which would better the customs which now produce vague, dull, halting and evasive observation of
actual social ties. We are not caught in a circle; we
traverse a spiral in which social customs generate some
consciousness of interdependencies, and this consciousness is embodied in acts which in improving the environment generate new perceptions of social ties, and so
on forever. The relationships, the interactions are for-

ever there as fact, but they acquire meaning only in the desires, judgments and purposes they awaken.

We recur to our fundamental propositions. Morals is connected with actualities of existence, not with ideals, ends and obligations independent of concrete actualities. The facts upon which it depends are those which arise out of active connections of human beings with one another, the consequences of their mutually intertwined activities in the life of desire, belief, judgment, satisfaction and dissatisfaction. In this sense conduct and hence morals are social: they are not just things which *ought* to be social and which fail to come up to the scratch. But there are enormous differences of better and worse in the quality of what is social. Ideal morals begin with the perception of these differences. Human interaction and ties are there, are operative in any case. But they can be regulated, employed in an orderly way for good only as we know how to observe them. And they cannot be observed aright, they cannot be understood and utilized, when the mind is left to itself to work without the aid of science. For the natural unaided mind means precisely the habits of belief, thought and desire which have been accidentally generated and confirmed by social institutions or customs. But with all their admixture of accident and reasonableness we have at last reached a point where social conditions create a mind capable of scientific outlook and inquiry. To foster and develop this spirit is the social obligation of the present because it is its urgent need.

Yet the last word is not with obligation nor with the future. Infinite relationships of man with his fellows and with nature already exist. The ideal means, as we have seen, a sense of these encompassing continuities with their infinite reach. This meaning even now attaches to present activities because they are set in a whole to which they belong and which belongs to them. Even in the midst of conflict, struggle and defeat a consciousness is possible of the enduring and comprehending whole.

To be grasped and held this consciousness needs, like every form of consciousness, objects, symbols. In the past men have sought many symbols which no longer serve, especially since men have been idolators worshiping symbols as things. Yet within these symbols which have so often claimed to be realities and which have imposed themselves as dogmas and intolerances, there has rarely been absent some trace of a vital and enduring reality, that of a community of life in which continuities of existence are consummated. Consciousness of the whole has been connected with reverences, affections, and loyalties which are communal. But special ways of expressing the communal sense have been established. They have been limited to a select social group; they have hardened into obligatory rites and been imposed as conditions of salvation. Religion has lost itself in cults, dogmas and myths. Consequently the office of religion as sense of community and one's place in it has been lost. In effect religion has been distorted into a possession—or burden—of a limited part of human nature, of a limited portion of humanity which finds no way to universalize religion except by imposing its own dogmas and ceremonies upon others; of a limited class within a partial group; priests, saints, a church. Thus other gods have been set up before the one God. Religion as a sense of the whole is the most individualized of all things, the most spontaneous, undefinable and varied. For individuality signifies unique connections in the whole. Yet it has been perverted into something uniform and immutable. It has been formulated into fixed and defined beliefs expressed in required acts and ceremonies. Instead of marking the freedom and peace of the individual as a member of an infinite whole, it has been petrified into a slavery of thought and sentiment, an intolerant superiority on the part of the few and an intolerable burden on the part of the many.

Yet every act may carry within itself a consoling and supporting consciousness of the whole to which it belongs and which in some sense belongs to it. With responsibility for the intelligent determination of particular acts may go a joyful emancipation from the burden for responsibility for the whole which sustains them, giving them their final outcome and quality. There is a conceit fostered by perversion of religion which assimilates the universe to our personal desires; but there is also a conceit of carrying the load of the universe from which religion liberates us. Within the flickering inconsequential acts of separate selves dwells a sense of the whole which claims and dignifies them.

In its presence we put off mortality and live in the universal. The life of the community in which we live and have our being is the fit symbol of this relationship. The acts in which we express our perception of the ties which bind us to others are its only rites and ceremonies.

INDEX

GREAT BOOKS IN PHILOSOPHY PAPERBACK SERIES

ESTHETICS

- ❏ Aristotle—*The Poetics*
- ❏ Aristotle—*Treatise on Rhetoric*

ETHICS

- ❏ Aristotle—*The Nicomachean Ethics*
- ❏ Marcus Aurelius—*Meditations*
- ❏ Jeremy Bentham—*The Principles of Morals and Legislation*
- ❏ John Dewey—*Human Nature and Conduct*
- ❏ John Dewey—*The Moral Writings of John Dewey, Revised Edition*
  (edited by James Gouinlock)
- ❏ Epictetus—*Enchiridion*
- ❏ Immanuel Kant—*Fundamental Principles of the Metaphysic of Morals*
- ❏ John Stuart Mill—*Utilitarianism*
- ❏ George Edward Moore—*Principia Ethica*
- ❏ Friedrich Nietzsche—*Beyond Good and Evil*
- ❏ Plato—*Protagoras, Philebus,* and *Gorgias*
- ❏ Bertrand Russell—*Bertrand Russell On Ethics, Sex, and Marriage*
  (edited by Al Seckel)
- ❏ Arthur Schopenhauer—*The Wisdom of Life*
  and *Counsels and Maxims*
- ❏ Benedict de Spinoza—*Ethics* and *The Improvement of the Understanding*

METAPHYSICS/EPISTEMOLOGY

- ❏ Aristotle—*De Anima*
- ❏ Aristotle—*The Metaphysics*
- ❏ Francis Bacon—*Essays*
- ❏ George Berkeley—*Three Dialogues Between Hylas and Philonous*
- ❏ W. K. Clifford—*The Ethics of Belief and Other Essays*
  (introduction by Timothy J. Madigan)
- ❏ René Descartes—*Discourse on Method* and *The Meditations*
- ❏ John Dewey—*How We Think*
- ❏ John Dewey—*The Influence of Darwin on Philosophy and Other Essays*
- ❏ Epicurus—*The Essential Epicurus: Letters, Principal Doctrines,
  Vatican Sayings, and Fragments*
  (translated, and with an introduction, by Eugene O'Connor)
- ❏ Sidney Hook—*The Quest for Being*
- ❏ David Hume—*An Enquiry Concerning Human Understanding*
- ❏ David Hume—*Treatise of Human Nature*
- ❏ William James—*The Meaning of Truth*
- ❏ William James—*Pragmatism*
- ❏ Immanuel Kant—*The Critique of Judgment*
- ❏ Immanuel Kant—*Critique of Practical Reason*
- ❏ Immanuel Kant—*Critique of Pure Reason*
- ❏ Gottfried Wilhelm Leibniz—*Discourse on Metaphysics* and the *Monadology*
- ❏ John Locke—*An Essay Concerning Human Understanding*

- ❑ George Herbert Mead—*The Philosophy of the Present*
- ❑ Charles S. Peirce—*The Essential Writings*
  (edited by Edward C. Moore, preface by Richard Robin)
- ❑ Plato—*The Euthyphro, Apology, Crito,* and *Phaedo*
- ❑ Plato—*Lysis, Phaedrus,* and *Symposium*
- ❑ Bertrand Russell—*The Problems of Philosophy*
- ❑ George Santayana—*The Life of Reason*
- ❑ Sextus Empiricus—*Outlines of Pyrrhonism*
- ❑ Ludwig Wittgenstein—*Wittgenstein's Lectures: Cambridge, 1932–1935* (edited by Alice Ambrose)

PHILOSOPHY OF RELIGION

- ❑ Jeremy Bentham—*The Influence of Natural Religion on the Temporal Happiness of Mankind*
- ❑ Marcus Tullius Cicero—*The Nature of the Gods* and *On Divination*
- ❑ Ludwig Feuerbach—*The Essence of Christianity*
- ❑ David Hume—*Dialogues Concerning Natural Religion*
- ❑ William James—*The Varieties of Religious Experience*
- ❑ John Locke—*A Letter Concerning Toleration*
- ❑ Lucretius—*On the Nature of Things*
- ❑ John Stuart Mill—*Three Essays on Religion*
- ❑ Friedrich Nietzsche—*The Antichrist*
- ❑ Thomas Paine—*The Age of Reason*
- ❑ Bertrand Russell—*Bertrand Russell On God and Religion* (edited by Al Seckel)

SOCIAL AND POLITICAL PHILOSOPHY

- ❑ Aristotle—*The Politics*
- ❑ Mikhail Bakunin—*The Basic Bakunin: Writings, 1869–1871* (translated and edited by Robert M. Cutler)
- ❑ Edmund Burke—*Reflections on the Revolution in France*
- ❑ John Dewey—*Freedom and Culture*
- ❑ John Dewey—*Individualism Old and New*
- ❑ John Dewey—*Liberalism and Social Action*
- ❑ G. W. F. Hegel—*The Philosophy of History*
- ❑ G. W. F. Hegel—*Philosophy of Right*
- ❑ Thomas Hobbes—*The Leviathan*
- ❑ Sidney Hook—*Paradoxes of Freedom*
- ❑ Sidney Hook—*Reason, Social Myths, and Democracy*
- ❑ John Locke—*Second Treatise on Civil Government*
- ❑ Niccolo Machiavelli—*The Prince*
- ❑ Karl Marx (with Friedrich Engels)—*The German Ideology,* including *Theses on Feuerbach and Introduction to the Critique of Political Economy*
- ❑ Karl Marx—*The Poverty of Philosophy*
- ❑ Karl Marx/Friedrich Engels—*The Economic and Philosophic Manuscripts of 1844* and *The Communist Manifesto*
- ❑ John Stuart Mill—*Considerations on Representative Government*
- ❑ John Stuart Mill—*On Liberty*
- ❑ John Stuart Mill—*On Socialism*

GREAT MINDS PAPERBACK SERIES

ART

CRITICAL ESSAYS

ECONOMICS

HISTORY

LAW

PSYCHOLOGY

❑ Sigmund Freud—*Totem and Taboo*

RELIGION

❑ Thomas Henry Huxley—*Agnosticism and Christianity and Other Essays*
❑ Ernest Renan—*The Life of Jesus*
❑ Upton Sinclair—*The Profits of Religion*
❑ Elizabeth Cady Stanton—*The Woman's Bible*
❑ Voltaire—*A Treatise on Toleration and Other Essays*

SCIENCE

❑ Jacob Bronowski—*The Identity of Man*
❑ Nicolaus Copernicus—*On the Revolutions of Heavenly Spheres*
❑ Marie Curie—*Radioactive Substances*
❑ Charles Darwin—*The Autobiography of Charles Darwin*
❑ Charles Darwin—*The Descent of Man*
❑ Charles Darwin—*The Origin of Species*
❑ Charles Darwin—*The Voyage of the* Beagle
❑ Albert Einstein—*Relativity*
❑ Michael Faraday—*The Forces of Matter*
❑ Galileo Galilei—*Dialogues Concerning Two New Sciences*
❑ Ernst Haeckel—*The Riddle of the Universe*
❑ William Harvey—*On the Motion of the Heart and Blood in Animals*
❑ Werner Heisenberg—*Physics and Philosophy:*
   The Revolution in Modern Science (introduction by F. S. C. Northrop)
❑ Julian Huxley—*Evolutionary Humanism*
❑ Edward Jenner—*Vaccination against Smallpox*
❑ Johannes Kepler—*Epitome of Copernican Astronomy*
   and *Harmonies of the World*
❑ Charles Mackay—*Extraordinary Popular Delusions*
   and the Madness of Crowds
❑ James Clerk Maxwell—*Matter and Motion*
❑ Isaac Newton—*The Principia*
❑ Louis Pasteur and Joseph Lister—*Germ Theory and Its Application*
   to Medicine and *On the Antiseptic Principle of the Practice of Surgery*
❑ William Thomson (Lord Kelvin) and Peter Guthrie Tait—
   The Elements of Natural Philosophy
❑ Alfred Russel Wallace—*Island Life*

SOCIOLOGY

❑ Emile Durkheim—*Ethics and the Sociology of Morals*
   (translated with an introduction by Robert T. Hall)